THE COMPLETE
MEDITERRANEAN
COOKBOOK

THE COMPLETE
MEDITERRANEAN
COOKBOOK

Tess Mallos

Food Photography by Rowan Fotheringham
Food Styling by Janet Mitchell

TUTTLE PUBLISHING
Tokyo • Rutland, Vermont • Singapore

A NOTE FROM THE AUTHOR ON MEASURES AND TEMPERATURES
Measures in recipes are given in both imperial and metric, with equivalent
cup measures where applicable for those, like myself, who prefer this
convenient way of measuring many ingredients. Because ovens use various heating systems, two temperatures are given; the lower temperature is for gas ovens and gas or electric fan-forced ovens, the higher
temperature is for conventional ovens.

Published by Tuttle Publishing, an imprint of Periplus Editions (HK) Ltd.

www.tuttlepublishing.com

Published in conjunction with Lansdowne Publishing Pty Ltd
3A Grandview Street, Naremburn NSW 2065. Australia

© Copyright text: Tess Mallos
© Copyright design: Lansdowne Publishing Pty Ltd

Chief Executive Publisher: Jane Curry. Publishing Manager: Deborah
Nixon. Production Manager: Sally Stokes. Project Co-ordinator: Kirsten
Tilgals. Editorial Assistant: Belinda Cudmore. Designer: Kathie Baxter-
Smith. Photographer: Rowan Fotheringham. Stylist: Janet Mitchell
Food Preparation: Myles Beaufort

Map on pages 10 to 11 illustrated by Dianne Bradley. Pictured on page 2
Parmigiana di Melanzane (recipe page 180), page 19 Spinaci alla Romana
(recipe page 192), page 298 Ratatouille (recipe page 176).

Set in Stemple Schneidler on Quark Xpress
ISBN 978-0-8048-4003-3

Distributed by

USA & Canada
Tuttle Publishing
364 Innovation Drive
North Clarendon, VT 05759-9436 U.S.A.
Tel: 1 (802) 773-8930; Fax: 1 (802) 773-6993
info@tuttlepublishing.com
www.tuttlepublishing.com

Japan
Tuttle Publishing
Yaekari Building, 3rd Floor
5-4-12 Osaki, Shinagawa-ku
Tokyo 141 0032
Tel: (81) 3 5437-0171; Fax: (81) 3 5437-0755
tuttle-sales@gol.com

Asia Pacific
Berkeley Books Pte. Ltd.
61 Tai Seng Avenue, #02-12, Singapore 534167
Tel: (65) 6280-1330; Fax: (65) 6280-6290
inquiries@periplus.com.sg
www.periplus.com

12 11 10   10 9 8 7 6 5 4 3 2

Printed in Singapore

TUTTLE PUBLISHING® is a registered trademark of
Tuttle Publishing, a division of Periplus Editions (HK) Ltd.

CONTENTS

INTRODUCTION

To intimately know even one cuisine of the Mediterranean region is to have an affinity with the whole. To accept the foods of one country makes it easier to accept those from countries in close proximity. Thus it has been all my life; although I was born in a country with a cuisine based on Anglo origins, the permeating essence of Mediterranean foods is so instilled in me that I have been waiting patiently for its wider acceptance to justify my preferences. That time has now come, not only because travellers to the region have fallen victim to the indefinable magic of its sun-kissed shores, nor due solely to an increased willingness to experiment and try new foods and dishes. It is in many cases simply a matter of caring more about our health.

Since the 1950s, health professionals have been studying the diets of the Mediterranean people, and the conclusions cannot be disputed. The people of Greece, particularly Crete, had the longest life expectancy in the world up into the 1960s, closely followed by southern Italy and France, then Spain. If the situation has changed a little more recently, it's due mainly to influences from outside the region causing changes within.

The important features of Mediterranean diets are the high intakes of cereals, grains, vegetables, dried beans, olive oil, garlic, fresh herbs, seafoods and fresh fruit. In the countries scrutinized, wine is taken with food in moderation, with red wine apparently more beneficial than white. Meat is used in moderation, with poultry, particularly chicken, served more frequently than red meat. Animal fats, in the form of butter, cream and lard, are not used excessively.

Mediterranean food and cooking is a multilayered experience, fashioned through its vast and fascinating history from antiquity, colored by its bright, shimmering, sometimes harsh landscapes, conditioned by the warmth of its climate, and nurtured by those who inhabit the shores of this sea "in the midst of lands".

There are two terms used throughout this book, each describing a region of the Mediterranean. The Levant is the eastern region, from Turkey-in-Asia, to Syria, Lebanon and Israel (not to be confused with the Levante region of Spain). The Maghreb, from the Arabic for "west" or "sunset", refers to Northwest Africa, from Morocco to Libya; where Egypt is included, the region is then referred to as North Africa.

It was on the shores of the Mediterranean that Western civilization had its beginnings, and during its burgeoning, established the olive, the vine and wheat — the foundations for its foods — supplemented with fruit, vegetables, herbs, seafoods and meat from sheep, goats, cattle and game, enhanced with spices brought to the region via the Arab spice traders from the East.

It was not far from its shores that Christopher Columbus set out on his voyage of discovery, to find an alternative route to the spice islands of the East Indies. Instead he discovered new lands, bringing to the Old World many New World foods, each weaving another color, another flavor, another texture, into the rich tapestry of Mediterranean foods. The region has a wealth of food history, and snippets of this are related throughout this book.

Certain dishes appear in somewhat similar form in the various countries. It has much to do with the history of the area; the Phoenicians, Greeks, Egyptians, Carthaginians, Persians, Romans and Byzantium all played a part in developing the region's foods. However, it was the Arabs, spreading forth under the banner of Islam, that had the greatest influence on their cuisines: the use of nuts in sauces (a recurrent theme), extending the cultivation and use of saffron (although known in the region from ancient times), and introducing rice, eggplant, spinach, sugar cane, sweet oranges and apricots, and the fragrant rose and orange flower waters to North Africa, Spain, southern France, southern Italy and Sicily.

Over the years I have absorbed the foods and cultures of the Mediterranean through travel and through many friends and acquaintances from the various countries. However, when formulating recipes, I have taken a little license and modernized methods.

Recipes have been chosen with regard to the availability of ingredients outside the region. For countries such as Spain, France and Italy, I have concentrated on dishes from the Mediterranean regions, avoiding those of regions such as central and northern Italy which do not reflect the Mediterranean style of cooking.

The recipes also cover the range of foods used most frequently in Mediterranean cuisines. There is some emphasis on vegetarian cooking throughout the book; this is necessary today, as there are many who eschew animal products. With Mediterranean cooking you can produce vegetarian dishes using natural foods, without the need to rely on manufactured foods that emulate meat.

Fortunately, we are familiar with most of the foods of the Mediterranean; it is how these ingredients are used that sets the cuisines of the region apart. This book's purpose is to guide you in their use, so embark now for your voyage of discovery into this fascinating world that is Mediterranean food.

TESS MALLOS

THE FOOD OF
THE MEDITERRANEAN

grapes

With such a long culinary history and with so many cultures involved, it would be an impossible task to cover every conceivable food used in Mediterranean cooking within the pages of one volume. Only those ingredients that are used in this book's recipes are covered in this chapter.

If a cookbook is going to be useful there is little point in suggesting ingredients that are difficult to obtain or unfamiliar to most cooks. Fortunately, most of the ingredients required for Mediterranean cooking are readily available today; if it is perceived that there might be some difficulty in obtaining certain ingredients, readily available substitutes are given.

OLIVE OIL

The single most distinguishing feature of Mediterranean cooking is its use of olive oil. It has been constant for thousands of years, and while other oils are used in the region nowadays, olive oil still reigns supreme.

It is believed that the cultivation of the olive tree began in the eastern Mediterranean lands some 6000 years ago. Originally the oil was used for lighting, as perfumed unguents, a cleanser for the body and for food. The pre-Greek Minoans traded olive oil from Crete about 2000BC, with subsequent Greek and Phoenician seafarers continuing the trade, carrying it as far west as Spain and today's Morocco. The Greeks, from 750BC,

planted olive trees in their colonies in eastern Spain, southern France, Italy and Sicily; where the Greeks did not plant them, the Carthaginians and the Romans did.

Today, the principal olive oil producer is Spain, followed by Italy and Greece; Tunisia, Turkey, Syria, Morocco and Algeria follow. However, Spanish and Italian olive oils dominate the market outside the Mediterranean. It is well worth the effort to track down Greek olive oil, however, as it is of excellent flavor and quality.

Extra virgin and virgin olive oils: These are from the first pressing, have a fruity flavor varying in intensity according to source and a greenish tinge which fades to a clear golden color in time. Because they are very low in oleic free fatty acid, they have a longer shelf life. They are high in antioxidants and remain more stable after repeated use in deep-frying; however, the fruity flavor of the oil is lost when subjected to high temperatures. Some extra virgin and virgin oils, having undergone minimal processing, tend to solidify to a certain extent when food is refrigerated. This does not affect the flavor of the oil or the food; and once brought to room temperature, the oil becomes liquid again. As these oils are more expensive, they should be used with discretion to complement foods.

Olive oil: A blend of refined olive oil with some virgin oil added to restore the distinctive flavor and color. It is the most widely used oil and is suitable for deep frying; it can be reused a number of times, providing it is strained through a double layer of cheesecloth (muslin) into a clean container and stored in a cool place between use.

Light and extra light olive oil: These are 100 percent olive oil, but refined and blended with just enough virgin oil to given them a light, subtle taste. These oils are excellent when the flavor of the foods with which they are used should not be masked. They are also worthwhile trying if you have had an aversion to olive oil in the past, but wish to use it for its health benefits.

Choosing an olive oil is very much a matter of taste. Some extra virgin olive oils from Italy, particularly Tuscany, are prized for their peppery bite, which may be a little strong for some palates. Other extra virgin olive oils have a distinctive fruity flavor which can vary from strong to subtle. It is recommended that you buy a small bottle to try an oil first, before investing in a larger bottle or can.

Because olive oil is high in monounsaturated fats, it is recommended by health professionals for inclusion in the diet. It contains a range of anti-oxidants, which are beneficial to coronary arteries, and on-going research indicates that these can reduce the incidence of breast and bowel cancers. Of course, excess consumption of any fat, including olive oil, is not desirable when controlling body weight, although research shows that the fatty acids contained in olive oil are metabolized by the body more readily than those found in other fats and oils.

OTHER FATS AND OILS

There are other fats that are traditionally used in the region: pork fat or lard in Spain, southern France and Italy; goose fat in the Languedoc; tail fat from the special fat-tailed sheep in the Maghreb; clarified butter in the Maghreb and the Levant; and butter in southern France, Malta, Cyprus, Turkey and Greece.

In Greek cooking, butter has more recently been replaced by a product called fytini, which was initially made from an olive oil base with sheep's milk butter giving the flavor without the high cost of pure butter. Unfortunately, fytini is now made with cottonseed oil, and palm oil which is twice as high in saturated fats as butter. I believe that this is a contributing factor in

toppling Greeks from international first place ranking with regard to longevity.

The following oils are also produced and used in the Mediterranean region.

Cottonseed oil: Produced in Egypt as a by-product of cotton-growing, it is refined and used for frying. Outside Egypt, cottonseed oil is not readily available for culinary use, but can be a component in vegetable oil blends and margarines. It is predominantly polyunsaturated, but it does not break down as quickly as other polyunsaturates when subjected to high heat.

Grapeseed oil: Extracted from grape seeds, it is a by-product of wine production in France and Italy, and is widely exported. It is used more widely as a salad and cooking oil outside the region, as it is considered to be healthy, particularly if cold-pressed. Although predominantly polyunsaturated, it is excellent for deep-frying.

Hazelnut oil: Produced in France, hazelnut oil is used in salad dressings and occasionally in cooking, where the nutty flavor complements the food. It is a monounsaturated oil.

Maize (corn) oil: Produced in Cyprus and Egypt but not used a great deal elsewhere, it is predominantly polyunsaturated.

Safflower oil: Produced in Spain and Turkey for local use and export, the safflower and its oil has been known in the region since ancient times (see saffron, page 20). The oil is polyunsaturated.

Sunflower oil: Because of its lower cost, sunflower oil is produced in many countries of the Mediterranean for local use. It is polyunsaturated, and therefore is not a good oil for high-temperature deep-frying as it breaks down quickly, and should only be used once. A plant of the New World, the sunflower's introduction to the Mediterranean has been recent; one probable reason being the perceived health benefits of polyunsaturated oils although experts now recommend monounsaturated oils such as olive oil.

Walnut oil: Produced in France, walnut oil is often used in salad dressings in place of olive oil, and occasionally in cooking, when its distinctive nutty flavor is desired. It is predominantly polyunsaturated.

Clarified butter: This is pure butter fat with water and milk solids removed. Ghee, refined butter fat, is a suitable substitute providing the pack also states that it is clarified butter; in some countries where food laws are not so stringent, ghee can contain other fats. It is particularly popular in the Levant for general cooking purposes, where it is known as samneh, not to be confused with the Maghreb smen. When using fillo pastry, clarified butter is preferred as the milk solids present in standard butter can cause dark patches on the cooked pastry, spoiling its appearance.

Either salted or unsalted butter can be clarified as the salt is effectively removed in the froth and sediment. Because the milk solids are removed, clarified butter has a higher smoke point, making it more suitable for frying.

To clarify butter: Cut up butter, place in a pan and melt over medium-low heat; excessive heating brings a lot of froth to the surface and should be avoided. Remove from heat and let stand for a few minutes. Skim any froth from the top and pour off the clear oil into a container, leaving the milky sediment behind.

Smen: In the Maghreb, clarified butter is left to simmer on low heat for about 40 minutes, with the milk solids browning lightly. Three teaspoons of coarse salt is placed in a cheesecloth (muslin)-lined strainer for every 8 oz (250 g) butter and the hot oil poured through this to salt it slightly. It is stored in a sealed container in the refrigerator. Smen can be quite strong and cheesy in aroma and is an acquired taste. Some versions are flavored with various herbs, and aged in earthenware jars. It is used to flavor couscous. Ordinary salted butter or clarified butter can be used in place of smen.

OLIVES

One of the most popular and simple appetizers is the olive, used as a food since ancient times. Archaeological evidence suggests that the Minoans of Crete ate olives around 1400BC, perhaps sooner, and the Phoenicians around 1200BC. Just how it was discovered that such a bitter fruit could be made palatable by soaking in brine remains a mystery; one can only guess, but it was probably more by accident than by design.

Brine-cured black or green olives are available, with the latter also sold stuffed with pimiento, anchovies or almonds. Black olives vary from the small, Niçoise olives of France, brownish-black and packed in olive oil, to the giant purple-black, brine-packed olives. Kalamata olives, oval in shape and with slits cut into them, are considered

the tastiest of all; they are pickled in a brine and red wine vinegar solution. There are also the shrivelled black olives, picked when totally ripe and cured with salt only, giving them a wrinkled appearance and intense flavor.

When olives are used in cooking, green olives in particular need to be blanched in boiling water for 1 to 2 minutes to remove excess salt. Black olives usually only require rinsing, unless very

salty; however, two or three blanchings do make the olive sweeter for inclusion in some recipes. Marinated olives are also available, flavored with various herbs, spices and orange or lemon rind — see page 34 for recipes.

ONIONS

Native to Central Asia, the first records of the cultivation of onions occur in Sumerian texts, written about 2400BC. Onions (*Allium cepa*) and other members of the genus Allium such as garlic and leeks were known in the Mediterranean, specifically Egypt, about 3000BC. It is through ancient Egyptian art that its presence in that region can be confirmed. Along with garlic, onions were essential food for the slaves building Egypt's pyramids, as it was believed that they increased strength. Even the soldiers of ancient

Rome were given a daily ration of onions for the same reason. Today, the onion is the most widely used vegetable in the world.

Unless otherwise specified, onions used in recipes in this book refer to dry brown or yellow onions (also known as Spanish onions in some countries). Where necessary, I specify either the white onion or the purple onion when a mild or sweet flavor is required. The latter is also known as the red or Italian onion, and erroneously as a Spanish onion in some regions.

Recipes are also specific about warming the oil, adding the onion and cooking it gently. Gentle cooking develops the flavorsome oils and softens the onion; with long, slow cooking, the sugar content of the onion caramelizes.

If you are particularly sensitive to onions, keep two or three in the refrigerator, and replace as they are used. Chilling prevents the irritating "fumes" from dissipating.

Scallions: There is quite a lot of confusion about this vegetable which is variously known as a spring onion and green onion in some regions, and erroneously as an eschalot or shallot in others (see below). The type used in these recipes is the fresh, green, immature onion, long and slender, white at the root, and gradually shading to green. When preparing, include some of the green top, unless the white part only is specified. These onions become bulbous at the end (pearl onions) when mature and the green tops become coarse — use the bulbs only in place of dry onions when small, whole onions are required.

Leeks: Probably originating in the Eastern Mediterranean or the Near East, as well as islands of the mid-Atlantic, England and Wales, leeks have been used as a food from ancient times. The cultivated leek is grown in furrows with the soil drawn up around the base to exclude light and keep it white. To prepare leeks for cooking, it is necessary to halve the trimmed leek lengthwise, leaving the root in place, then wash thoroughly between the leaves to remove all traces of soil. Trim off root after washing and complete preparation according to recipe.

Shallots: Native to the eastern Mediterranean, shallots were more appreciated in that region in earlier times than they are today. The botanical name, *Allium ascalonicum*, is a clue to its origins in the Philistine city of Ascalon. Because the ascalonicum onion was regarded as good for sauces, French knights carried it back to France from the Crusades. In some countries, it is still referred to as a French shallot. Favored for its special flavor — a cross between onion and garlic — it is used in southern France, but not elsewhere in the region, except by professional chefs. The shallot is a small, hard, reddish-brown-skinned onion which grows in clusters, something like garlic, but with larger cloves. The papery skin can be difficult to remove; if so, cover with boiling water and leave 1 minute — the skins then slip off easily.

GARLIC

This aromatic bulb is believed to be native to Central Asia, with its use probably dating back before recorded history. Certainly the ancient world knew it well, with mention of it in Sumerian texts, dating from before 2300BC. It has been claimed to have many therapeutic properties, amongst them preventing colds, lowering high blood pressure, curing rheumatism and as an antiseptic. Attributed with antibacterial qualities, during World War I its juice was placed on sterile wound dressings to prevent infection; we now know that garlic contains two sulphur compounds, which explains its antibiotic qualities. Experiments also suggest that it can increase the beneficial HDL-cholesterol in the blood, while decreasing LDL-cholesterol, which makes garlic a sensible part of a healthy heart diet.

The use of garlic is a major characteristic of Mediterranean cooking, and has been identified as one of the elements of the diet that could account for the lower incidence of heart disease in the region. Unfortunately, it was shunned by the uninitiated for many years because of its assertive flavor and odor, but it is now one of the most widely-used aromatics, and popular natural health remedies, often in the form of odor-free capsules.

There are two major types of garlic readily available — the white-skinned, mildly-flavored bulbs, and the stronger purple-skinned ones, often called Italian garlic and preferred in the Mediterranean.

The flavor of garlic is strong when raw, pleasantly aromatic if gently heated in oil for a short while, more assertive if lightly browned, and quite strong if allowed to become very brown.

Green garlic or garlic shoots are immature garlic that have not formed bulbs and resemble small leeks. They have a fresh, pungent flavor. Recently appearing in specialized markets outside the Mediterranean, green garlic is only used occasionally in Mediterranean cooking, mainly in Spain where ajos tiernos, as they are called, are used during their brief season to flavor tortilla (see page 40).

Whole bulbs of garlic are roasted in Provence, and used with meats, especially roast lamb, and vegetables. The resultant puree from roasted garlic is creamy and sweet, without the assertiveness of raw or lightly fried garlic. Toss roasted garlic through steamed green beans, boiled young beets (beetroot) or boiled new potatoes with olive oil, or mix into potato puree. It is also good tossed through hot pasta with olive oil and pepper or spread onto toasted slices of baguette.

To roast garlic: New season's garlic should be used, without shoots developing in the cloves. Simply rub whole bulbs with olive oil, wrap in foil and roast for 45 minutes in a moderate oven. Slice off the root end, place on a plate and press bulb with a fork to squeeze out the soft garlic.

Using garlic: If garlic is to be pressed (crushed), chopped or merely bruised, the cloves can be easily peeled by placing the flat of a heavy kitchen knife on the clove and pressing with the heel of your hand. The skin then slips off easily. If cloves need to be left intact, cut the top of the clove and pull off the papery skin, trimming the base. For pressed (crushed) garlic, use a garlic press, or chop roughly, sprinkle with a little salt and work into a paste with the tip of a knife or the tines of a fork. Traditionalists would use a pestle and mortar.

Always choose firm garlic bulbs with no sign of softness. Store in a cool, dark place for up to 8 weeks, longer for the purple-skinned variety.

Eating raw garlic (which features in many Mediterranean sauces, such as aioli) can result in the dreaded "garlic breath". Long ago, a Greek singer gave me her solution: before eating a dish laden with raw garlic, swallow a whole garlic clove. Take a small clove from the center of the knob, about the size of a large vitamin pill, peel it without cutting or crushing the clove, carefully trim the rough end, and swallow with a gulp of water. It works! Chewing fresh parsley afterwards is another antidote.

TOMATOES

Mediterranean cooking without tomato? Not all that long ago, that was the case, but Christopher Columbus and the Spanish Conquistadors changed all that, and more. The tomato as we know it — named tomate by the Spaniards from the Nahuatl tomatl — is extensively used today, yet is a relative newcomer to the kitchens of the region, and to the world in general, even North America.

The Spaniards brought back the tomato from the New World, where it was found growing wild in Aztec Mexico and Peru. Apparently natives of Peru used the fruit, but from all accounts the somewhat bitter flavor and perishability were not conducive to cultivating the plant. However, in Aztec Mexico it was cultivated incidentally; as a weed growing in the fields, it benefited from the cultivation of maize, and developed into a palatable food plant. It was used with chilies to add flavor to beans and maize cakes.

The first tomatoes taken to the Old World were yellow, and named pomo d'oro (apple of gold) by the Italians. Both the small, round or pear-shaped yellow tomato and the cherry tomato are grown today, the closest relatives to the wild tomatoes of South America.

In Spain, and in Italy where it made its appearance early in the sixteenth century, the tomato was first grown as an ornamental plant; recognised as belonging to the nightshade family, it was thought to be poisonous (in fact, the stems and leaves are noxious). When the tomato was eventually bred into an acceptable food item, it was subject to long cooking in the belief that this was necessary to make the fruit safe for eating, a practice that continued into the mid-nineteenth century in many countries.

The Italians are credited with breeding the tomato away from the original, producing red, pear-shaped fruit; the round, fluted variety followed. By the end of the eighteenth century, the tomato was well-established in Italian and Spanish kitchens, and had spread to other Mediterranean countries, France and Northern Europe. Early in the nineteenth century, the British and North Americans cast aside their suspicions and grew it in their kitchen gardens.

Fresh tomatoes: Because of today's marketing methods, and the need to have tomatoes capable of withstanding the rigors of harvesting and travel to the market place, flavorsome, juicy tomatoes are not so easy to come by. Skins have to be tougher, the flesh firmer, and the fruit is picked before it ripens.

Vine-ripened tomatoes are recommended where the flavor of the tomato is important to a particular recipe, although flavorsome tomatoes are available during the summer months.

Plum (egg-shaped) tomatoes are readily available and these are also recommended for certain recipes because they are fleshier with fewer seeds, and have good flavor.

Growing your own, of course, solves such problems as there are many cultivars from which to choose.

When tomatoes are purchased, ripen them at room temperature if necessary, stem side down, then store in the refrigerator for up to 1 week. Bring to room temperature if the tomato is to be eaten raw, so that the flavor is at its best. Out of season, good quality canned tomatoes should be used in place of fresh tomatoes in cooking.

Peeling and seeding: Place tomatoes in a bowl, cover with boiling water and let stand 30 seconds. Drain and cover with cold water. Drain and pull off the skin. To seed, halve crosswise and either squeeze out seeds or flick out with a small spoon.

Canned tomatoes: These are recommended in many recipes because they are convenient and have been picked and canned at their peak. The varieties grown for canning are often different to those available fresh. As canneries are usually in close proximity to tomato crops, portability is not a major factor in choosing the species to be cultivated, but flavor usually is.

Look for tomatoes canned in Italy, especially the San Marzano plum tomatoes (with a nipple on the end), but do try those grown in your region as major canneries endeavor to emulate the Italian tomatoes. The best canned tomatoes are always packed in tomato juice, which should be incorporated into the dish being prepared.

Tomato paste: The Italians were probably the first to find that extracting the pulp and removing most of the moisture was a way to have a tomato concentrate year-round. Available in jars, cans or tubes, tomato paste, or puree as it is also known in the UK, can accentuate the tomato flavor of a dish, even though the flavor of the paste is different to that of fresh tomato. Add a little sugar when using the paste.

Passata: Italians also like to prepare a fresher-tasting tomato puree, with a consistency somewhere between tomato paste and tomato juice. Fresh tomatoes are cooked to a pulp — uncovered so that excess moisture is evaporated — then put through a food mill or sieve to separate pulp from seeds and skins. Passata is available in bottles, usually flavored with basil or garlic and a little salt, but canned tomato puree is a convenient substitute for both the bottled passata or the home-made version.

Sun-dried tomatoes: Italian in origin, sun-dried tomatoes are just that, and can be packed in oil with or without flavorings. They are also sold in dried form; soak these briefly in boiling water until softened, drain and press between paper towels to remove excess moisture, then pack in olive oil with flavorings (e.g. garlic, basil, oregano, peppercorns) and refrigerate until required. Sun-dried tomatoes are chewy and have an intense tomato flavor. They can be served as an antipasto; used in focaccia or sandwich fillings; chopped or pureed and added to prepared dishes such as salads, pasta or pizza.

CUCUMBERS

The cucumber is believed to have been cultivated in the Burma-Thailand region about 9750BC, according to the carbon-dating of seeds found in a cave in 1970. Over such a long period, it had time to spread east and west. It is mentioned as a food crop in Sumerian texts of about 2400BC, and its entry into the Mediterranean area could well have occurred around the same period. Certainly the ancient Romans enjoyed the cucumber, and wrote about it. Crisp, cool cucumbers are now essential to many Mediterranean cold dishes, especially salads.

The standard green cucumber available in most markets is only worth using if it is young, slender and very firm. How I detest those large, green monstrosities — bigger is not better! To make them palatable, the seeds must be scooped out. To my taste, the small seeds of a well-chosen cucumber add a little extra flavor.

I like to use the small, tender-skinned, vivid green cucumber which goes under various names in various regions — Lebanese, European, Greek, Cypriot and burpless. Again, don't go for the largest and make sure they are firm.

The gherkin or pickling cucumber is small and always firm and crisp, but it is only available in summer. It can be used like other cucumbers, except the skin is thick and requires peeling.

The other variety I like, because it keeps a little longer in the refrigerator, is the hot-house, English or telegraph cucumber — long and slender, slightly to moderately ridged, with very few seeds. This is similar to the long variety grown in the Mediterranean, slightly curved or hooked on the end, and known as the Italian cucumber. In general, leave the skin on cucumber providing it is tender and not waxed, as it gives an extra crispness, besides containing most of the vitamins. Avoid scooping out the seeds, but do so if you find the cucumber is more mature than you desire.

EGGPLANT
Native to South East Asia, probably India, the eggplant or aubergine was used in Persia in ancient times. With the expansion of the Persian Empire, its use extended westwards to Asia Minor and south to Egypt. Well-established in the region of today's Near and Middle East, history is not clear who actually spread its use throughout the Mediterranean. It could have been through the expansion of the Roman and Byzantine Empires — more likely the later, as eggplant was a favored food in Constantinople. Because the Arabs had such a passion for eggplant, they would certainly have introduced it into North Africa, Spain, parts of Italy and Sicily from about 660AD. Nevertheless, the eggplant is one of the most important vegetables in Mediterranean cooking.

The oval or globe eggplant is widely used, but the long, slender variety, also known as Japanese eggplant, is recommended as it is regarded as sweeter than its fat relative. Tiny eggplants, purple, white or striated, are used for making pickles and even sweet preserves in Greek cooking.

The large eggplant needs to be salted to dégorge any bitter juices. The slender or small varieties do not require this treatment. Dégorging does not prevent eggplant from soaking up oil during cooking; it will do so whether salted or not. Broiling (grilling) eggplant, after lightly brushing the slices with oil, is a better alternative to frying if you find the oiliness of eggplant dishes not to your taste.

When choosing eggplant, check that there are no holes in the skin — look under the green calyx as well, just to be certain that no grub has set up house in it. The eggplant should feel heavy in relation to its size, smooth, firm and blemish-free. Store in the vegetable compartment of the refrigerator for up to 1 week.

PEPPERS AND CHILIES
We have Columbus to thank for many things, not the least of which is confusing us about the word "pepper". When the Caribbean Indians flavored his food with a hot spice, he named it "pimienta", Spanish for the spice "pepper". The name remained for the chilies and other peppers of the genus Capsicum that he took back to Spain. The sweet bell peppers became known as "pimiento" in Spanish; pulverized, dried red peppers are "pimenton dulce" or "pimenton piquante", depending on whether they are sweet or hot. The English word "chili" (or "chilli") is derived from the Latin-American Spanish "chile", which in turn comes from the Nahuatl "chili". In Spain, hot red chilies are known as "guindillas".

All peppers and chilies, of which there are some 200 varieties, are of the genus Capsicum. There is a great range of shapes and colors, and a varying degree of pungency, from sweet to extremely hot. The sweet and mild varieties are widely used in Mediterranean cooking, with chilies popular in Spain, North Africa (Tunisia in particular), and southern Italy (especially in Basilicata where dried chilies are steeped in olive oil to make the fiery olio santo or holy oil, which is used as a condiment).

Sweet peppers can be bell-shaped and fleshy (the bell pepper or capsicum), with colors ranging from green (unripe) to red (ripe) or can be yellow or purple-black. They can also be long, tapering, slightly curved and less fleshy and known simply as sweet green pepper, green banana pepper or bull's horn. Multi-colored long, mild peppers are usually used for pickles. In southern France, a small red, heart-shaped pepper, about 3 to 4 inches (8 to 10 cm) long and medium-hot in flavor, is also used. However, the bell pepper is the variety of pepper most favored in cooking, in particular for roasting.

Identifying specific peppers and chilies is a daunting task, as each particular country outside the region has its own range of readily-available fresh and dried peppers and chilies. Finding the romesco pepper used in Catalan is almost impossible; it is a small, round dark red pepper, full of flavor and with a touch of heat. The nearest equivalent in Mexican chilies would be the fresh poblano (ancho when dried).

For this reason, the recipes are quite basic in directing which peppers and chilies to use, but the results are more than acceptable. While dried whole chilies are not usually given, these can be used as a substitute if fresh are not available; cover with water, bring to boil and simmer for 5 minutes. Let steep until very soft. Drain and remove stems and seeds before using.

Cayenne pepper, made from various red chilies, is specified in recipes in this book as it is a universally known ingredient. Ground chili pepper made entirely from hot chilies can be used instead, providing it contains no other spices.

Spanish paprika can be sweet and a little lighter in color than Hungarian paprika, or it can be quite pungent; it is used widely in the Maghreb. In Turkey a ground red pepper with a mild pungency is used. For recipes in this book, the desired flavor has been taken into account and a hot ingredient such as cayenne pepper has been added where applicable; when paprika is needed, use the readily available Hungarian variety.

HERBS OF THE MEDITERRANEAN

The heady fragrance of dew-kissed wild herbs warmed by the sun is one of the unforgettable smells of morning in the fertile, rural regions of the Mediterranean. We tend to forget that the region is home to most of our culinary herbs, so far have they travelled over time, so valuable are they to the kitchens of the world. All the herbs listed are native to the Mediterranean or the nearby Middle East with few exceptions, and have been used for culinary and medicinal purposes since ancient times.

While it is ideal to grow your own, most fresh herbs purchased at the markets can be stored in the refrigerator, either in a container of water with a plastic bag fitted loosely over the top to prevent the leaves from drying out, or wrapped in paper towels and stored in a plastic bag.

Anise: Native to the Middle East and known in ancient Egypt, Greece and Rome. The seed, aniseed, is preferred for use, especially as a digestive. Nowadays, aniseed is used to flavor liqueurs of the region, such as the pastis of Provence, Galliano and anisette of Italy, the ouzo of Greece and the raki and arrack of the Levant. The seed is also used in the cakes, sweet breads and confections of the Maghreb, as well as added to some soups and spice mixes for fish and game.

Basil: Native to India and a member of the mint family. Basil is an essential ingredient in Italian and southern French cooking, especially for the pesto of Genoa and its French counterpart, pistou, and for tomatoes with which it has a special affinity.

Sweet basil, with its large, fleshy leaves, is the most widely available in the marketplace, but according to herb nurserymen, it is the smaller-leafed bush basil Italians buy for their kitchen gardens, as it is considered better in flavor. Ask for the bush basil selected by Italian clients as there are a few varieties of bush basil available. The particular cultivar that is most popular is known in Italy as piccolo fino verde. Bush basil is also the type grown in almost every Greek household, rarely for cooking, but for its perfume and its religious significance.

To keep cut basil, trim the ends of the stems with a sharp knife and stand in a container of water in the kitchen — refrigeration will turn the leaves black unless used within 2 to 3 days.

Bay leaves: The leaves of the bay laurel tree are used in all the countries on the northern side of the Mediterranean, and on most islands. Fresh or dried, they are added to soups, meat, poultry, game and seafoods, marinades and preserves and are essential in bouquet garni (see page 17).

Borage: While native to the Middle East, borage is not used in that part of the Mediterranean, but in France it is finely chopped and added to salads, and fresh leaves are used to flavor herb teas. Borage also grows all over Italy where it is used as a flavoring and as a vegetable, either cooked like spinach or the leaves dipped in batter and fried. Ligurians appreciate its cucumber-like flavor and use it frequently with vegetables, in soups and worked into fresh pasta (the pansotti recipe on page 212 often includes borage according to the whim of the cook).

Bouquet garni: A bunch of flavoring herbs, usually comprising 2 sprigs each parsley and thyme, 1 bay leaf, and the leafy top of a celery stalk (rib), tied together. Marjoram sprigs are sometimes added. Dried bouquets garnis are also available, tied in little cheesecloth (muslin) bags, but fresh herbs should be used when possible.

Caraway: While native to Europe, caraway is also believed to be native to North Africa, where the seeds are used in spice blends, especially in Tunisia. It is not used elsewhere in the region.

Chamomile: Native to Europe, chamomile grows wild from Spain to Turkey. In all these countries, the flower heads are harvested and dried for making tea, claimed to have relaxing qualities and a soothing effect on digestion. The Spanish word for chamomile tea is manzanilla, which is also the name of a light, dry sherry, and a type of small black olive — be warned!

Chervil: Much loved in southern French cooking, especially as a salad herb, chervil is an essential ingredient of fines herbes (used generally in French cuisine), together with chives, tarragon and parsley. You may have to grow this herb yourself as it is not readily available in markets.

Chives: Believed to be native to Britain, chives were known in the Mediterranean prior to Christian times. Used in French cuisine, and essential for fines herbes, they are occasionally added to salads and used as garnish in modern Mediterranean cooking.

Coriander: The naming of this plant could be enough to put off the uninitiated, as coriander is derived from the Greek koreos for "bug"; the ancient Greeks thought the leaves and green seeds had a smell similar to crushed bugs, and there are some who might agree. A more acceptable description of the aroma of the leaves is a combination of lemon zest and sage.

The leaves are widely used in the cooking of the Maghreb and Cyprus, but not used elsewhere in the region. Strangely, it is rarely used in Spain (but adored in Portugal) yet it was probably the Spaniards who introduced coriander into the New World, where it has become an important herb in Mexican cooking. The alternative name, cilantro, is from the Spanish.

Coriander seeds, with their warm, spicy fragrance, are used in North Africa (especially in spice blends), Cyprus and the Levant, but not used elsewhere in the region.

Dill: Popular in Greece, Cyprus and Turkey, especially for flavoring spinach dishes, lamb or kid fricasees (with egg and lemon sauce) or adding to globe artichokes, broad beans, yogurt salads and carrot dishes.

Fennel: Popular from southern France to Turkey, some of the islands and Tunisia, fennel is rarely used elsewhere. Both the leaves and the seeds are used in France and parts of Italy, especially for fish dishes, with dried fennel stalks either placed under fish when baking it, used to flambé fish, especially sea bass, and sometimes added to fish soups. In Tunisia, the feathery leaves are used with fish, and a large quantity is used in a regional herb couscous; seeds are added to Tunisian spice mixes.

Herbes de Provence: A mixture of dried herbs and other aromatics grown in Provence, it usually contains dried rosemary, thyme, bay leaves, summer savory, marjoram and lavender flowers. It is often available in gourmet food stores packed in little clay pots or cellophane bags. Use this combination to flavor grilled or broiled fish, meats, poultry, and add to marinades and vegetable dishes.

Lavender: The flowers of the variety known as English lavender (even though all lavenders are native to the Mediterranean) are dried and used as a culinary herb, especially in herbes de provence. Also grown in Grasse for the perfume industry, a natural by-product is lavender honey which is used in Provençal desserts.

Marjoram: Popular in southern France and Italy, marjoram is little used elsewhere, except as a substitute for rigani (see the entry on page 18).

Mint: Fresh or dried mint is widely used in the cooking of the Levant, with spearmint the favored variety. It is also used in Greece, Cyprus and North Africa, but little used elsewhere. In North African countries, from Morocco to Lybia, mint tea is a popular beverage.

Oregano: While closely related to marjoram, the flavor of oregano is different. Use fresh if possible as it is superior to dried and is much used in Italian cooking, although dried oregano is used out of season.

Parsley: Most of the Mediterranean countries use flat-leaf parsley, also known as Italian and continental parsley. Its flavor is superior to the curled parsley, which is only suitable for garnish; However, if the curled variety is your only option, use a good portion of the finer stalks in cooking and add the thick stalks to a bouquet garni.

Rigani: This is actually wild marjoram, *Origanum heracleoticum*, Greece's very special herb. It grows wild and sprigs with flower heads are always dried for use as the flavor is better. It has a different taste to dried oregano, which should not be substituted if rigani is not available. Far better to use dried marjoram with a tiny pinch of dried sage to add the desired pungency. Dried rigani is available at Greek markets. Crumble to a coarse powder and sprinkle on grilled or roast meats and fish before cooking.

Rosemary: Used from France to Greece, and on many of the islands, rosemary is always used fresh. Dried rosemary is a poor substitute; if you have to use it, make sure it is not stale.

Sage: This herb is very popular in Italian and French cooking and used occasionally in Greek dishes. Use dried sage (powdered or crushed leaves) with care as it far more pungent than the fresh herb. Dried leaves are widely used for sage tea in Greece and Cyprus.

Savory: Both the summer and winter savory are widely used in the cooking of Provence, either fresh or dried. Savory has a sharp, hot flavor and it can be used as a substitute for pepper. As it is difficult to purchase fresh savory of either type, use the dried, ground herb.

Sorrel: The variety known as French sorrel is native to southern France, where it also grows wild. It has an acidy, lemon-like flavor and is a little bitter, making it a popular addition to mixed salad greens. It is used to make sorrel sauce and soup, and to flavor some Provençal fish soups. As sorrel is also a northern European herb, its use has entered Israeli cooking in the form of a soup.

Tarragon: The variety known as French tarragon is used in southern France to flavor sauces, vinegar, poultry and salads, and included in fines herbes. Other varieties are not suitable; if the fresh herb is not available, use dried French tarragon.

Thyme: Popular from southern France across to Greece and on most islands, thyme is used fresh as well as dried for winter. Where wild thyme is in profusion, thyme-flavored honey is produced.

OTHER FLAVORINGS

Allspice: This is the berry of a tree native to Central America and the West Indies. Columbus was the first to write about it in his journal, and the Spaniards took it back to the Old World. The spice is also known as pimento, which causes some confusion with pimiento, the English (via Spanish) name for the preserved sweet red pepper. With a flavor of cinnamon, nutmeg and cloves, it is often used in place of spice mixes used in Arabic and Turkish cooking.

Capers: These are the tiny buds of *Capparis spinosa*, native to barren areas of the Mediterranean where they thrive in the dry conditions. They have been used in the region since ancient times. Caperberries are a recently "discovered" food outside the region. These are the seed pods formed after the flower dies. Both pods and seeds are left to wilt in the air, then pickled in a strong, lightly salted white wine vinegar.

Cinnamon: Native to Sri Lanka, cinnamon is one of the most-used spices in Mediterranean cooking, added to both savory and sweet dishes. The sticks or quills are used whole in recipes in this book unless otherwise specified; the usual size is 2 inches (8 cm) long. Ground cinnamon can vary in flavor as some manufacturers include cassia, *Cinnamomum cassia,* in the blend.

Citron: The fruit of *Citrus medica*, native to China, is believed to have been introduced into the Mediterranean about 500BC. It is important in the Jewish festival of Sukhot, grows in Greece where it is made into a preserve and a liqueur, and in Sicily where it is prepared as candied or glacé citron peel. It is also grown for candying in southern France and in Corsica where it is also used in a liqueur called cedratine.

Juniper: These ripe berries have a particular affinity to game, and are used in stuffings or sauces for game birds, in pâtés and occasionally in stews of pork, venison or veal. Juniper grows wild in the mountainous regions of southeastern France and Corsica, and is used in Corsica, Provence and Languedoc.

Orange flower water: Distilled from orange blossoms, this fragrant liquid is used to flavor sweets and pastries. The strength varies from mild to strong, so use carefully or dilute with water. Orange flower water is readily available at Middle Eastern and gourmet food stores.

Rose water: Distilled from fragrant rose petals, it is used in a similar way to orange flower water (see earlier entry).

Saffron: The stamens of the purple crocus flower have become the world's most expensive spice; 5,000 flowers are needed to yield one ounce of dried saffron, which is available in threads or powdered. Threads are usually pounded in a mortar then soaked in hot water before adding to dishes. In the Maghreb, imitation saffron powder or turmeric is often added for color, as the delicate flavor of saffron could be lost among stronger flavors. In Turkey, the dried deep orange petals of the safflower, known as haspir, are used as a saffron substitute for the color rather than flavor; also known as saffron thistle, Mexican saffron and bastard saffron outside the region.

SHELLFISH

Shellfish such as clams, cockles or mussels should be alive before cooking. They close tight when being handled and open up when cooked. As a general rule, throw out any that do not close while handling (it indicates they are dead). Also discard any that do not open after cooking as this indicates they were dead before being cooked.

Clams and cockles: Dissolve a small handful of rough salt in a bucket of cold water. If the shellfish are very sandy, place a round cake rack in the base of the bucket so there is less chance of sediment re-entering the shells. Add shellfish and leave for several hours to allow them to open and disgorge any sand or grit. Lift them out carefully so that the sediment is not stirred up — the shells close as soon as they are handled, taking in any sand that might be disturbed in the water. They can be stored in the water in a cool place (but not the refrigerator), for 3 to 4 days until required for use — this is recommended if the shells are very sandy. Scrub if necessary before cooking.

Mussels: These are not usually sandy, but if necessary treat and store using the method described above. Just before cooking, scrub if necessary. Scrape mussel shells to clean off any marine growth, and tug off beards by pulling them towards the pointed end of the shell.

Squid: Also called calamari, squid is so popular that prepared rings are readily available. Use these if they are all you can obtain, but freshly prepared squid is much tastier. In addition to the rings (cut from the bodies), you will have the tentacles, which curl up into rosette shapes when cooked, adding interest to the finished dish.

Preparation: Pull head and attached tentacles gently from the body, drawing out the gut. Pull out transparent quill and discard. Clean and rinse the body. Cut off tentacles just below the head, and push out beak located where the tentacles join. Discard head and entrails. Cut the two long feelers to remove the scaly ends and make them the same length as the tentacles. If squid is large, tentacles can be divided into sections. Pull off fine skin covering body, if desired; it can be left on. Cut off flaps and cut into strips. Slice body into rings. If the body is to be stuffed, leave flaps on. Rinse prepared squid and drain well.

Cuttlefish: The ink from the cuttlefish, from which the dye sepia was once obtained, is used in the Veneto for risotto nero, and is now used to color and flavor fresh pasta. In Greece and Spain, the cuttlefish is stewed in its own ink. Because chefs have "discovered" the pleasant peppery flavor of cuttlefish ink, it is available at specialty markets in small plastic pouches (which could account for the ink missing from your purchase of fresh cuttlefish).

Preparation: Slit open the body on the soft side, taking care not to rupture the ink sac if it is intact (keep the ink sac aside if intact as it can be used in cooking; usually contents of one or two sacs is sufficient for a dish). Lift out gut with head and tentacles and remove cuttlebone. Cut tentacles from head, just below the eyes, and remove beak. Pull skin from body and cut body pieces into strips, or leave whole. Rinse and drain.

Octopus: Similar to squid preparation, except that the body does not contain any quill or cartilage. Separate tentacles into pairs or according to recipes. For baby octopus, cut off the head and body below the eyes and discard it, as the body can be rather chewy. Push out and remove beak located in the center of the tentacles. Large octopus is usually tenderized before being sold.

NUTS AND SEEDS

The hunter-gatherer of pre-recorded history used wild nuts as a food, and valued them for their keeping qualities. Through recorded food history, nuts have been used, not only as a food, but for the oil that could be extracted from them. In recent times, nuts in the Western diet have been primarily a snack food, with the majority of cookery uses confined to baking. Not so in the Mediterranean where nuts have always been more highly regarded. They were, and still are, used to thicken sauces and add texture and interest to savory dishes, as well as being widely used in cakes, cookies and pastries. With the trend to more natural foods in our diets, nuts are regaining importance as a food in their own right, especially for those who eschew animal products.

All unsalted nuts need careful storage because of their high oil content. If used frequently, store in a cool, dry place in a sealed container; for longer storage, pack in plastic bags and refrigerate to prevent rancidity. The exception is fresh chestnuts which are perishable; they can only be stored in a cool place for 3 to 4 days, or refrigerated in a sealed container for up to 1 week.

Almonds: Native to the Near East, the almond tree gradually spread westwards and the nuts were used in Crete from about 3500BC. However, it was the Arabs who, totally captivated by the almond's attributes, ardently carried it as far west as Morocco and Spain and points in between, late in the fifth century. Today it is the most widely used nut in the Mediterranean. Almonds are classified as sweet or bitter; the sweet almond is the type used, while the bitter almond is actually the kernel of the apricot, used in the commercial manufacture of Italian amaretti (macaroon-style cookies) and amaretto liqueur. As the bitter almond contains prussic acid, it requires heat treatment to make it safe to eat in quantity.

You can buy almonds shelled, blanched, flaked, slivered and ground (almond meal), although nuts in the shell, or shelled but unblanched, are recommended as they keep better.

To blanch: Pour boiling water on almonds, let stand 2 to 3 minutes, drain, rinse with cold water and slip off the skins. Dry in a cloth. If they appear soft, dry further in a slow oven, especially if they are to be ground in a food processor.

Pistachio nuts: Native to Western Asia and the Mediterranean, we know the pistachio nut has definitely been used as a food since at least 6750BC, thanks to the carbon dating of remains found in a cave in northeastern Iraq. The pistachio tree was grown in the Hanging Gardens of Babylon; the Persians of antiquity adored it. It has been said that the pistachio was so highly regarded by Darius the Great of Persia, that he instructed his satraps to plant the tree in their satrapies in the Persian Empire, which extended to northern Greece. Perhaps long cultivation had improved the Persian variety, which could add credence to the story. Certainly the Persians were responsible in using the pistachios in savory sauces and sweets, a practice copied and spread by the Arabs.

For cooking, unsalted pistachios in the shell are plumper and fresher-tasting; the shells are easily prised apart to extract the kernel. Otherwise purchase shelled, unsalted pistachios.

To blanch: Recipes in this book use chopped or ground pistachios, and while it is preferrable to blanch them, this is time-consuming. Besides, the fine skins do add to fiber intake. Blanching, however, does intensify the green color of the nut, and is recommended in some recipes. Place the shelled nuts in a bowl, cover with boiling water and leave for 2 to 3 minutes, drain, rinse with cold water and tear off skins.

Hazelnuts: Also known as cobnuts and filberts, hazelnuts are native to the temperate zones of Europe and America. They are particularly popular in Turkish cookery and are widely used for baking and desserts throughout the region.

To skin: Place hazelnuts in a baking dish and heat in moderate oven for 5 to 6 minutes until skins begin to split; if required toasted, heat for a further 5 to 6 minutes, stirring occasionally. Place in a rough cloth, twist cloth into a bundle and rub nuts together to loosen the skins. Pick out the skinned nuts; it does not matter if they are not completely skinned. Because it is difficult to remove all traces of skin, you can blanch hazelnuts, as you would almonds, if they are to be used in tarator (see page 120).

Walnuts: The various species of walnuts are native to a number of regions, including the Mediterranean, where the nut has been used for thousands of years. The light-skinned, yellow-brown Persian walnut is reputedly native to Persia, and it is this walnut that is preferred for Mediterranean cooking, not the black walnut. It is used in savory sauces in Turkey, Greece and Italy, as well as being used in cakes, cookies and pastries. Green walnuts, so immature that the shell inside the green husk has not hardened, are

used in Greece and Cyprus to make a preserve.

Try to purchase walnuts in the shell when in season, as their flavor is so much better; shell and store in the refrigerator (see page 21). Otherwise, purchase walnuts packed in cans; these are the preferred light variety.

Pine nuts: Also known as pignolia and pinon, the best pine nut comes from the stone or parasol pine native to the Mediterranean and has been used as a food from ancient times. It takes a tree 75 years before it begins to produce (the reason why production is so limited). The pine nut is a seed rather than a nut, extracted from the mature pine cones. Torpedo-shaped, it is delicate in flavor and widely used throughout the region. The triangular-shaped pine nut is stronger in flavor, is much less expensive than the Mediterranean pine nut, and comes from other species of pine trees native to other regions. These can be used in recipes as a substitute, as can slivered almonds.

Chestnuts: Besides growing in the wild, chestnuts are also cultivated in France, Italy, Greece and Turkey. The nuts are nutritious and low in fat, and have been an important food for the underprivileged for hundreds of years. During winter, chestnuts often replace potatoes in the diet and are added to soups and meat stews, and used in stuffings for poultry.

Fresh chestnuts appear from mid-fall (autumn) to mid-winter. They should be glossy and firm when pressed. Even if they yield slightly to pressure, they will still be good. Dull nuts with brittle shells should be avoided.

To shell: Cut a cross on the flat side of the shell of each nut if roasting over an open fire or barbecue. If it is to be used in cooking, cut a cross into flat side and cut completely around rim of nut between flat and rounded sides. Put prepared nuts in a saucepan and cover with cold water. Add 1 teaspoon salt per 1 lb (500 g) nuts — this helps to remove inner skin. Bring to boil, and boil 1 minute. Remove from heat but do not drain. Wearing rubber gloves, remove one chestnut at a time and strip off shell and inner skin. Any nuts which are difficult to skin may be returned to the pan and left to be skinned later — reheat if necessary. Use as directed in recipes.

To roast: Prepare chestnuts as described above and place in a large frying pan. Roast on an open fire or on barbecue until shells split open. Peel and eat while hot.

Tahini: Also known as tahina, this is an oily paste made from ground sesame seeds. Used in both savory and sweet dishes, it has a nutty taste, a little like peanut butter. The oil separates on standing, so stir well before using. Once a jar or can is opened, store in the refrigerator.

BREADS

Many of the recipes in this book give instructions to "serve with bread", as this is one of the most important elements of a Mediterranean meal. To list all the breads of the Mediterranean would fill a book, as there are literally hundreds of different types. With the range available today, it is easy to complete a Mediterranean-style meal with a suitable bread. You could use almost any bread except for pre-sliced, packaged white bread or Northern European breads using rye flour. White bread is the most popular in the region, but you can use wholemeal (whole wheat) if preferred.

Recipes have been given for basic bread dough and some ways in which to use it, especially for breads that have no counterpart readily available in the marketplace (see page 231).

In recipes using bread, I have referred to pita bread, country-style bread and the long French bread stick known as the baguette. The baguette must be used on the day of baking; if you need to shop ahead, freeze the baguette, suitably wrapped, then thaw and heat briefly in a moderate oven before using it. Stale baguette and other white bread can be used for crumbing (see below) or for croûtes (bread slices, with or without crusts, fried until crisp and golden in olive oil, which can be flavored with a whole garlic clove) or croutons (cubes of bread similarly prepared).

Country-style bread refers to an Italian, French or Greek white bread with a crisp or soft crust and a coarse crumb. Torpedo- or oval-shaped bread is preferred as it gives slices of the right size and shape for bruschetta or for placing into soup bowls before adding the soup. Sour-dough bread of this shape is also good as it has the right texture and flavor. These breads can also be used for the Italian crostini (slices of bread served as an antipasto with a savory topping). Crostini can also be buttered or brushed with olive oil and toasted, or fried in oil as for croûtes.

Pocket pita breads should be used if ingredients are to be inserted but note that not all types have a pocket. Other flat breads, such as lavash (very thin flat bread), can be used in place of pita breads where a pocket is not required.

To make soft breadcrumbs: Choose a loaf with a coarse crumb; round or torpedo-shaped loaves of country-style bread are good. Leave at room temperature for 2 to 3 days to allow it to become stale. Remove crusts and crumb the bread in a food processor, or use the large shredder holes of a grater. Store in a sealed plastic bag in the freezer to have on hand when required.

To make dry breadcrumbs: Dry out bread in the oven, then roll or pound to fine crumbs or break it up and process in a food processor. These crumbs are also available commercially but, unfortunately, many look and taste synthetic and are no substitute for the real thing. Good quality commercial crumbs should resemble home-made ones in flavor and texture; if not, make your own.

GRAINS

Burghul: Also known by the Turkish bulgar or bulghur, this is steamed, cracked wheat. It is popular in the Levant, Cyprus (where it is known as pourgouri) and Tunisia (where it is called alica). Available in fine or coarse grades.

Couscous: Known as seksu (Morocco), naama and maach (Algeria) and kouski (Tunisia), this durum wheat semolina product is of Berber origin. The names refer to both the grain itself and the cooked dish. The grain is also used in Sicily, where it is known as cuscusu. Semolina granules are moistened with lightly salted water, sprinkled with semolina flour and rolled into pellets, traditionally by hand, but also by machine. In the Maghreb, couscous is also made with cracked barley, roasted and cracked green barley and green wheat. Instant couscous is now available, shortening the traditionally lengthy process of soaking and steaming.

Semolina: Made from the inner endosperm of durum or hard wheat, semolina is coarsely grained in texture and is usually used for porridge. Fine-grained semolina flour is used for making dry pasta products. In the Mediterranean, the coarse-grained semolina is used for couscous, gnocchi (see page 224), halva, cakes and sweet pastries.

PASTRY

Fillo pastry: A paper-thin pastry used in the Eastern Mediterranean. The name comes from the Greek phyllon, meaning "leaf", and is also spelt phyllo and filo. Fresh, chilled or frozen pastry is readily available. Always bring the sealed package

TO ROLL PASTA OR PASTRY THINLY

If making pasta without the benefit of a pasta machine, or making pastry that has to be rolled out thinly, the dough in both instances has to have elasticity. Because of this, rolling by conventional means with a conventional rolling-pin is very hard work. In Italy, Greece and Turkey, they use long rolling-pins or lengths of wooden dowelling with a smaller diameter; in Italy, the recommended diameter is 1½ in (4 cm); in Greece, Cyprus and Turkey, dowelling of ¾ in (2 cm) diameter is preferred, but the larger diameter can be used; length should be about 30 in (75 cm). Your work surface should have an area about 3 feet (90 cm) wide and 3 to 4 feet (90 to 120 cm) long.

When rolling, do not grip pin as you would a conventional one. Place palms of hand on each side of the pastry on the pin, letting pin roll under your hands. Your hands should move outwards as dough stretches.

Shape the dough into either a ball or square. Dust work surface and dough with flour and roll out to a roughly 8 in (20 cm) round or square. Dust surface and dough again with flour and place rolling pin on end nearest you. Roll dough onto pin, pressing down firmly as you roll to end. Unroll carefully, turn dough round 180°, dust surface and dough again with flour and roll dough again onto pin.

For really thin pasta or pastry, after first rolling, flour dough and work surface and roll dough onto pin to within 2 in (5 cm) of end. Place palms of hands, fingers spread out, on top of dough and roll back and forth with 4 or 5 quick, short movements, moving hands outwards along the dough as you roll. Roll up to end of dough, then unroll carefully. Turn dough 180°, dust again with flour and roll again.

Recipes in this book give an indication of what quantity of dough should be rolled each time.

---

of pastry to room temperature before attempting to open it out. When working with fillo, keep it covered with thick plastic or a folded dry cloth covered by a moistened one. Never place a moistened cloth in direct contact with the pastry as it causes the delicate sheets to stick together.

Warkha: Also spelled ouarka, this paper-thin pastry is used for bisteeya (see page 234) and other pies in Morocco. In Algeria it is called dioul, in Tunisia malsouqua, where it is used for the popular brik (see page 249). A ball of sticky dough is tapped lightly on the base of an upturned large metal pan heated over a pot of boiling water. Each tap on the pan leaves a small circle of dough, and with frequent tappings, the surface of the pan is covered with a flat, paper-thin round of pastry. This is peeled off and the process repeated. Expertise is required, but there are substitutes. Asian egg roll skins (spring roll wrappers) are made in a somewhat similar fashion, and can be substituted if the pastry is to be fried. Fillo pastry can be used for bisteeya and other pies which require baking, as warkha is better fried than baked.

PRESERVED MEATS

The Mediterranean region is rich in preserved meats, sausages and salamis. A few of the important ones are detailed here.

Chorizo: A Spanish pork sausage flavored with paprika, hot chili pepper, herbs and garlic. It is smoke-cured and can be served sliced if well-dried; less firm chorizo is left whole or sliced and fried when included in recipes or served as a tapa. The chorizo of Mexico is a fresh, spiced pork sausage and is not an appropriate substitute; however, if it is the only type available, prick well and fry slowly in a greased pan until cooked through, then slice and use as directed in recipes.

Jamón serrano: Spanish salt-cured and air-dried ham, similar to prosciutto crudo. It is usually used in cooked dishes, diced, julienned or minced, or served in fairly thick, small slices topped with pimiento as a tapa.

Pancetta: Belly pork, salted and cured, but not smoked. It may be a flat slab or rolled, sold thinly or thickly sliced. It is usually diced and fried with onion and garlic as a basis for soups and stews. Bacon is often given as a substitute, but it should be green or unsmoked bacon. If neither pancetta nor green bacon is available, use smoked streaky bacon, boiled in water for 2 to 3 minutes, then drained. To store pancetta, wrap in waxed paper, overwrap in foil and store in refrigerator for 2 to 3 weeks.

Prosciutto crudo: Also known as Parma ham after its place of origin, it is also prepared in neighbouring regions and many countries outside Italy. Uncooked pork leg is salt-cured, pressed and air-dried. (Prosciutto cotto is cooked ham.) It is usually sold in paper-thin slices, but can be purchased in thicker slices on request. Store as for pancetta.

CHEESE

The cheeses of the Mediterranean are many and varied. Mediterranean Spanish cheeses use sheep and goats' milk. They are not mentioned in this book because they are difficult to obtain outside the region, and cheese-making is still a developing industry in Spain (the cheese is usually served at the end of a meal with fruit).

Mediterranean France has roquefort and many farmhouse chevres (goats' milk cheeses) — the best known being banon. In cooking, parmesan, emmental and gruyère are widely used.

Mediterranean Italy makes wide-use of mozzarella, provolone, parmesan, pecorino and ricotta, the latter recommended as a substitute in Greek, Cypriot and Turkish recipes when similar cheeses are called for. Parmesan is also used in many Greek recipes where a grana-type cheese is required i.e. a hard cheese with a grainy texture, suitable for grating. Following are some of the cheeses mentioned in this book.

Bocconcini: Small, round white balls of fresh mozzarella cheese. It was made from buffalos' milk (hence the name buffalo mozzarella in some countries) but is now made with cows' milk, especially outside Italy. It only takes 24 hours to make, and is packed in its whey for sale; it could be labelled as fresh mozzarella. Store in refrigerator and use as soon as possible.

Feta: A Greek cheese made from sheeps' or goats' milk matured in a brine solution. It is soft, white and crumbly with a pleasant tang. Feta is made in countries outside Greece and the Balkans, often with cows' milk. Cows' milk feta can be used for cooking purposes but it does not melt as well as traditional feta. For the recipes in this book, try to purchase Greek feta, although Bulgarian feta is a good substitute.

Haloumi: A salty sheeps' milk cheese made in Cyprus and Lebanon. It is a cooked cheese, kneaded, sprinkled with mint (in Cyprus) or black cumin (in Lebanon) folded in three and matured in brine. Slice thickly and cook on an oiled griddle or serve as a table cheese. Outside the region haloumi is made with cows' milk.

Kasseri: A Greek hard cheese made from sheeps' or goats' milk with a pronounced tang. It is a table cheese and also used in cooking. Kaser is the Turkish equivalent.

Kefalograviera: A Greek cheese made from cows' milk, similar to gruyère, which can be used as a substitute. It is a table cheese, used for grating onto pasta, and melts when heated.

Kefalotiri: A Greek, grana-style cheese made from cows' milk. It too is used as a table cheese and for grating onto pasta. Parmesan cheese can be used as a substitute.

Mascarpone: Made from fresh cream, this cheese is slightly acidic and resembles thick, clotted cream. Originating in Lombardy, it is now made in other regions in Italy and is usually sold in cheesecloth (muslin) bags to be used as an accompaniment to fresh fruit. With modern production methods, mascarpone that has a longer shelf life is readily available and, although it is made in other countries, Italy also exports it.

Parmesan: A hard, grana-type cheese with a thick crust, aged at least 2 years. The best is parmigiano-reggiano, from Parma and Reggio-Emilia, but many other good parmesan cheeses are made in Italy and other countries. Use fresh parmesan for the best flavor.

Pecorino: Made from sheeps' milk, there are a number of pecorino cheeses made in southern Italy, Sardinia and Sicily. Pecorino romano is the best; used mainly for grating and cooking. Pecorino pepato (with peppercorns) and pecorino fresco (young pecorino) are good table cheeses.

YOGURT

Yogurt from the eastern Mediterranean uses milk from cows, sheep and goats. It is now used in most countries in the region.

Greek or country-style yogurt is usually very thick and does not require draining; to check if it is necessary, scoop a little hollow in surface and leave for about 1 hour — if free liquid does not fill the hollow, yogurt does not require draining.

To drain plain (natural) yogurt: Line a plastic or stainless steel sieve with a piece of cheesecloth (muslin), spoon in yogurt and set over a bowl. Cover top with a plate and leave in the refrigerator to drain for 3 to 6 hours until it is thick — draining time depends on whether full-cream or low-fat yogurt is used.

BASIC RECIPES

ROASTED PEPPERS

Roasted peppers (capsicums) are popular through-out the Western Mediterranean — Spain, Southern France, Italy, Morocco, Algeria and Tunisia. They are particularly essential for Spanish tapas and Italian antipasti, and are so popular that they are preserved in oil or vinegar. Red peppers preserved in a light brine are called pimientos, and are very convenient when a small quantity is required for a recipe. However, oil preservation is best left to the experts. If you want to taste roasted peppers at their best, prepare them yourself when required.

Choose fleshy red, yellow or black-purple sweet bell peppers. Green bell peppers can also be prepared in this way but their flavor is not as rewarding. Wash well and pat dry with paper towels before cooking.

Oven roasting: Preheat oven to 425–450°F (220–230°C/Gas 7). Place whole bell peppers directly onto oven rack with a tray placed on next rack underneath to catch drips. Roast until skins are blistered and lightly charred, about 20 to 30 minutes, turning frequently.

Flame charring: Spear a whole bell pepper on a two-pronged cooking fork and hold over a gas flame until skin is blistered and charred, about 10 minutes, turning frequently.

Broiler grilling: Place bell pepper (whole, halved or cut into strips) on foil-lined broiler (grill) tray. Cook under a hot broiler, until skin is blistered and charred, about 10 to 15 minutes, turning frequently if whole.

Barbecue grilling: Place whole or halved peppers on grid over glowing coals or on gas barbecue. Cook until skin is blistered and charred, about 20 minutes, turning frequently if whole.

To finish: Place blistered peppers in a paper or plastic bag, close and let stand 15 minutes to steam. Pull off and discard skin, scraping off any charred flesh. Avoid rinsing. Remove cores, seeds and white membrane and cut into wide strips. Use as directed in recipes, or place in a dish, cover with olive oil and serve immediately. To store, cover and refrigerate up to 4 days. If oil solidifies, it will liquidize once brought to room temperature.

Slata Mechouia (page 206)

DRESSING SALADS

Bottled dressings have fostered a misconception that salads are dressed with a mixture shaken or beaten together before being poured over a salad. In Mediterranean countries, dressing a salad is so much a part of their food culture that they do so by instinct and taste alone; careful measuring of ingredients is left to food communicators. These are some of the methods used.

The salad greens should be washed then dried in a salad spinner, or wrapped in a cotton cloth and refrigerated for about 1 hour to crisp and dry. Meanwhile, prepare other ingredients you might like to add to the salad.

The French way: Rub the salad bowl with a cut clove of garlic. Pour a small amount of vinegar into the bowl and add about three times that amount of extra virgin olive oil. Add a good pinch of salt and a grinding or two of pepper, a small spoon of Dijon or other prepared mustard and a pinch of sugar. Beat well with a fork until creamy. Taste and, if necessary, add more of any ingredient to give the flavor you require. When the dressing is to your satisfaction, add prepared greens and any other ingredients desired, toss lightly and thoroughly to coat leaves — often this process is carried out at the table so that the salad can be served as soon as it is tossed.

The Italian way: Have the salad ingredients ready in a serving bowl. Salt is first sprinkled on the salad with a light hand; pepper is seldom added. Drizzle over sufficient extra virgin olive oil to lightly coat leaves or other salad vegetables. Add a small splash of balsamic or red wine vinegar, or a squeeze of lemon juice, and toss lightly. Taste and, if necessary, add more of any ingredient to give the flavor you require. Serve immediately. If garlic is used in an Italian dressing, either a cut clove of garlic is added to the oil and allowed to steep, then discarded, or a piece of bread is rubbed with a cut garlic clove, added to the salad, tossed then discarded.

The Greek way: Have the salad ingredients ready in a serving bowl. Sprinkle lightly with salt and freshly ground pepper. Splash on a small amount of wine vinegar, toss lightly, then drizzle generously with a fruity olive oil. Toss well and serve immediately. Greek cooks claim that the vinegar should be added first; if oil is added first, it coats the ingredients and does not allow the vinegar to do its work. Often lemon juice is used in place of vinegar, particularly for winter salads using shredded cabbage.

HAMAD M'RAKAD

Preserved Lemons (Morocco)

Recipes for preserved lemons are often vague about the actual proportion of salt used. My first efforts resulted in the lemons spoiling, the next effort had them far too salty. Consultation with a food scientist resulted in a formula which gives lemons that are not too salty, and that keep well at room temperature, as they are meant to be kept until opened.

Select fresh firm lemons with no blemishes. In Morocco, they use the fragrant lemon called doqq (the Meyer lemon), and the more tart boussera. Eureka, Lisbon or Villa Franca lemons may be used providing their skins are not too thick. Ripe (yellow) limes may also be used.

1. Choose jars which will take amount of lemons to be salted; smaller jars (about 16 fl oz/ 500 ml capacity) are recommended and will take 2 lemons, plus extra peels. Measure the capacity of each jar in which lemons are to be packed. Sterilize jars and plastic lids by boiling.

2. For each 8 fl oz (250ml) capacity, use 5 level teaspoons (1 oz/30 g) cooking salt, not table salt.

3. Wash lemons and wipe dry with a clean cloth. If very firm, soak lemons in warm water 3 days to soften them, changing water daily.

4. Measure out salt required for each jar and set it aside with its jar. Halve and juice 3 lemons to begin. Strain juice and cut lemon skins in half (these can also be preserved). More lemons can be juiced as required. Cut lemons to be preserved almost through into quarters from stem end, leaving them joined at the base.

5. Pack one jar at a time — sprinkle cut surfaces of lemons with some of the salt allocated to their jar, and press lemons back into shape. Place about 1 tablespoon of remaining salt into base of jar. Add 1 lemon, fill spaces with 2 to 3 pieces of peel and sprinkle with a little more salt. Add another lemon and more peel to fill spaces, squashing the whole lemons as much as possible into the jar so they may release their juice. Fill jar in this manner. Add any remaining salt, half-fill jar with strained lemon juice and fill to top with cooled, boiled water. Place a piece of lemon peel on top, then seal tightly with plastic lid. Jar should be filled to capacity with lemons, lemon peels and liquid.

6. Wipe outside of jar and store in cool, dark cupboard, occasionally tilting back and forth for first 3 to 4 days to dissolve salt. Lemons will be ready to use in 4 weeks, and can be kept for 6 months.

Note: If any mold does form, it will do so on the piece of lemon peel on top — simply skim off mold and discard the piece of peel. Do not add any oil to jar, and do not use oily utensils to remove lemon from jar — use a clean fork.

To use: Remove a lemon to a clean plate, cut off amount required and return remainder to jar and reseal. Discard all pulp and membrane from piece of lemon, leaving peel with pith intact. Rinse peel well under cold water and chop, dice or slice as directed in recipes. Once jar is opened, store in refrigerator.

Pasta all'Uovo

Fresh Egg Pasta (Italy)   MAKES ABOUT 1 LB (500 G) PASTA

While it is fascinating to see an Italian cook prepare pasta in the traditional manner, I have given only food processor instructions as it saves so much time and effort. A manual pasta machine is desirable even though there are electric models available, including machines that also make the dough. It is also preferable to use unbleached flour. As flours vary in their ability to take in moisture, and egg sizes may vary a little, always hold back some of the flour in the initial stage.

2 cups (10 oz/300 g) all-purpose (plain) flour
3 large eggs
2 teaspoons light olive oil
1 tablespoon milk (optional)

Place about 1½ cups flour in food processor with steel blade fitted and process briefly. Break eggs onto flour and add oil. Add milk only if making pasta that will be stuffed (e.g. ravioli). Process until dough gathers on blades, pulsing the motor at first. If dough is too sticky, add a little more flour and process about 1 minute to knead. Turn out onto a board and knead in remaining flour only if dough is still too sticky. Shape into smooth ball. If rolling by hand, wrap in plastic and let rest 30 minutes. If using a machine, cut dough into 6 equal "slices" and cover with plastic wrap — dough does not have to rest.

Pasta Verde (Spinach and Egg Pasta) Variation: Thaw and drain 2½ oz (75 g) frozen chopped spinach. Spread out on two paper towels, top with another two paper towels and press well to remove excess moisture. Replace top paper towels with dry ones, turn over and replace bottom layers of towel and press again. Scrape spinach off towels with spatula — you should have about 2 tablespoons well-drained spinach. Add spinach to flour with eggs and oil and proceed as directed above.

Pasta machine method: Spread a little flour on work surface. Take a piece of pasta and dip cut sides in flour, shaking off excess. Set rollers on machine at widest point and pass dough through. Fold dough into thirds, dust lightly with flour and pass through next setting on machine. Repeat until dough passes through setting you require, dusting lightly with flour each time. If pasta is to be stuffed, dough should be rolled as thinly as possible; if it is to be used for fettuccine or linguine, it can be thicker. For lasagne, use second narrowest setting.

Hand-rolling (also see page 24): After resting dough, divide in half and keep one portion wrapped in plastic. Sprinkle rolling area on clean dry work surface with flour (a large wooden table is ideal). Shape dough into a ball and flatten with your palm. Dust top with flour and roll out to desired thickness, giving dough a quarter turn after each rolling. For lasagne, cut into large pieces. For strips, dust lightly with flour, roll up into a long sausage shape and cut into thin or thick pieces with a floured knife, unrolling each strip onto a floured cloth. For pasta that will be stuffed, follow specific recipe directions. Roll out remaining dough and repeat.

To cook fresh pasta: Bring large pot of water to boil and add about 1 tablespoon each salt and oil. Add pasta and stir gently with a wooden fork or spoon until water returns to the boil. Boil until al dente, about 3 to 5 minutes, longer for pasta that has been stuffed.

Depending on the capabilities of your machine, you can substitute fresh pasta for any recipe using pasta strips, sheets or other shapes.

To cook fresh lasagne: Leave pasta as wide as it emerges from pasta machine but cut into squares for easier handling. Spread clean cotton cloths on work surface. Bring large pot of water to boil over high heat and add about 1 tablespoon each salt and oil. Add 5 to 6 lasagne sheets at a time, return water to the boil and cook about 5 seconds more. Remove with large skimmer and drop into large bowl of cold water. Lift out pasta sheets separately, spread out on cloth and leave until required for assembling.

STOCKS

In most countries, commercial preparations of stocks are available. For small quantities, stock or bouillon cubes or granules (powder) may be used, dissolved in hot water. For large quantities, make stock as they do in the Mediterranean. It can be reduced and stored in the freezer for convenience.

Freezing stock: When stock is ready, strain through a fine sieve into a clean pan. Return to high heat, bring to boil and boil rapidly until reduced by half. Let cool. Skim off fat and pour in 1 cup quantities into rigid containers, leaving 3/4 in (2 cm) headspace to allow for expansion. Seal, label and store in the freezer for up to 3 months. When using, dilute with equal quantity of water.

FISH

In some countries, commercial preparations of fish stock are available or bottled clam juice may be substituted.

3 lb (1.5 kg) fish trimmings (heads, backbones etc.)
7 cups (56 fl oz/1.75 L) water
1 onion, quartered
1 carrot, sliced
1 leafy celery top
4 parsley stalks
1 teaspoon salt
6 whole black peppercorns

Rinse fish trimmings well, removing all traces of blood from heads and bones. Place in a large pot and add remaining ingredients. Bring to a simmer, skimming off froth as it rises. Cover and simmer over low heat 30 minutes. Strain stock through a fine sieve into a bowl and discard fish and flavoring ingredients. If not required immediately, cover and store in refrigerator for up to 4 days.

Rich Fish Stock Variation: Replace 1 cup water with dry white wine, omit celery top from vegetables and add 1 sliced well-washed leek, 2 sprigs thyme, 1 small sprig fennel or 1/4 teaspoon fennel seeds (optional) and thinly peeled strip of orange rind (optional).

MEAT

This is a light meat stock, popular in Mediterranean cooking. Have your meat retailer cut bones into small pieces so they fit into the pot. Use lamb or veal bones, or a combination of the two.

4 lb (2 kg) meaty lamb or veal bones
2 onions, chopped
2 carrots, chopped
1 stick celery, chopped
bouquet garni (3 sprigs each parsley and thyme, 2 bay leaves, tied together)
2 teaspoons salt
1/2 teaspoon peppercorns

Place bones in pot with vegetables, bouquet garni, and water to cover. Bring slowly to the boil, skimming off froth as it rises. Add salt, cover and simmer over low heat 3 hours, adding peppercorns during last 20 minutes. Strain stock through a fine sieve into a large bowl and discard chicken and flavoring ingredients. If not required immediately, cover and store in refrigerator for up to 4 days. Remove solidified fat before using.

CHICKEN

3 lb (1.5 kg) chicken carcases, wing tips and necks
1 carrot, sliced
1 onion, quartered
bouquet garni (4 parsley stalks, 2 sprigs thyme, 1 bay leaf, 2 sprigs celery leaves, tied together)
8 cups (64 fl oz/2 L) water
2 teaspoons salt
1/2 teaspoon peppercorns

Rinse chicken pieces well, removing all traces of blood. Place in a large pot with carrot, onion, bouquet garni and water. Bring to boil, skimming off all froth as it rises. Add salt, cover and simmer over low heat 2 hours, adding peppercorns during last 20 minutes. Strain stock through a fine sieve into a large bowl and discard chicken and flavoring ingredients. If not required immediately, cover and store in refrigerator for up to 4 days. Remove solidified fat before using.

SUGO DI POMODORO

Tomato Sauce (Italy)   MAKES ABOUT 4 CUPS (36 FL OZ/1 L)

This is an easy version of tomato sauce for any type of pasta and for use in other recipes. It is convenient to have on hand for quick-to-prepare meals. Italian or other good quality canned tomatoes should be used; often they have a better flavor, particularly in winter when fresh tomatoes are not at their sun-ripened best.

2 x 15 oz (425 g) cans tomatoes, chopped but undrained
2 medium onions, quartered
2 bay leaves
2 cloves garlic, peeled and pressed (crushed)
3 tablespoons olive oil
1 teaspoon sugar
salt and freshly ground black pepper
2 tablespoons chopped flat-leaf (Italian) parsley
1 tablespoon chopped fresh basil

Combine all ingredients except herbs in a heavy pan. Bring to boil, cover and simmer gently 40 minutes. Add herbs and simmer 15 minutes more. Puree in food processor or blender or pass through a food mill fitted with medium screen set over a bowl.

If using sauce immediately, return to pan and bring to boil again.

To store, pour into warmed sterilized jars, let cool and seal with sterilized plastic lids. Refrigerate for up to 2 weeks.

SALTSA DOMATA

Tomato Sauce (Greece/Cyprus)   MAKES ABOUT 4 CUPS (32 FL OZ/1 L)

The tomato sauce of Greek and Cypriot cooking is flavored with cinnamon and whole cloves and butter is preferred to olive oil. It tastes quite different to Italian tomato sauces and is excellent served over pasta with grated kefalotiri or parmesan cheese or over rice pilaf, or serve with keftethes (see page 146). It is always a problem fishing out the cloves so cut a thickish slice from the root end of the onion and insert cloves into this — it is easy to locate and discard.

4 lb (2 kg) ripe tomatoes
4 oz (125 g) butter
1 large onion, finely chopped
1 cup (8 fl oz/250 ml) water
3-in (8 cm) cinnamon stick
3 whole cloves
1 bay leaf
1 to 1 1/2 tablespoons sugar
salt and freshly ground black pepper

Peel, seed and chop tomatoes. Melt butter in a saucepan. Add onion and cook gently until transparent, about 10 minutes. Add tomatoes, water, cinnamon, whole cloves, bay leaf and sugar to taste. Cook gently until tomato is soft and thick, about 35 to 45 minutes. Season to taste with salt and pepper and discard cinnamon stick, cloves and bay leaf. Use immediately or transfer to sealed, sterilized jar and store in refrigerator for up to 2 weeks.

SALSA DE TOMATES

Tomato Sauce (Spain)　　　　　　　　　　　　MAKES ABOUT 2 CUPS (16 FL OZ/500 ML)

Spanish tomato sauces can vary greatly, according to the region and the sauce's use. This is a Mediterranean version containing pimientos (sweet red bell peppers) and sherry. It can be served with barbecued meat or poultry, or over pasta or rice.

3 tablespoons olive oil

2 large onions, chopped

2 cloves garlic, crushed

2 red bell peppers (capsicums), cored, seeded and chopped

15 oz (425 g) can tomatoes, chopped but undrained

2 tablespoons chopped fresh parsley

1 teaspoon chopped fresh thyme

salt and freshly ground black pepper

2 tablespoons fino (dry) sherry

Warm olive oil in saucepan. Add onion and cook gently until transparent, about 10 minutes. Add garlic and cook 1 minute. Add bell pepper, cover and cook over low heat 15 minutes.

Add tomatoes with their liquid, parsley, thyme and salt and pepper to taste and cook, covered, until thick, about 20 minutes. Puree with a hand-held blender in the pan or in food processor or food mill. Return to pan, add sherry, adjust seasoning and warm through. Use immediately or transfer to sealed, sterilized jar and store in refrigerator for up to 2 weeks.

HARISSA

Hot Pepper Sauce (Tunisia)　　　　　　　　　　MAKES 1/2 CUP (4 FL OZ/125 ML)

This fiery condiment is used widely in Tunisian cooking, and has crossed borders to Algeria and Morocco. It is available in tubes and cans at some specialty food stores; if using commercially prepared harissa, add with caution to recipes as it is much hotter than the version given below. While most versions call for dried chilies or hot chili or cayenne pepper, make it with fresh red chili whenever possible. Because chilies come in many varieties and sizes, I have given weight as an indication. If you can tolerate very hot condiments, use the whole chilies, otherwise remove seeds as their inclusion increases the fieriness of the finished harissa. When handling fresh chilies, do not touch eyes or mouth as they can be very irritating and wash hands immediately after preparation.

1 whole or 4 tablespoons chopped canned pimiento

2 oz (60 g) fresh hot red chilies or 3 teaspoons dried red pepper flakes

1/2 teaspoon salt

3 cloves garlic, chopped

1 teaspoon ground coriander

1 teaspoon ground cumin

olive oil (optional)

If using whole canned pimiento, drain well and pat dry with paper towels. Seed fresh chilies and remove membranes if desired. Chop roughly. Process chili, pimiento, salt, garlic, coriander and cumin in food processor to finely textured, thick puree. Use immediately as directed in recipes or transfer to a sterilised jar, cover with a film of olive oil, seal and store in the refrigerator for up to 2 weeks.

MARINATED OLIVES

Adding flavorings to olives makes them even more appealing as appetizers. While many are available already marinated, it is easy to make your own. These are some of the ways in which cured olives are prepared in various countries of the region. For all olives, rinse and drain well before preparing.

CYPRUS

1 lb (500 g) green olives, cracked

2 tablespoons coarsely crushed coriander seeds

2 cloves garlic, pressed (crushed)

juice of 1 lemon

1/4 cup (2 fl oz/60 ml) olive oil

Crack olives by hitting sharply with flat of a cleaver or meat mallet. Place in bowl or jar and add remaining ingredients. Mix well and marinate 1 to 2 hours. Serve or store in sealed jar in refrigerator for up to 2 weeks and bring to room temperature before serving.

ITALY

1 lb (500 g) black olives (shrivelled variety are excellent)

2 to 3 cloves garlic, peeled and halved

olive oil

Place olives and garlic in jar with oil to cover. Seal and let stand at room temperature 2 to 3 days. Serve or refrigerate for up to 2 weeks.

TUNISIA

1 lb (500 g) black or green olives

2 teaspoons harissa (see page 33)

1/2 cup (4 fl oz/125 ml) olive oil

Mix olives with harissa and oil and refrigerate in sealed jar 1 to 2 days before use. Bring to room temperature before serving. Olives can be stored in refrigerator for up to 1 month, shaking jar occasionally to distribute marinade.

MOROCCO

1 lb (500 g) black, purple or green olives

2 tablespoons finely chopped flat-leaf (Italian) parsley

2 tablespoons finely chopped fresh coriander leaves (cilantro)

2 cloves garlic, finely chopped

1 tablespoon finely chopped preserved lemon rind (see page 29)

1 teaspoon finely chopped fresh hot red chili

1/2 teaspoon ground cumin

1 tablespoon juice from preserved lemon jar

2 tablespoons fresh lemon juice

1/2 cup (4 fl oz/125 ml) olive oil

Place all ingredients in bowl and mix well. Transfer to jar, seal and refrigerate 1 to 2 days. Bring to room temperature before serving. If you do not have preserved lemons, use 2 teaspoons finely shredded fresh orange rind (no pith) and increase lemon juice to 3 tablespoons.

SPAIN

1 lb (500 g) black or green olives

3 cloves garlic, peeled and halved

1 teaspoon ground cumin

1 teaspoon each chopped fresh thyme, marjoram and rosemary

1/2 teaspoon fennel seeds

2 bay leaves, crumbled

1/4 cup (2 fl oz/60 ml) sherry vinegar

1/4 cup (2 fl oz/60 ml) olive oil

Place all ingredients in bowl and mix well. Transfer to jar, seal and let stand at room temperature 2 days before using, shaking occasionally to distribute marinade. Bring to room temperature before serving. Olives can be stored in refrigerator for up to 1 week.

PESTO

Genoese Basil Sauce (Italy)   MAKES ABOUT 2 CUPS

The Ligurians insist that their famous basil sauce can only be made in a marble mortar with a wooden pestle, and it is the crushing action that gives pesto its name. Provence has adopted it as their own pistou, the ingredients of which can vary but it seldom contains pine nuts and sometimes contains cheese. I prefer to use a food processor to make this sauce as it takes but a minute or two. The flavor is still excellent and it still retains texture, unlike using a blender which I do not recommend. The quantity of sauce given below is generous as it has other uses besides serving on pasta — in Liguria, the favored pasta is trenette (thin ribbon pasta). Dress boiled potatoes, or spoon over fish or potato gnocchi, or on top of minestrone alla genovese (see page 70). A little more or less basil than amount specified will not adversely affect the sauce but the leaves must be dry before processing in order for the sauce to keep.

2 cups (4 oz/125 g) fresh basil leaves, tightly packed
1/2 cup (21/2 oz/75 g) pine nuts
3 cloves garlic, chopped
1 cup (8 fl oz/250 ml) virgin olive oil
1/2 cup (2 oz/60 g) freshly grated parmesan cheese
1/4 cup (1 oz/30 g) freshly grated pecorino cheese
salt and freshly ground black pepper
olive oil, to store

Rinse basil gently and remove leaves, discarding any damaged ones. Spin leaves dry in salad spinner, or spread on cloth and let stand 1 hour. Measure leaves and place in food processor.

Toast pine nuts in a dry, heavy frying pan over medium heat until lightly colored, stirring often. Transfer to a plate to cool. Add to food processor with garlic and process to a coarse puree, adding a little oil to facilitate processing. Add cheeses and process to a paste. With motor running, gradually pour in remaining oil. Season with salt and pepper.

If not required immediately, transfer to sterilized jar, cover with a film of olive oil, seal and store in refrigerator for up to 4 days.

CRÈME FRAÎCHE

Cultured Cream (France)   MAKES 11/2 CUPS (12 FL OZ/375 ML)

While crème fraîche might belong in the cooking of northern France (Normandy in particular), its use has spread throughout France and beyond. It is available commercially, but if you cannot find it in your market, the ingredients are easy to obtain so that you can make it in your kitchen. If the cream you use is 35% fat content, use commercially purchased sour cream for the culture; if higher in fat content, use buttermilk.

1 cup (8 fl oz/250 ml) heavy cream (35–45% milk fat)
1/2 cup (4 fl oz/125 ml) sour cream or buttermilk (see note above)

Mix cream and sour cream/buttermilk in a bowl, cover and let stand at room temperature until it has thickened and tastes slightly acid, about 5 to 6 hours. Refrigerate until required; it keeps for up to 1 week. Serve with desserts, stir a little into soups and sauces, or use as directed in recipes.

MAYONNAISE

The Spaniards claim the sauce as their own. It is said to have been invented by a French chef on the island of Minorca to commemorate its capture by the Duc de Richelieu in 1756, and it is generally accepted that the name was derived from the original spelling mahonnaise, meaning "of Mahon", capital of Minorca. Mayonnaise is used in all the countries on the northern side of the Mediterranean.

Do not use extra virgin olive oil as it is too strong in flavor; even olive oil should be diluted with the bland extra light olive oil, or another bland oil. Mayonnaise should not be left at room temperature for longer than 4 hours as there is a risk of spoilage, undetected by smell or taste, due to the inclusion of raw egg yolks. The lukewarm water prevents the mayonnaise from separating under refrigeration.

3 egg yolks
1 teaspoon salt
1/2 teaspoon mustard powder
1 tablespoon lemon juice or white wine vinegar
1 cup olive oil (8 fl oz/250 ml)
1/2 cup extra light olive oil (4 fl oz/125 ml)
freshly ground white pepper
1 tablespoon lukewarm water

Process egg yolks in food processor with salt, mustard powder and half the lemon juice or vinegar until yolks are light. With motor operating, gradually add olive oils in the early stages — start by pouring in a thin stream with motor pulsing then, as mayonnaise begins to thicken, pour oil in a steady stream with motor running constantly. Stop processing as soon as oil is added. Add white pepper and more lemon juice or vinegar to taste. Add water and process briefly. Transfer to a bowl, cover and refrigerate until required, or transfer to a sealed sterilized jar and keep for up to 1 month.

AÏOLI

Garlic Mayonnaise (France)

Garlic mayonnaise is also known as alioli in Spain. The Spaniards used to make it without egg yolks, but generally include them nowadays. The French usually add much more garlic than the amount used in this recipe. Aioli has a more lemony flavor than mayonnaise — both go well with cold, steamed fish, cooked crustaceans such as crab, shrimp (prawns) and lobster, and raw vegetable pieces (crudites).

3 egg yolks
1 teaspoon salt
4 to 6 cloves garlic, pressed (crushed)
2 tablespoons lemon juice
1 cup (8 fl oz/250 ml) olive oil
1/2 cup (4 fl oz/125 ml) extra light olive oil
freshly ground white pepper
1 tablespoon lukewarm water

Process egg yolks in food processor with salt, garlic and half the lemon juice until yolks are light. With motor operating, gradually add olive oils in the early stages — start by pouring in a thin stream with motor pulsing then, as aioli begins to thicken, pour oil in a steady stream with motor running constantly. Stop processing as soon as oil is added. Add white pepper and more lemon juice or vinegar to taste. Add water and process briefly. Transfer to a bowl, cover and refrigerate until required. Transfer to a bowl, cover and refrigerate until required, or transfer to a sealed sterilized jar and keep for up to 1 month.

SEKSU

Couscous (Morocco)   SERVES 6

To prepare couscous in the traditional manner requires much effort — pre-soaking, steaming, transferring to a dish, sprinkling with water, rubbing butter or smen through it, then back to steaming. Instant couscous is a must for modern cooks, but ignore instructions on the pack and follow the directions below if you want to prepare it as close as possible to the traditional. Couscous may also be steamed over a separate pot of boiling water, particularly if your pan is full. The bottom of the steamer must not sit in the broth or water — there must be sufficient space for steam to rise and pass through the grains. The foil seal described here is safer than using the traditional cloth. In Morocco, the couscous is steamed uncovered but it is covered with a lid in Algerian and Tunisian cooking.

2¹/₂ cups (1 lb/500 g) instant couscous
2¹/₂ cups (20 fl oz/625 ml) water
1 teaspoon salt
3 oz (90 g) butter

Place couscous in a baking dish. Place water, salt and 1 oz (30 g) butter in saucepan and bring to boil. Pour boiling water evenly over couscous. Spread couscous evenly, cover with baking sheet or foil and let stand 5 minutes. Stir with a fork, cover and let stand 5 minutes more. Stir with fork and separate any lumps with your fingers.

To heat, choose a steamer or metal colander which fits snuggly over pan of food being cooked or boiling water and line with a piece of muslin (cheesecloth). Drape long piece of foil around rim of pan, fit steamer into place on pan, and scrunch foil to seal. Spread couscous evenly in steamer and steam over the boiling food until steam rises through couscous grains, about 20 minutes, occasionally forking it lightly so that it heats evenly.

Meanwhile, melt remaining butter. When couscous is hot, transfer to heated platter, pour over melted butter and fork it through. Pile up and serve immediately.

BEYAZ PILAV

Plain Pilaf (Turkey)   SERVES 6

There are many instances when serving a Mediterranean meal that a rather plain boiled rice is required. No country of the region would ever cook rice just in boiling water — a stock is used that complements the dish with which it is to be served. This Turkish pilaf is a good basic recipe; medium-grained rice can be substituted for the long-grain. You can use a home-made stock, a commercial preparation, or stock cubes dissolved in water. Fish or meat stock can be used in place of chicken stock, according to the meal it is to accompany.

2 cups (14 oz/420 g) medium- or long-grain rice
2 tablespoons butter
1 small onion, finely chopped
3¹/₂ cups (28 fl oz/875 ml) chicken stock (see page 31)
salt and freshly ground black pepper

Wash rice in sieve and drain well. Melt butter in a large saucepan. Add onion and cook gently until transparent, about 10 minutes. Add rice and cook over low heat until rice looks opaque, stirring occasionally. Add stock and season with salt and pepper to taste. Increase heat and bring to boil, stirring. Reduce heat, cover and simmer over low heat until water is absorbed and holes appear on surface of rice, about 15 minutes. Remove from heat and let stand, covered, 5 minutes. Fluff up with fork and transfer to warmed serving dish.

APPETIZERS AND LIGHT MEALS

The Mediterranean is more than a region, it is a state of mind and there is no better way to experience this euphoric state than by nibbling on fresh, visually-appealing appetizers in the right setting, with a good wine, congenial company and stimulating conversation. Often appetizers are presented in such variety that they can be a satisfying meal. While the antipasti of Italy and the hors d'oeuvres of southern France are meant to precede a meal, usually lunch, and served to whet the appetite, not satisfy it, one can get rather carried away when all the right elements are present.

Spanish tapas, the word's literal meaning is "cover", originated in the bars of Andalusia, where a small plate containing either olives, slices of jamon serrano or chorizo was placed on top of a glass of sherry or wine with the compliments of the establishment. These days it is rarely free, and it has become part of the social life to call into more than one tasca, or tavern, to sample the specialties of the house. Their popularity is such that tascas now serve such a wide range of dishes that it is possible to dine on tapas in the one establishment. As well as the recipes in this chapter, other dishes which can be served as tapas are identified in other chapters.

The mezethakia of Greece and Cyprus and the meze/mezza of the Levant are local versions of appetizers; where alcohol is allowed, again it is not taken without something to nibble on. The number of dishes can be few or, as in the Levant, of bewildering array, more of a continuing feast than appetite-appeasers. In the Maghreb, the appetizer course is called mukabalatt, with a variety of salads plus fried pastries and tiny kebabs placed on the table before the main meal.

Besides prepared dishes, you can serve sliced preserved meats, plain or marinated olives, crisp young radishes, nuts, cheese, pickled vegetables and boiled shrimp (prawns). Don't forget the bread.

Other recipes included in this chapter are traditional first course dishes for special dinners, or light meals for lunch or supper. They all reflect the rich mosaic of Mediterranean foods and set the scene for relaxed eating.

Gambas al Ajillo (page 46)

Tortilla Española

POTATO OMELETTE (SPAIN)   SERVES 4

No tapas would be complete without this ubiquitous Spanish omelette. The cold omelette is cut into small squares for the purpose and this recipe will then serve eight. However, tortilla española is also excellent served hot as a light meal with salad. Other ingredients may be added, such as chopped chorizo sausage and sliced bell peppers (capsicums). The potatoes are usually sliced, but are easier to handle diced, if you prefer.

1½ lb (750 g) potatoes
⅓ cup (3 fl oz/80 ml) olive oil
2 large onions, sliced
salt
6 eggs
freshly ground black pepper

Peel and cut potatoes into ¼ in (5 mm) thick slices. Reserve about 1 tablespoon oil and heat remainder in large frying pan with sloping sides, preferably nonstick. Add potatoes and onions, season lightly with salt, cover and cook over medium-low heat until vegetables are tender, about 15 minutes — toss occasionally during cooking with a spatula. Let cool 10 minutes.

Beat eggs with ½ teaspoon salt and pepper to taste in large bowl. Fold in potato and onion mixture. Wipe frying pan with paper towels and add most of reserved oil. Heat well and pour in egg mixture. Flatten top with spatula and cook over medium-low heat until omelette is browned underneath and top is set around edges, about 5 to 8 minutes. Loosen edge of omelette with spatula and shake pan to check that it has not stuck. Slide out onto plate. Brush pan with remaining oil, about 1 teaspoon. Place pan over top of plate and invert omlette back into pan. Return to heat and cook until base is lightly browned, about 3 to 4 minutes.

Alternatively, leave partly cooked omelette in frying pan and place under a heated broiler (grill) — protect handle with foil. Broil (grill) until lightly browned and slide onto serving plate. Serve hot cut in wedges, or bring to room temperature, cut into 1 in (2.5 cm) cubes and serve as tapa dish.

BAGNA CAUDA

HOT ANCHOVY SAUCE WITH VEGETABLES (FRANCE)   SERVES 6 TO 8

While bagna cauda is from Piedmont in northern Italy, and uses butter in the sauce, this version has been adopted into Provençal cuisine, with olive oil replacing the butter. Any selection of tender vegetables may be used; cooked baby beets (beetroot) and small potatoes are often added, particularly if served as a light meal. The vegetables are dipped into the hot sauce at the table before eating.

8 oz (250 g) slender green asparagus spears

8 oz (250 g) young cauliflower

3 celery stalks

2 medium carrots

1 bunch small radishes

12 to 16 scallions (spring onions/green onions)

2 Belgian endive (witloof)

1 red bell pepper (capsicum), cut into strips

1 green or yellow bell pepper (capsicum), cut into strips

baguette (long French bread), sliced, to serve

Bagna Cauda:

1 cup (8 fl oz/250 ml) olive oil

3 cloves garlic, thinly sliced

3 tablespoons mashed, drained anchovy fillets

Break off woody ends from asparagus. Cut cauliflower into florets. Cut celery and carrots into 3 in (8 cm) long strips. Wash and trim radishes, leaving part of tops to use as "handles". Clean and trim scallions, retaining part of green tops. Separate endive into leaves. Arrange vegetables in groups on large platter or in basket.

For bagna cauda: Warm oil in fondue pot or similar flame-proof dish over gentle heat. Add garlic and cook until barely colored. Add anchovies and cook until dissolved. Transfer pot to table-top burner alongside vegetables.

Serve with bread.

PEPERONI ARROSTITI

ROASTED PEPPERS (ITALY)   SERVES 6 TO 8

This dish uses roasted bell peppers in their simplest form. Use three yellow peppers (if available) with three red for a more colorful dish. Choose firm, fleshy peppers and roast either in the oven or on a barbecue, steam and clean as directed. Use a fruity virgin olive oil. Some oils solidify when chilled, but once brought to room temperature, revert to a liquid state.

In Spain, pimientos al ajillo are prepared in the same manner to serve as a tapa — red bell peppers are sprinkled with thin slices of garlic (3 to 4 cloves), and then oil, salt and black pepper are added to taste.

6 red bell peppers (capsicums), roasted (see page 27)

salt

freshly ground black pepper

1/2 cup (4 fl oz/125 ml) virgin olive oil

Cut roasted peppers into wide strips and place in shallow dish. Season lightly with salt and pepper and cover with olive oil. Serve immediately, or cover and refrigerate until required. Bring to room temperature before serving as an antipasto.

Pipel Adom im Yogurt veh Nana

RED PEPPERS WITH YOGURT AND MINT (ISRAEL)   SERVES 4

This is often served as a breakfast in Israel, but makes a pleasant light meal.

1¹/2 cups (12 fl oz/375 ml) plain
(natural) yogurt

4 red bell peppers (capsicums),
roasted (see page 27)

¹/2 cup (2 oz/60 g) coarsely chopped
pecan nuts

2 tablespoons finely chopped
fresh mint

salt and freshly ground
black pepper

pita bread, to serve

Spread thick layer of yogurt in serving dish or on individual plates. Cut roasted pepper into strips and place on top of yogurt. Sprinkle with chopped pecan nuts and mint. Season to taste, if desired. Serve with warm bread.

Ricotta al Forno

BAKED RICOTTA (ITALY)   SERVES 10 TO 12

Baked ricotta is a popular item at many delicatessens and gourmet food stores, but it can be easily made at home. Accompaniments are only limited by the availability of ingredients, and the imagination of the cook! Purchase fresh ricotta in a block or cut into a wedge from the large rounds on sale — don't use the tub-packed ricotta. The browning of the cheese depends very much on the type of oven and the cheese itself.

1 lb (500 g) block or wedge fresh
ricotta cheese

3 tablespoons olive oil

freshly ground black pepper

paprika

To Serve:

sun-dried tomatoes

sun-dried red bell peppers
(capsicums)

olives

sliced cucumber

pesto (see page 35)

crusty Italian bread or focaccia

Preheat oven to 350–375°F (180–190°C/Gas 4).

Handling ricotta gently, pat dry with paper towels. Pour half the oil into casserole dish and add ricotta. Sprinkle top with pepper and a light dusting of paprika, and drizzle over remaining oil. Cover and bake 10 minutes.

Remove lid and bake until top is golden brown, about 10 minutes, basting twice during cooking with oil in casserole dish. If ricotta has not browned, place under hot broiler (grill) until top is brown, about 3 to 4 minutes. Serve hot, or let cool in casserole dish to room temperature. Can be stored, covered, in refrigerator until required.

To serve, place ricotta to one side of large platter and arrange tomatoes, bell peppers, olives and cucumber on platter. Place pesto in small bowl with spoon. Provide cheese knife for ricotta. Serve bread in basket.

Ricotta al Forno

SAGANAKI

FRIED CHEESE (GREECE)   SERVES 4

A saganaki is a small two-handled frying pan in which the cheese is traditionally fried. Any presentable frying pan will do. Gruyère cheese may be used in place of the Greek kefalograviera and parmesan in place of the kefalotiri. Kefalotiri and haloumi hold their shape when shallow-fried, and can be taken onto plates, but the kefalograviera or gruyère, and the parmesan, melt, and these are scooped directly from the pan with bread. Extra lemon juice is squeezed on, if desired. If taken from the pan, the olive oil is soaked up by the bread in the process, adding to the enjoyment of the dish. If you prefer individual serves, use cheese that retains its shape and lift out with a spatula onto individual warmed serving plates, pouring the oil evenly over each serve.

8 oz (250 g) kefalograviera, kefalotiri
or haloumi cheese
(see page 25)

all-purpose (plain) flour,
for coating

olive oil, for shallow frying

freshly ground black pepper

lemon juice

lemon wedges, to serve

crusty bread, to serve

Cut cheese into slices or wedges 1/2 in (1 cm) thick. Moisten with water, shake off excess, and coat with flour.

Pour oil into frying pan until 1/4 in (5 mm) deep. Heat over medium-high heat until almost smoking. Add cheese in single layer and shallow fry until golden brown, about 2 minutes each side. Sprinkle with pepper and lemon juice. Serve immediately, directly from pan, with lemon wedges and bread.

SALADE DE CHÈVRE CHAUD

WARM GOATS' CHEESE SALAD (FRANCE)   SERVES 4

Warm salads did not originate in Provence, but the idea has filtered to the sunny region. The two main elements of this salad are very definitely of Provençal origins — mesclun (mixed wild and cultivated salad greens and herbs) and chevres. Choose bread that is a little larger in diameter than the cheese rounds.

8 slices French bread e.g. baguette

1/4 cup (2 fl oz/60 ml) olive oil

1 clove garlic, bruised

6 oz (180 g) mesclun (e.g. oak leaf
lettuce, young spinach, chervil,
arugula/rocket, curly endive,
dandelion, watercress, borage)

8 x 1/2 in (1 cm) slices goats' cheese

Dressing:

1/2 cup (4 fl oz/125 ml) walnut oil

1 tablespoon red wine vinegar

1 tablespoon fresh lemon juice

1 teaspoon Provençal or other
herbed mustard

salt and freshly ground black pepper

Preheat oven to 350–375°F (180–190°C/Gas 4).

Cut bread into 3/4 in (2 cm) thick slices. Heat oil in frying pan with garlic. When garlic is brown, remove and add bread slices. Fry until golden brown and crisp, about 1 minute each side. Drain on paper towels.

Rinse mesclun and dry in salad spinner, or roll in clean cloth and place in refrigerator. Combine dressing ingredients in screw-topped jar. Shake well and set aside.

Place goats' cheese slices onto garlic croûtes on baking sheet, and bake until cheese is slightly melted, about 8 to 10 minutes. Alternatively, cook under heated broiler (grill). Meanwhile, toss mesclun with dressing and divide salad between four small serving plates. Top each salad with 2 goats' cheese croûtes and serve immediately.

GVINAT EZIM METOUGENET IM SALAT NANA

FRIED GOATS' CHEESE WITH MINTED SALAD (ISRAEL)   SERVES 4

Israel is beginning to find its culinary identity, with many new food industries broadening its scope. Cheese-making is one of these, and chefs are quick to give these foods an Israeli identity, reflecting the indigenous foods and the developing new cuisine. Shred mint leaves at the last possible moment before serving as mint discolors quickly. Don't peel the cucumber.

8 x 1/2 in (1cm) thick slices round goats' cheese (chevre)

fine matzo meal or dried breadcrumbs

1 egg, beaten

olive oil, for shallow frying

Mint Salad:

2 cups (1 1/2 oz/45 g) fresh mint leaves, lightly packed

small bunch watercress

1 small cucumber (see page 14), thinly sliced

1 small purple onion, thinly sliced

3 tablespoons olive oil

1 tablespoon red wine vinegar

salt and freshly ground black pepper

Coat cheese slices carefully with matzo meal or breadcrumbs, dip into beaten egg, then coat again with meal or crumbs. Place on a paper towel-lined tray and refrigerate at least 10 minutes.

For mint salad: Rinse mint leaves and dry in salad spinner or wrap in clean cloth to dry. Pick tender sprig tips and leaf brackets from watercress, rinse and dry separately to mint. Place watercress, cucumber and onion rings in bowl. Beat oil and vinegar in small bowl, add salt and pepper to taste. Just before serving, gently shred mint leaves with a sharp knife and add to salad, pour over dressing and toss lightly.

Pour oil into large frying pan until 1/4 in (5 mm) deep. Heat on medium-high, add cheese and shallow fry quickly until golden brown, about 1 to 2 minutes each side. Drain on paper towels.

Divide salad between four serving plates and top with 2 rounds of hot fried cheese. Serve immediately.

OLIVE ALLA SICILIANA

SICILIAN FRIED OLIVES (ITALY)   SERVES 4

Hot olives make a very interesting appetizer, and if you can obtain the Italian Gaetas, then use these, otherwise use large Greek black olives or kalamatas. Serve the olives from the pan for informal eating — the bread can be dunked in the juices. Or divide the olives into warmed individual bowls placed on small plates, with slices of crusty bread on the side.

40 black olives

4 tablespoons olive oil

2 to 3 cloves garlic, pressed (crushed)

3 tablespoons red wine vinegar

2 tablespoons finely chopped fresh marjoram

crusty bread, to serve

Rinse olives; drain well on paper towels. Heat oil in frying pan. Add garlic and cook several seconds. Add olives and cook 1 minute, stirring frequently. Add vinegar and cook until most of the liquid has evaporated. Sprinkle with marjoram, toss well and serve piping hot with bread.

GAMBAS AL AJILLO

GARLIC SHRIMP (SPAIN)   SERVES 4 TO 6

In Spain, shrimp are quickly cooked in small flame-proof dishes of glazed earthenware, called cazuelas, over direct heat. This is one of the most popular tapas served in seaside bars and restaurants. In the domestic kitchen, it is easier to cook the shrimp in a frying pan, and transfer to heated, individual bowls for serving. While not traditional, you can leave the shrimp unshelled; provide fingerbowls and a plate for the discarded shrimp shells. The bread is served to sop up the flavorsome oil in the dish.

1¹/₂ lb (750 g) large uncooked jumbo shrimp (large prawns)

¹/₄ cup (2 fl oz/60 ml) olive oil

3 cloves garlic, thinly sliced

1 hot red chili pepper, seeded and finely chopped (optional)

salt

crusty bread, to serve

Peel and devein shrimp, leaving tails intact. Rinse and pat dry with paper towels.

Heat oil in large frying pan over high heat. Add shrimp, garlic and chili, and sprinkle lightly with salt. Stir or shake over high heat until shrimp are pink, about 3 to 4 minutes, taking care garlic does not burn. Turn immediately into warmed, individual bowls, dividing oil between bowls. Serve with crusty bread.

CHAMPIÑONES CON AJO Y PEREJIL

MUSHROOMS WITH GARLIC AND PARSLEY (SPAIN)   SERVES 4 TO 6

This popular tapa dish can also be served as an accompaniment to poultry and meat dishes. In Catalan, picking wild mushrooms is a way of life. Spanish varieties of mushroom may not be available in your region but you can use a selection from your market: oyster, saffron or delicious milk cap, Swiss brown, boletus (also known as cepe or porcini), chantrelle and morel, for example. Or simply use the cultivated field mushrooms that are readily available — the caps should be opened but not flattened out. If you do go mushroom hunting, please invest in a color-illustrated guide that covers poisonous mushrooms.

1 lb (500 g) mixed fresh mushrooms

¹/₃ cup (3 fl oz/80 ml) olive oil

3 cloves garlic, thinly sliced

1 tablespoon lemon juice

salt and freshly ground black pepper

3 tablespoons finely chopped parsley

Only wash mushrooms if they are wild. Otherwise, wipe over mushrooms with slightly moistened cloth. Trim stems and leave mushrooms whole or, if large, slice thickly.

Heat oil in large frying pan. Add mushrooms and garlic and cook over high heat, stirring often, until lightly browned, about 5 minutes — do not allow garlic to burn. Add lemon juice and salt and pepper to taste. Transfer to warmed dish and sprinkle with parsley. Serve hot or at room temperature.

Champiñones con Ajo y Perejil

Baba Ghannouj

EGGPLANT AND TAHINI PUREE (LEBANON, SYRIA)   MAKES ABOUT 2 CUPS

In Syria, this delicious dip is known as mutabbal. It is also popular in Israel.

2 medium oval eggplants
(aubergines)

2 cloves garlic, chopped

juice of 1 lemon

1/2 cup (4 fl oz/125 ml) tahini
(sesame paste)

salt

To Serve:

olive oil

chopped fresh parsley

pita bread, cut into wedges, or
savory crackers or crusty bread

Leave stems on eggplants and roast over glowing coals on barbecue until soft, about 30 to 40 minutes — turn often, and allow skin to char lightly all over. Alternatively, cook on middle shelf in oven preheated to 400–425°F (200–220°C/Gas 6), turning occasionally.

Peel off skin while hot, and remove stems. Chop flesh roughly, place in colander and shake well to remove excess moisture. Transfer to food processor with garlic and process to coarse puree. Add lemon juice and tahini and process to a thick puree. Add salt to taste, and more lemon juice, if necessary. Transfer to bowl, cover and refrigerate until required.

To serve, place puree in shallow bowl, swirling it with back of spoon. Drizzle with olive oil and sprinkle lightly with parsley. Serve with bread.

Tapenade

OLIVE PASTE (FRANCE)   MAKES ABOUT 1 1/2 CUPS

Tapenade can be served in a small pot as an accompaniment to crudites (raw vegetable pieces), or used as a spread on slices of toasted or fresh baguette (long French bread), or in pan bagnat (see page 61). It is available commercially but is easy to make with a food processor and keeps for weeks in the refrigerator; pack into small, sterilized jars, cover with a thin layer of olive oil, and seal with sterilized plastic lids.

8 oz (250 g) flavorsome black olives,
drained

2 tablespoons (1 1/2 oz/45 g)
chopped, drained, canned
anchovy fillets

3 tablespoons (1 1/2 oz/45 g)
drained capers

1 clove garlic, chopped

freshly ground black pepper

2 teaspoons red wine vinegar

1/4 cup (2 fl oz/60 ml) olive oil

Rinse olives if packed in brine and drain brine or oil-packed olives well. Pit olives by pressing with the flat of a heavy knife to smash, then remove pit.

Place olives in food processor with all other ingredients except oil. Process to coarse puree. With motor operating, gradually pour in olive oil in thin stream. Transfer to bowl, cover and refrigerate until required. Bring to room temperature before serving.

ANCHOÏADE

ANCHOVY PASTE (FRANCE)   MAKES 3/4 CUP

2 oz (60 g) drained anchovy fillets,
packed in oil

milk

1/2 cup (4 fl oz/125 ml)
extra-virgin olive oil

2 cloves garlic, chopped

2 teaspoons chopped fresh thyme
or winter savory

1 tablespoon red wine vinegar

freshly ground black pepper

1 loaf French country-style bread,
sliced, to serve

radishes, to serve

Belgian endive (witloof), to serve

black olives, to serve

Blot anchovies well with paper towels before weighing. Place in bowl and cover with milk. Let stand 2 minutes to reduce saltiness, drain and rinse carefully in cold water. Pat dry with paper towels. Place anchovies in food processor with oil, garlic, thyme and vinegar and process to smooth puree, adding pepper to taste. Transfer to serving bowl.

To serve in the traditional way, toast bread on one side under hot broiler (grill), spread untoasted side with anchoïade and return to broiler until anchoïade is bubbling. Serve with radishes, endive leaves and olives.

TZATZIKI

YOGURT AND CUCUMBER SPREAD (GREECE, CYPRUS)   MAKES ABOUT 3 CUPS

This popular dip is called talattouri in Cyprus, and cacik in Turkey (see page 81), and can also be served as a sauce for fried fish. Having the right cucumber is important (see page 14), but if the types suggested are not available, choose a small, slim, firm regular cucumber. If you cannot obtain Greek yogurt, use 3 cups (24 fl oz/750 ml) plain (natural) yogurt and drain as instructed on page 25.

2 small green or
1/2 hothouse cucumber

salt

2 cups (16 fl oz/500 ml) thick
country-style Greek yogurt

2 cloves garlic, pressed (crushed)

2 teaspoons dried mint flakes

2 tablespoons olive oil

mint sprigs, to garnish

crusty bread or pita bread,
to serve

salad vegetables
(e.g. celery and radishes),
to serve

Wash cucumbers and shred on coarse side of grater (the skin doesn't have to be removed unless waxed). Alternatively, quarter cucumbers lengthwise and cut into fairly thin slices. Place in colander, sprinkle with 2 teaspoons salt, toss well and let stand 1 hour. If grated, press well with back of spoon to remove as much moisture as possible. If sliced, shake well.

Combine yogurt, cucumber, garlic, mint flakes and oil in bowl. Mix well, cover and refrigerate. Serve in bowl, garnished with mint sprigs, and use as a dip with bread and salad vegetables.

*Pages 50 to 51: Tzatziki (page 49), Anchoïade (page 49),
Hummus bi Tahini (page 52), Taramosalata (page 53)*

TARATOUR BI TAHINI

TAHINI SAUCE (LEBANON, SYRIA)   MAKES ABOUT 2 CUPS

Tahini is very much a part of Lebanese and Syrian cuisine — they use this sauce like a mayonnaise, with falafel or baked or grilled fish, or as a dip. The first liquid added to tahini thickens it, the second thins it down so it is best to get the flavor right with lemon juice and then add water to adjust the consistency.

2 cloves garlic

salt

1 cup (8 fl oz/250 ml) tahini (sesame paste)

1/2 cup (4 fl oz/125 ml) lemon juice

2 to 3 tablespoons cold water

pita bread, to serve

Chop garlic roughly and mix with 1/2 teaspoon salt. With a knife-tip, squash garlic and mix to smooth paste.

Combine garlic paste, tahini, lemon juice and cold water in bowl. If too thick, add a little more water until a sauce-like consistency is reached. Add about 1/2 teaspoon salt or to taste. Serve as a dip with bread, or as a sauce.

For Bakdounis bi Tahini (Parsley and Tahini Sauce) Variation: Stir in 1/2 cup (1 oz/30 g) finely chopped flat-leaf (Italian) parsley and serve as a dip or as a sauce.

HUMMUS BI TAHINI

CHICKPEA AND TAHINI DIP (LEBANON, SYRIA)   MAKES ABOUT 3 CUPS

To make this in the traditional way, soak 1 cup (7 oz/210 g) dried chickpeas in 3 cups (24 fl oz/750 ml) water for 12 hours in the refrigerator. Purists would remove the fine skins from the chickpeas but this is not necessary. If you do want to skin them, place soaked dried chickpeas in a large quantity of cold water. Rub handfuls of the peas together, drop them back in the water and repeat (removing skins as they accumulate on top of the water). Then, to cook, simply drain the chickpeas and boil in water to cover (no salt) for 1 1/2 to 2 hours until very soft. This dip keeps for several days in the refrigerator.

2 x 15 oz (425 g) cans chickpeas (garbanzos)

2 cloves garlic, chopped

juice of 1 lemon

1/2 cup (4 fl oz/125 ml) tahini (sesame paste)

1/2 teaspoon ground cumin

pinch of cayenne pepper

salt

olive oil, to garnish

paprika, to garnish

pita or lavash bread, to serve

Drain chickpeas, reserving liquid and 3 to 4 whole chickpeas. Place in food processor bowl with garlic and process to smooth puree, adding a little lemon juice. Add tahini, cumin and cayenne and process, adding more lemon juice. When mixture is too thick to process, add about 3 tablespoons reserved chickpea liquid; consistency should be thick but creamy. Check flavor, and add more lemon juice if necessary and salt to taste. Transfer to bowl, cover and refrigerate until required.

To serve, place hummus in shallow dish. Drizzle with olive oil and dust with paprika. Garnish with reserved chickpeas, and serve with bread.

TARAMOSALATA

FISH ROE DIP (GREECE)   MAKES ABOUT 3 CUPS

While I tend to use a food processor to make this dip, an electric mixer gives a light result. The bread used is very important; choose a Greek or Italian-style bread with a dry crumb, and keep it for two to three days so that it is nicely stale before making the crumbs.

1 small onion

2 cups (4 oz/125 g) soft white breadcrumbs, packed

about ¼ cup (2 fl oz/60 ml) strained lemon juice

½ cup (4 fl oz/125 ml) olive oil

¼ cup (2 fl oz/60 ml) extra-light olive oil

1 clove garlic

1 egg yolk

4 oz (125 g) tarama (fish roe)

freshly ground white pepper (optional)

black olive, to garnish

crusty bread, crackers, thin toast, radishes or celery, to serve

Grate onion onto a plate. Strain through sieve into a bowl, pressing well to extract juice. Combine 1 tablespoon onion juice, breadcrumbs, 2 tablespoons lemon juice, and oils in bowl of electric mixer. Stir and let stand until bread is very soft, about 20 minutes.

Press (crush) garlic to a paste. Add to bowl and, with mixer, beat until very light. Beat in egg yolk, gradually adding tarama. Continue beating until light and fluffy, adding more lemon juice if necessary. If mixture is still too thick, and lemon flavor is satisfactory, beat in a little cold water. Beat in pepper to taste, if desired, and transfer to bowl. Cover and refrigerate until required.

Garnish with olive and serve with choice of accompaniment.

PÂTÉ DE VOLAILLE AUX CHAMPIGNONS

CHICKEN LIVER AND MUSHROOM PÂTÉ (FRANCE)   SERVES 8 TO 10

1 lb (500 g) chicken livers

1 cup (8 fl oz/250 ml) milk

4 oz (125 g) slice bacon, roughly chopped

8 scallions (spring onions/green onions), white part only, sliced

1 bay leaf, halved

1 clove garlic, pressed (crushed)

4 oz (125 g) wild or cultivated mushrooms, chopped

1 teaspoon fresh thyme leaves

2 tablespoons olive oil

¼ teaspoon ground nutmeg

2 tablespoons brandy or cognac

salt and freshly ground black pepper

baguette (long French bread), sliced, to serve

Clean chicken livers thoroughly to prevent bitterness, removing any threads and gall. Place in a bowl, cover with milk and let stand 2 hours. Drain well, then pat dry with paper towels. Chop roughly and set aside. Heat large frying pan over medium-low heat, add bacon and cook until fat melts and bacon is cooked but not browned. Add scallions and bay leaf and cook gently until scallions are soft, about 10 minutes. Add garlic, mushrooms and thyme and cook over medium heat until mushroom liquid evaporates, about 5 minutes, stirring often. Discard bay leaf. Transfer to food processor bowl and let cool. Wipe pan with paper towels, add oil and place over high heat. Add livers and cook quickly, stirring often, until livers are browned but still slightly pink inside — cut a piece to check. Let cool and add to food processor with nutmeg and brandy and process to a paste. Add salt and pepper to taste and process briefly. Transfer pâté mixture to earthenware or china pot. Smooth top, cover with plastic wrap and refrigerate several hours or overnight. Serve with fresh or toasted bread.

Fiori di Zucca Fritti

ZUCCHINI FLOWER FRITTERS (ITALY)   SERVES 6

The zucchini plant produces both male and female flowers. The male flowers usually wither and die but not in some countries of the Mediterranean. They are used in the cooking of southern France, Italy, Greece and Cyprus — either stuffed, added to omelettes or rice dishes, or simply fried in batter. If you do not grow zucchini plants yourself, you may find the flowers in Italian and Greek markets in their season — from spring to late summer. Zucchini flowers can be fried in a simple batter or filled with an anchovy stuffing, if desired. Rather than the usual batter containing water, oil and egg white, I find that club soda gives a batter that is much crisper and lighter.

30 (about 4 oz/125 g) zucchini (courgette) flowers

3/4 cup (3 1/2 oz/110 g) all-purpose (plain) flour

1/2 teaspoon salt

3/4 cup (6 fl oz/180 ml) club soda (soda water)

oil, for deep frying

lemon wedges, to serve

Anchovy Stuffing (optional):

8 canned anchovy fillets, drained

1 cup (2 oz/60 g) soft white breadcrumbs

1 tablespoon chopped flat-leaf (Italian) parsley

freshly ground black pepper

2 teaspoons lemon juice

2 to 3 tablespoons water

Gently part petals of zucchini flowers and pull out pistils. Trim stems to 3/4 in (2 cm). Rinse flowers, shake gently and place on cloth. Let stand about 1 hour to dry.

Sift flour and salt into bowl. Make well in middle and add most of soda. Using a fork, gradually stir in flour until incorporated, using remaining soda if necessary to give thickish cream consistency.

Heat oil almost to smoking point — drop in a little batter, it should begin to sizzle immediately. Holding each flower by stem, dip into batter, scraping off excess on side of bowl. Drop five or six at a time into hot oil and deep fry, turning to brown evenly. Remove to crumpled paper towels to drain. Pile onto heated serving platter and serve hot with lemon wedges.

For anchovy stuffing variation: Finely chop anchovies and combine with remaining stuffing ingredients in bowl, adding enough water to hold mixture together. Gently part flower petals and insert a teaspoon of stuffing in each flower. Press petals together. Dip in batter and deep fry as above.

Fiori di Zucca Fritti

DOMATOKEFTETHES

TOMATO FRITTERS (GREECE)   MAKES ABOUT 30

These tasty tomato fritters are from the island of Santorini, where it is claimed that the volcanic soil is responsible for the superb flavor of their tomatoes. A little sugar and tomato paste added to the mixture improves the flavor of mass-produced tomatoes.

1 lb (500 g) firm, ripe tomatoes

6 scallions
(spring onions/green onions)

2 tablespoons chopped flat-leaf
(Italian) parsley

2 teaspoons chopped fresh mint

3 teaspoons tomato paste

1 teaspoon sugar

salt and freshly ground
black pepper

1 cup (5 oz/150 g) all-purpose
(plain) flour

1 teaspoon baking powder

olive oil, for shallow frying

Peel and seed tomatoes and chop finely; place in bowl. Trim scallions, retaining part of green tops, and chop finely. Add to tomatoes with parsley, mint, tomato paste, sugar, and salt and pepper to taste. Mix well. Just before cooking, sift flour and baking powder and add to tomato mixture, mixing to fairly stiff batter.

Pour olive oil into frying pan until 1/4 in (5 mm) deep. Heat well over medium heat and drop generous tablespoons of fritter mixture into oil — fritters should be about 2 in (5 cm) in diameter. Shallow fry until deep golden brown, about 3 minutes each side. Drain on crumpled paper towels and serve hot as an appetizer.

MELANZANE MARINATE

MARINATED EGGPLANT (ITALY)   SERVES 4 TO 6

Eggplant is prepared similarly throughout the Mediterranean, but is usually fried. In Greece, Cyprus and Turkey, for example, they would serve fried eggplant with a garlic sauce as in skorthalia (see page 94) or tarator (see page 120). I prefer to broil (grill) the eggplant for this recipe — using a vegetable oil with a bland, unobtrusive flavor — with the olive oil in the marinade imparting its fruity flavor.

4 medium eggplants (aubergines),
stems removed

salt

vegetable oil

1/2 cup (4 fl oz/125 ml) extra
virgin olive oil

2 tablespoons red wine or
balsamic vinegar

2 cloves garlic, finely chopped

2 tablespoons finely chopped
fresh basil

freshly ground black pepper

Cut eggplant into 1/4 in (5 mm) thick slices. Place in colander, sprinkling each layer with salt. Let stand 30 minutes. Rinse and press dry in a clean cloth.

Preheat broiler (grill) until very hot. Place a layer of eggplant on lightly oiled baking sheet and brush with vegetable oil. Cook under broiler, turning to brown evenly. Transfer to shallow dish and cook remaining eggplant.

Combine olive oil, vinegar, garlic, basil and pepper to taste. Pour over eggplant and refrigerate 2 to 3 hours or overnight. Serve at room temperature as an antipasto.

FALAFEL

CHICKPEA AND BURGHUL PATTIES (ISRAEL)   MAKES ABOUT 30

The Israeli version of these popular dried bean patties is indigenous to the area, originating with the Arabs. Lebanon and Syria make a somewhat similar version without the burghul or bulghur and combining chickpeas with dried fava (broad) beans. The tameya of Egypt use only fava beans. As fava beans need lengthy soaking, and skins have to be removed unless ready-skinned dried fava beans are available, the following version is by far the easiest to make. The chickpeas (or fava beans) must only be soaked; if cooked, they disintegrate when fried.

1¼ cups (8 oz/250 g) dried chickpeas (garbanzos)

3 cups (24 fl oz/750 ml) cold water

½ cup (3 oz/90 g) burghul (steamed cracked wheat)

2 cloves garlic, chopped

4 scallions (spring onions/green onions), roughly chopped

3 tablespoons chopped flat-leaf (Italian) parsley

1 teaspoon ground coriander

1 teaspoon ground cumin

¼ teaspoon cayenne pepper

1 tablespoon lemon juice

1½ teaspoons salt

freshly ground black pepper

½ teaspoon baking soda (bicarbonate of soda)

oil, for deep frying

To Serve:

taratour bi tahini (see page 52)

pita bread (optional)

salad vegetables (e.g. shredded lettuce, sliced tomato and cucumber) (optional)

tabbouleh (see page 201) (optional)

Pick over chickpeas and remove any that are damaged. Place in large bowl and add cold water. Soak in refrigerator 24 hours.

Place burghul in sieve and rinse under cold water. Transfer to bowl, cover and let stand 20 minutes to swell and soften.

Drain chickpeas and place in food processor with burghul and remaining ingredients. Process until ground to coarse paste-like consistency. (Alternatively, mix ingredients and pass through meat grinder twice, using fine screen; then transfer to bowl and knead to paste). Cover and let stand 30 minutes.

With moistened hands, shape tablespoons of mixture into thick patties about 1½ in (4 cm) in diameter. Heat oil for deep frying to 375°F (190°C) or until cube of bread turns golden in 1 minute. Deep fry six or seven falafel at a time, turning to brown evenly, about 5 minutes. Drain on paper towels. To check if falafel are cooked, cut one in half — the color should be even through to middle; if not even, increase cooking time by 1 minute.

Serve hot as an appetizer with taratour bi tahini, or serve in warm pita bread with taratour bi tahini and salad vegetables or tabouleh.

ÇILBIR

POACHED EGGS WITH YOGURT AND SAGE (TURKEY)   SERVES 4

Placing the yogurt in warmed dishes and topping it with hot eggs makes it warm enough for serving. Alternatively, you can top the eggs with yogurt. Don't hold in a warm oven or the yogurt could separate.

1 cup (8 fl oz/250 ml) thick, country-style plain (natural) yogurt at room temperature

2 cloves garlic, pressed (crushed)

1 teaspoon salt

8 eggs

vinegar, for poaching

2 oz (60 g) unsalted butter

1/2 teaspoon paprika

1/4 teaspoon cayenne pepper

12 small fresh sage leaves

pita or crusty bread, to serve

Combine yogurt, garlic and salt. Divide mixture between four warmed individual serving dishes or plates, spreading mixture evenly over bases.

Poach eggs in water with a little vinegar added.

Meanwhile, melt butter in small frying pan. Add paprika, cayenne and sage and cook until butter sizzles, but do not let it burn. When eggs are poached as desired, remove with slotted spoon and place two in each dish. Pour a little sizzling butter mixture over each serving. Serve immediately with warm bread.

UOVA SODE RIPIENE

STUFFED EGGS (ITALY)   SERVES 6

Ideally, a hard-cooked (boiled) egg should be simmered for 15 minutes to prevent the egg white from becoming rubbery. However, it is difficult to separate the shell from the white when shelling them. Cooking eggs just at boiling point, without boiling so vigorously that they knock together, is the answer to having smooth, easily shelled boiled eggs. Have the eggs at room temperature before cooking.

6 large eggs

4 canned anchovy fillets, drained and finely chopped

31/2 oz (100 g) can tuna, drained and flaked

2 teaspoons drained capers, chopped

1 tablespoon finely chopped parsley

salt and freshly ground black pepper

Place eggs in pan and cover well with cold water. Bring to boil and boil gently, uncovered, 15 minutes. Drain and cover with cold water. Take one egg out at a time, roll it on hard surface to crack shell and return to pan — this allows air into the egg and prevents dark rings forming around yolks. Change water 2 to 3 times as eggs cool. Shell eggs, halve lengthwise and remove yolks to bowl. Set whites aside.

Add anchovies, tuna, capers, parsley and salt and pepper to taste to yolks. Mix just enough to combine so various ingredients are visible. Fill egg whites with mixture, mounding smoothly. Cover dish with plastic wrap and refrigerate until required for serving.

Antipasti including Uova Sode Ripiene

DOLMATHAKIA LATHERA

GRAPE VINE LEAVES WITH RICE STUFFING (GREECE)   MAKES 6 DOZEN

These delectable rolls are one of the most popular mezethes in Greece, originally devised for serving during times of fasting when animal foods are not permitted. They also appear in Turkish cuisine, known as yalanci asme yapraği. If using preserved leaves, select those packed in a plastic bag if possible, or use jar-packed leaves; canned leaves are not recommended as they tend to be damaged in the canning process. Do not roll the leaves too tightly as the rice filling swells during the final cooking. The rolls should be fairly long and slender.

1 lb (500 g) preserved grape vine leaves or 7 dozen fresh

3/4 cup (6 fl oz/180 ml) olive oil

3 tablespoons pine nuts

1 large onion, finely chopped

6 scallions (spring onions/green onions), finely chopped

1 cup (7 oz/210 g) medium-grained rice

3 tablespoons chopped flat-leaf (Italian) parsley

2 teaspoons chopped fresh mint

1 tablespoon chopped fresh dill

3 tablespoons dried currants

salt and freshly ground black pepper

2 cups (16 fl oz/500 ml) water

juice of 1 lemon

To Serve:

lemon slices

thick country-style plain (natural) yogurt (optional)

Rinse leaves. Blanch in boiling water 2 to 3 minutes. Drain in colander and rinse under cold water. Snip off any stems.

Heat 1/2 cup oil in pan. Add pine nuts and stir until lightly golden. Add onion and scallions and cook gently, stirring occasionally, until transparent, about 10 minutes. Add dry rice and stir over heat 2 minutes. Stir in herbs, currants, salt and pepper to taste, and half the water. Cover tightly and cook over low heat until water is absorbed, about 10 minutes. Set aside.

To fill rolls, place leaf, smooth-side down, on plate and place heaping teaspoon of stuffing in middle. Fold stem end over stuffing, fold in sides and roll to end of leaf.

Line base of heavy saucepan with whole or damaged leaves and pack rolls closely in layers, with end of leaf facing down. Sprinkle each layer with a little remaining olive oil and lemon juice. When completed, pour in remaining water, cover with more leaves and invert heavy plate on top. Cover pan, bring to boil, reduce heat and simmer gently 50 minutes. Let cool, covered.

Remove rolls carefully to serving dish. Cover and refrigerate several hours before serving. Garnish with lemon slices. Serve with yogurt for dipping, if desired.

PAN BAGNAT

NIÇOISE SANDWICH (FRANCE)   SERVES 6

Olive oil is undoubtedly the butter of the Mediterranean, and nothing illustrates this fact more deliciously than the famous pan bagnat of Nice. Foods indicative of the region are combined to produce a delicious, moist sandwich. Not all filling ingredients need be used, but one type of fish and the eggs should be included. The lettuce or endive too close to the oil will become soggy very quickly so when constructing the sandwich place leaves away from bread surface.

2 cloves garlic

2/3 cup (5 1/2 fl oz/160 ml) extra
virgin olive oil

1 baguette (long French loaf) or
6 crusty white bread rolls

Filling:

1 green bell pepper (capsicum),
thinly sliced

1 cucumber, peeled and sliced

1 purple onion, thinly sliced

crisp butter head lettuce or
curly endive leaves

3 ripe tomatoes, sliced

1 roasted red bell pepper
(capsicum) (see page 27), or
1 canned pimiento, thickly sliced

3 hard-cooked (boiled) eggs, sliced

12 drained canned anchovy fillets
and/or 6 oz (180 g) can tuna,
drained and flaked

12 black olives, pitted and halved
or 4 tablespoons tapenade
(see page 48)

Bruise garlic cloves by pressing with flat of heavy knife and place in clean jar with olive oil. Seal and let stand several hours or overnight, shaking jar occasionally.

If loaf is very long, halve it, then split each half horizontally. If using bread rolls, split into halves. Remove a little crumb from inside to make hollows. Brush each cut side generously with garlic-flavored oil.

Layer filling ingredients into loaf or rolls, beginning with bell pepper or cucumber. Top with olives, or spread top half of bread with tapenade. Wrap in plastic wrap and flatten between two boards 1 to 2 hours if desired. If using for a picnic, refrigerate, then keep chilled until required. If using loaf, cut each half into 3 pieces before serving.

BRUSCHETTE CON RUCHETTA

GARLIC TOASTS WITH ARUGULA (ITALY)   SERVES 6

The bruschette of Italy inspired the ubiquitous garlic bread, but the original, drizzled with fruity olive oil, is far more enjoyable. Toppings can vary but simple tomato and arugula is hard to beat. I like to add sun-dried tomatoes to intensify the tomato flavor but these can be omitted if your tomatoes are sweet and flavorful. Use an oval-shaped loaf of Italian bread. You can also serve the bruschette individually, two to a plate, to be eaten with a knife and fork.

1/2 cup (4 fl oz/125 ml) extra-virgin olive oil

2 cloves garlic, halved

4 oz (125 g) small arugula (rocket) leaves

6 to 8 medium vine-ripened tomatoes

12 thick slices Italian bread

salt

freshly ground black pepper

3 tablespoons chopped, drained sun-dried tomatoes

Combine olive oil in jug with garlic and let stand 30 minutes. Rinse arugula leaves and dry in salad spinner, or roll loosely in clean cloth and place in refrigerator to crisp and dry. Wash tomatoes, dry and halve lengthwise. Carefully cut out stem section of each half. Cut into thin wedges.

Toast bread slowly under broiler (grill) using moderate heat so it dries as well as toasts on each side. Overlap tomato wedges on each bruschetta, season with salt and pepper and sprinkle lightly with sun-dried tomatoes. Top each with 3 or 4 arugula leaves. Arrange bruschette slightly overlapping on platter. Garnish with remaining arugula. Strain olive oil evenly over bruschette and serve immediately.

PA AMB TOMAQUET

TOASTED BREAD WITH TOMATO (SPAIN)   SERVES 6

I first tasted this popular bread on the Costa Brava, relishing its simple flavors — the tomatoes were warm from the sun, yielding to the touch, and tasting as a tomato should. Any close-textured, crusty country-style bread can be used for this Catalan version of the Italian bruschetta. Choose an oval loaf so that the slices are of manageable size. If your tomatoes seem to lack flavor and are very firm, halve and place cut-side up under a moderate broiler (grill) 3 to 5 minutes to soften slightly. Sprinkle with a little sugar before rubbing into bread. In Catalonia, the guests would rub the tomato into the bread themselves. Serve as a snack, tapa or as an accompaniment to main meals.

12 x 1/2 in (1 cm) thick slices country-style bread

3 cloves garlic, halved (optional)

6 soft, vine-ripened tomatoes

olive oil

salt and freshly ground black pepper

paper-thin slices ham, to serve (optional)

Toast bread under hot broiler (grill) or on barbecue grid over glowing coals. While warm, rub each slice on one side with cut garlic clove.

Halve tomatoes crosswise and rub each side of toast with tomato half, allowing juice, seeds and pulp to soak into bread. Drizzle with olive oil and season with salt and pepper. Serve topped with ham, if desired.

Bruschette con Ruchetta

POMODORO RIPIENI

STUFFED TOMATOES (ITALY)   SERVES 6

12 medium-sized ripe tomatoes
sugar
salt and freshly ground black pepper
1/2 cup (4 fl oz/125 ml) olive oil
1 onion, finely chopped
1 clove garlic, finely chopped
1 cup (7 oz/210 g)
medium-grain rice
3 tablespoons chopped fresh basil
1 1/2 cups (12 fl oz/375 ml) water
2 tablespoons tomato paste

Slice tops from tomatoes and reserve. Scoop out pulp with melon baller or teaspoon, and reserve. Sprinkle cavities with sugar and set aside. Place pulp in saucepan with salt, pepper and 1/2 teaspoon sugar and simmer until soft. Press through sieve or food mill with fine screen into bowl and reserve.

Warm half the oil in frying pan. Add onion and cook gently until soft, about 10 minutes. Add garlic and cook gently several seconds. Add tomato pulp, rice, half the basil and half the water. Stir well, cover and simmer gently until rice is half-cooked and liquid is absorbed, about 10 minutes. Season with salt and pepper to taste.

Preheat oven to 325–350°F (160–180°C/Gas 3). Spoon mixture loosely into tomatoes and cover with tops. Pour a little oil in baking dish, arrange tomatoes on base and spoon remaining oil over. Combine tomato paste with 1 teaspoon sugar, remaining water, and salt and pepper to taste. Pour around tomatoes. Bake uncovered until rice is cooked, about 30 to 35 minutes. Serve hot or at room temperature.

ROLLATA DI ZUCCHINE

ROLLED ZUCCHINI WITH RICOTTA (ITALY)   SERVES 4 TO 6

5 large, evenly-shaped
zucchini (courgettes),
about 7 in (18 cm) long
salt
1/2 cup (4 fl oz/125 ml) olive oil
1 clove garlic, bruised
1 1/2 cups (12 oz/375 g)
ricotta cheese
4 tablespoons grated
parmesan cheese
2 tablespoons finely chopped
parsley
2 tablespoons finely chopped
fresh basil
4 scallions (spring onions/green
onions), including some green tops,
finely chopped
freshly ground black pepper

Trim stems and rounded ends from zucchini and cut lengthwise into 1/8 in (3 mm) thick slices; discard skin-covered side strips. Place in colander, sprinkling each layer lightly with salt. Let stand 20 minutes to soften. Rinse, drain and dry slices with cloth. Pour some of the olive oil into frying pan to just cover base. Add garlic and heat until garlic is lightly browned; discard. Add single layer of zucchini to pan and fry each side until golden brown. Set aside. Fry remaining zucchini in batches.

Mash ricotta with fork in bowl. Mix in parmesan, herbs, scallions, and salt and pepper to taste.

Brush shallow baking dish with a little oil. Preheat oven to 325–350°F (160–180°C/Gas 3). Place strip of zucchini on plate and spread with 1 tablespoon cheese mixture. Roll up from stem end and place fold-side down in baking dish. Repeat with remaining ingredients, placing rolls close together in dish. Drizzle remaining olive oil over rolls and bake until golden, about 30 minutes. Serve hot as an antipasto.

Soufflés au Roquefort

ROQUEFORT SOUFFLÉS (FRANCE)   SERVES 4

The home of roquefort cheese is Roquefort-sur-Soulzon in the northern hills of Languedoc. So great is the demand for this king of cheeses that the base sheep's milk cheeses arrive from many parts of Languedoc, the Pyrenees, and from Corsica, to be finished and matured in the famous caves. Perhaps the natives of Roquefort-sur-Soulzon may not approve, but the cheese makes a delicious soufflé. These soufflés can be served as a first course, accompanied by a mesclun salad, dressed with walnut oil and wine vinegar. If you make the sauce in advance, press a piece of plastic wrap over the surface before completing and cooking soufflés.

2 tablespoons unsalted butter

2 tablespoons all-purpose (plain) flour

1 cup (8 fl oz/250 ml) milk

3 oz (90 g) roquefort cheese, crumbled

freshly ground black pepper

grating of fresh nutmeg

4 egg yolks

5 egg whites

Melt butter in saucepan, stir in flour and cook gently 2 to 3 minutes without allowing it to color. Remove pan from heat, add milk all at once and stir well with wooden spoon. Return to medium heat and stir until thickened and bubbling. Boil gently 1 minute. Mix in cheese, pepper and nutmeg, remove from heat and stir until smooth. Beat in egg yolks and set aside until ready to cook soufflés.

Preheat oven to 375–400°F (190–200°C/Gas 5). Butter four soufflé dishes, 1 cup (8 fl oz/250 ml) in capacity.

Beat egg whites in bowl until stiff peaks form, but do not over-beat. Fold 2 heaped tablespoons egg white into cooked sauce then pour sauce down side of egg white bowl. Using large metal spoon, combine egg whites and sauce lightly and thoroughly, using an over-and-under folding action rather than stirring. When completely combined, pour into soufflé dishes and run round-tipped knife blade around soufflé, 1/2 in (1 cm) in from edge. Place dishes on baking sheet. Bake until risen and golden brown, about 15 minutes. Transfer dishes to plates and serve immediately.

grapes

SOUPS

Mediterranean soups range from virtual meals in a pot, such as the minestrone of Italy or the fasoulatha of Greece and Cyprus to the therapeutic aigo boulido of southern France. There are also cold soups; the Andalusian gazpacho, a chilled salad soup bursting with the flavors of summer, ajo blanco con uvas malaga, a white garlic and almond gazpacho-style soup, and the refreshing cacik, a chilled yogurt soup from Turkey; all are ideal for serving on a hot day.

One characteristic of southern French and Italian soups is serving them over bread slices or adding bread to the ingredients. Bread is the roux of the Mediterranean, adding body as well as nourishment to the soups, and a very handy way to use up stale bread.

Lunch is the main meal of the day in the Mediterranean, taken in the early afternoon and followed by siesta, an enviable practice in hot climates. Soups, therefore, are often served at night with whatever is left over from lunch. Soups containing dried beans and peas and/or grains and pasta are ideal for serving as a meal, many of them meatless for those who follow a vegetarian diet.

One of my favorite soups is the Greek psarosoupa avgolemono. It is made with fish stock but can also utilize chicken, lamb or veal stock, and is the Greek equivalent of the Jewish mother's proverbial panacea, chicken soup. Italy also has its version in stracciatella alla romana. I was too young to remember my first taste of it, but it is spooned into the mouths of toddlers and dished up to any family member who is not feeling well. The delicious, light soup with its lemony tang is special enough to serve as a dinner party soup course; it can also be served chilled.

Many other soups work well as a separate course. The French soupe de tomates au pistou tastes as good as it looks; the potage purée de marrons and soupe au potiron, the Italian passato di spinaci, and the Israeli marak avocado are also excellent for such service.

Ajo Blanco con Uvas Malaga (page 80)

67

Soupe de Tomates au Pistou

TOMATO SOUP WITH PISTOU (FRANCE)   SERVES 6

Pistou, Provence's version of the Genoese pesto, is usually added to a vegetable soup. However, it is extremely good stirred into a fresh tomato soup, whether served hot or chilled. Tomato paste and sugar intensify the flavor of commercially-grown tomatoes. Wash the basil leaves and spin in a salad spinner to remove excess water before measuring.

2 tablespoons olive oil

1 large onion, chopped

2 cloves garlic, pressed (crushed)

3 lb (1.5 kg) ripe tomatoes, peeled, seeded and chopped

2 tablespoons tomato paste

3 sprigs flat-leaf (Italian) parsley

2 sprigs fresh thyme

1 cup (8 fl oz/250 ml) water

3 teaspoons sugar

salt and freshly ground black pepper

Pistou:

1 cup (2 oz/60 g) packed basil leaves

2 cloves garlic, chopped

1/4 cup (2 fl oz/60 ml) extra virgin olive oil

Warm oil in large saucepan. Add onion and garlic and cook gently until onion is transparent, about 10 minutes. Add tomatoes, tomato paste, herb sprigs (tied together), water, sugar, and salt and pepper to taste. Cover and simmer gently until tomatoes are very soft, about 30 minutes.

For pistou: Puree basil and garlic in food processor. Gradually add olive oil in thin stream while processing. Season with salt to taste.

Remove herbs from soup and discard. Puree soup in saucepan with hand-held blender or puree in batches in food processor. Return to pan and bring soup to boil. Adjust seasoning, and pour into soup bowls. Place 1 tablespoon pistou in middle of each bowl and swirl with fine skewer. Serve hot, or if desired chill soup and serve with pistou.

SOUPE AU POTIRON

PUMPKIN SOUP (FRANCE)   SERVES 6

Pumpkin is used to some extent in the region, particularly in the cooler months when it is in season. A firm, heavy pumpkin is superior to one that is light for its size, as its flesh could be watery and tasteless.

2 lb (1 kg) butternut pumpkin (squash) or other firm pumpkin

1 tablespoon olive oil

1 large onion, chopped

2 cloves garlic, chopped

1/4 cup (1 1/2 oz/50 g) medium-grain rice

2 sprigs each parsley and thyme

4 cups (32 fl oz/1 L) chicken stock (see page 31)

1/4 teaspoon grated nutmeg

salt and freshly ground black pepper

1/2 cup (4 fl oz/125 ml) light (single) cream

snipped fresh chives or chopped parsley, to garnish

extra light (single) cream, to serve

Peel pumpkin, remove seeds and chop into cubes. Warm oil in large saucepan. Add onion and cook gently until soft, about 5 to 6 minutes. Add garlic and cook several seconds. Add pumpkin, rice, herbs (tied together), stock, nutmeg, salt and pepper. Cover and simmer until pumpkin is soft, about 15 to 20 minutes. Discard herbs.

Puree soup with a hand-held blender in saucepan, or puree in batches in food processor. Return to pan and bring to gentle simmer. Stir in cream and heat gently. If too thick, add a little water. Serve hot, garnished with chives or parsley. A little extra cream may be swirled in middle of each bowl before garnishing, if desired.

MARAK AVOCADO

AVOCADO SOUP (ISRAEL)   SERVES 6

The avocado was introduced into the Mediterranean region by the Israelis, and even features in Lebanese cuisine, where its cultivation has spread.

3 scallions (spring onions/green onions), finely chopped

2 oz (60 g) margarine or butter

1/4 cup (2 oz/60 g) all-purpose (plain) flour

5 cups (40 fl oz/1.25 L) chicken stock (see page 31)

2 egg yolks

2 large avocados

juice of 1/2 lemon

salt and freshly ground white pepper

extra sliced avocado and lemon rind, to garnish

Melt margarine in medium saucepan and gently fry scallions until soft. Stir in flour and cook 2 minutes without allowing it to color. Gradually add stock and bring to boil, stirring constantly. Beat egg yolks in a bowl and whisk in 1 cup hot stock. Stir egg mixture into simmering stock in pan and stir over low heat just long enough to cook egg, about 1 to 2 minutes — do not boil. Remove pan from heat.

Peel avocados and puree in food processor or push through sieve. Stir into soup. Add lemon juice and salt and pepper to taste. Return to heat and stir contantly until just heated through — do not boil or heat for too long as avocado will become bitter. Serve hot, garnished with thin slices of avocado and julienned lemon rind.

MINESTRONE ALLA GENOVESE

MINESTRONE WITH PESTO (ITALY)   SERVES 6 TO 8

This is the Genoese version of the hearty vegetable, bean and pasta soup known throughout most of Italy. The soupe au pistou of Provence is similar, except that pine nuts are omitted from the pistou (which is, in turn, copied from the pesto of Genoa). To reduce preparation and cooking time, a 15 oz (425 g) can of cannellini beans may be used in place of the dried beans. Add drained canned beans with potatoes then proceed with recipe.

3/4 cup (5 oz/150 g) cannellini beans
1/4 cup (2 fl oz/60 ml) olive oil
2 onions, chopped
2 cloves garlic, finely chopped
8 cups (64 fl oz/2 L) water
2 medium carrots, diced
1 celery stalk, chopped
1 large potato, peeled and diced
15 oz (425 g) can tomatoes, chopped but undrained
2 tablespoons tomato paste
1/2 teaspoon sugar
salt and freshly ground black pepper
4 oz (125 g) green beans, cut in short lengths
2 zucchini (courgettes), diced
4 green cabbage leaves, ribs removed and shredded
4 oz (125 g) soup pasta or broken spaghetti
2 tablespoons pesto sauce (see page 35)

To Serve:
extra pesto sauce
freshly grated parmesan cheese

Wash beans well. Place in large bowl with three times their volume of cold water and soak overnight in refrigerator. Drain and rinse.

Warm oil in large saucepan. Add onion and cook gently until transparent, about 10 minutes. Add garlic and cook several seconds. Add drained beans, water, carrots and celery. Bring to boil, cover and simmer 1 hour.

Add potato, tomatoes with their liquid, tomato paste, sugar, and salt and pepper. Cover and simmer 30 minutes. Add green beans and zucchini and simmer, uncovered, 15 minutes. Add shredded cabbage and pasta and simmer until pasta is tender, about 15 minutes. Stir in pesto and serve hot with extra pesto and parmesan served separately.

Minestrone alla Genovese

70

ACQUACOTTA

TUSCAN VEGETABLE SOUP (ITALY)   SERVES 4 TO 6

A soup for vegetarians, as the name "cooked water" implies. Meat stock isn't used in this simple soup, but the eggs add body.

1/4 cup (2 fl oz/60 ml) olive oil

3 medium onions, sliced

2 celery stalks, diced

1 red bell pepper (capsicum), diced

15 oz (425 g) can tomatoes

2 tablespoons tomato paste

2 teaspoons sugar

5 cups (40 fl oz/1.25 L) water

salt and freshly ground
black pepper

3 eggs

To Serve:

8 to 12 thin slices country-style
bread, toasted

finely chopped parsley

grated parmesan cheese (optional)

Warm oil in large saucepan. Add onions and cook gently until transparent, about 10 minutes. Add celery and bell pepper and cook gently 5 minutes. Pass undrained tomatoes through food mill or press through sieve directly into saucepan. Stir in tomato paste, sugar, water, and salt and pepper to taste. Cover and simmer until vegetables are tender, about 30 minutes.

Bring soup to boil. Beat eggs in bowl with pinch of salt. Pour into warmed soup tureen or large serving bowl and gradually beat in boiling soup. Cover and let stand 5 minutes.

To serve, place 2 slices toast into wide soup bowls, spoon soup over and garnish with chopped parsley. Serve with bowl of grated parmesan, if desired.

CIPOLLATA

TUSCAN ONION SOUP (ITALY)   SERVES 6

This is one of a number of onion soups in Italian regional cooking. Milder, white onions are preferrable to the stronger brown onions. The method used in preparation makes the onions easier on the digestion.

4 large white onions

salt

3 oz (90 g) pancetta, thickly sliced

1/4 cup (2 fl oz/60 ml) olive oil

6 cups (48 fl oz/1.5 L) meat or
chicken stock (see page 31)

freshly ground black pepper

6 thick slices coarse-textured bread,
toasted

3 tablespoons grated parmesan
cheese

Cut onions in half then into half-moon slices. Place in deep saucepan, cover with water and add 1 teaspoon salt. Bring to boil and boil 5 minutes. Drain in colander.

Coarsely chop pancetta. Heat oil in same saucepan. Add pancetta and cook gently 5 minutes. Add drained onions and cook gently over low heat, until golden, not browned, about 10 minutes, stirring often. Add stock and salt and pepper to taste. Bring to boil, cover and simmer gently 30 minutes.

Place a slice of toast in each soup bowl. Ladle in soup and sprinkle with parmesan.

MINESTRA AI FUNGHI

MUSHROOM SOUP (ITALY)   SERVES 6

Wild mushrooms are traditionally used in this Ligurian soup — porcini and ovoli (Caesar's mushroom) are particularly popular. You can use cultivated mushrooms — choose ones with the caps beginning to open — and add dried porcini to boost the flavor. If using vermicelli, choose long strands, not nests.

1 oz (30 g) dried porcini mushrooms (boletus/cepes) (optional)

8 oz (250 g) cultivated mushrooms

3 tablespoons olive oil

6 cups (48 fl oz/1.5 L) chicken stock (see page 31)

6 oz (180 g) spaghettini or vermicelli pasta

salt and freshly ground black pepper

2 tablespoons finely chopped flat-leaf (Italian) parsley

If using dried porcini, soak in warm water to cover 20 minutes. Drain, rinse and pat dry with paper towels. Cut into thin strips. Trim cultivated mushroom stems. Wipe off any soil with damp cloth but do not wash. Cut into thin slices.

Heat oil in large saucepan. Add mushrooms and cook, stirring constantly, until liquid begins to run. Add stock and bring to boil. Cover and boil 5 minutes. Add pasta, stir well and boil, uncovered, until pasta is tender, about 10 minutes. Add salt and pepper to taste, ladle into bowls and sprinkle with parsley. Serve hot.

ZUPPA DI ZUCCHINE

ZUCCHINI SOUP (ITALY)   SERVES 6

One would expect a soup of this type, delicate and nourishing, to feature in the Italian kitchen although it is not widely used. It is important to stir the soup after removing from heat — this prevents curdling from the stored heat in the saucepan.

1½ lb (750 g) small zucchini (courgettes)

2 oz (60 g) butter

1 large onion, chopped

1 clove garlic, finely chopped (optional)

6 cups (48 fl oz/1.5 L) chicken stock (see page 31)

2 large eggs

1 tablespoon chopped fresh basil

1 tablespoon chopped flat-leaf (Italian) parsley

2 tablespoons grated parmesan cheese

toasted country-style bread, to serve

grated parmesan cheese, to serve

finely chopped flat-leaf (Italian) parsley, to serve

Cut stems and round ends from zucchini, and slice thinly.

Melt butter in large saucepan. Add onion and cook gently until transparent, about 10 minutes. Add garlic and zucchini and cook gently, 5 minutes, stirring occasionally. Add stock and bring to boil. Cover and simmer over low heat until zucchini is very tender, about 20 minutes.

Puree in pan with hand-held blender, or in batches in food processor. Return to pan and bring to boil.

Beat eggs in bowl with herbs and cheese. Beat in 1 cup boiling soup. Remove pan from heat. Using wooden spoon, slowly add egg mixture to soup, stirring constantly. Return to medium heat and stir 1 to 2 minutes — do not allow soup to boil. Remove from heat and keep stirring 1 to 2 minutes to prevent curdling.

Place slice of toast in each wide soup bowl, pour in soup and sprinkle parmesan and parsley on top. Serve hot with extra parmesan in separate bowl.

Minestra di Ceci e Linguine

CHICKPEA AND LINGUINE SOUP (ITALY)   SERVES 6

Fasting days in Italy call for foods without animal products. As with all fasting recipes, this dish is excellent for those following a vegetarian diet. Chickpeas and pasta, two different sources of vegetable proteins, combine to give complete protein, as good as animal protein. Other pasta such as broken thin spaghetti or tagliatelle ribbon pasta may be used in place of the linguine.

1 cup (7 oz/210 g) dried chickpeas (garbanzos)

6 cups (48 fl oz/1.5 L) water

1 large sprig fresh rosemary

1/3 cup (3 fl oz/80 ml) olive oil

1 medium onion, sliced

2 cloves garlic, chopped

2 tablespoons tomato paste

salt and freshly ground black pepper

6 oz (180 g) linguine, broken into short lengths

To Serve:

1 tablespoon chopped fresh rosemary (optional)

crusty bread

extra virgin olive oil

Place chickpeas in sieve and pick over to remove any extra matter. Rinse under cold running water. Place in bowl with 3 cups water, cover and soak overnight in refrigerator.

Place chickpeas and their soaking liquid in large saucepan with 3 cups water and rosemary sprig. Bring to boil, cover and simmer until tender, about 1 1/2 hours. Discard rosemary.

Heat oil in frying pan. Add onion and cook gently until transparent, about 10 minutes. Add garlic and cook several seconds. Add tomato paste and 1 cupful of liquid from cooked chickpeas, stir well and add to saucepan of chickpeas. Season with salt and pepper to taste and bring to boil. Stir in pasta and boil gently until pasta is tender, about 10 minutes.

Transfer to individual soup bowls and garnish with chopped rosemary, if desired. Serve with crusty bread and a small jug of olive oil.

bell pepper

Minestra di Ceci e Linguine

FAKI SOUPA

LENTIL SOUP (GREECE, CYPRUS)   SERVES 6

Croutons of bread fried in olive oil are often served with this vegetarian soup, particularly in Cyprus.

1³/₄ cups (12 oz/375 g) brown lentils

8 cups (64 fl oz/2 L) water

¹/₄ cup (2 fl oz/60 ml) olive oil

1 large onion, chopped

2 cloves garlic, finely chopped

1 celery stalk, chopped

2 carrots, diced

15 oz (425 g) can tomatoes

1 bay leaf

2 small sprigs fresh rosemary

salt and freshly ground black pepper

1 to 2 tablespoons red wine vinegar (optional)

2 tablespoons chopped parsley

Place lentils in sieve and pick over to remove extra matter. Rinse under cold running water. Place in large saucepan, add 8 cups water and bring slowly to the boil, skimming when necessary.

Heat oil in small frying pan. Add onion and garlic and cook gently until transparent, about 10 minutes. Add to saucepan of lentils with celery, carrots, chopped tomatoes with their liquid, and bay leaf and rosemary tied together. Cover and simmer over low heat 45 minutes. Uncover and simmer until soup is thick, about 15 minutes more — do not stir during cooking or lentils could stick to base of saucepan.

Discard rosemary and bay leaf. Add salt and pepper and vinegar to taste. Serve sprinkled with parsley.

HARIRA HARA BI KESKOU

SPICY SOUP WITH COUSCOUS (ALGERIA)   SERVES 6

As this soup is made without meat stock, it is ideal for vegetarians. If you have traditional couscous, it will require longer cooking and should be added 15 minutes before end of cooking time.

4 tablespoons olive oil

1 small onion, finely chopped

2 cloves garlic, pressed (crushed)

1 teaspoon harissa (see page 33)

1 tablespoon paprika

15 oz (425 g) can tomatoes, chopped but undrained

6 cups (48 fl oz/1.5 L) water

salt and freshly ground black pepper

2 medium potatoes (about 12 oz/350g)

¹/₂ cup (3¹/₂ oz/100 g) instant couscous

3 tablespoons finely chopped fresh coriander leaves (cilantro)

Heat oil in large saucepan. Add onion and cook gently until transparent, about 10 minutes. Add garlic and cook several seconds. Add harissa to taste and cook gently, stirring, 1 to 2 minutes. Add paprika, tomatoes with their liquid, water, and salt and pepper to taste. Bring to boil.

Peel potatoes, cut into ¹/₂ in (1 cm) cubes and add to soup. Cover and simmer until potatoes are tender, about 20 minutes. Stir in couscous and boil gently, uncovered, until couscous has swelled and softened, about 10 minutes.

Adjust seasoning, adding more harissa if desired. Stir in coriander, cover and let stand 5 minutes. Serve hot in deep soup bowls with bread.

FAVA

SPLIT PEA PUREE (GREECE)   SERVES 4 TO 6

Although the word fava is used to describe broad beans elsewhere, in Greece it means a puree made from yellow split peas. This simple dish, eaten with a spoon, is filling and nourishing. Do not add more water than amount given. A good fava should be a thick puree and if water covers the peas throughout the cooking period, the result is too liquid. If your water is hard, use filtered or bottled water for quicker cooking. Do not add salt until the end. Avoid stirring during cooking or peas will stick to the pan, but do stir the top of the peas to distribute heat more evenly, otherwise some peas may not soften adequately.

2¹/₂ cups (1 lb/500 g) yellow
split peas
6 cups (48 fl oz/1.5 L) water
1 medium onion, chopped
salt

To Serve:
olive oil
lemon wedges
sliced purple onion
olives
country-style bread

Place peas in sieve and pick over to remove extra matter. Rinse under running cold water. Place in large, heavy saucepan, add 6 cups water and bring to boil, skimming off surface froth as it rises. Add onion and simmer, covered, over low heat until thick, about 50 to 60 minutes.

Remove from heat and let stand, covered, 10 minutes. Season with salt to taste.

To serve, spoon fava into wide soup bowls and trickle 1 tablespoon olive oil onto each serve. Serve with lemon wedges, purple onion, olives and bread.

SHOURBAT EL ADS

LENTIL AND VERMICELLI SOUP (EGYPT)   SERVES 6 TO 8

Soup made with red lentils is popular in the eastern part of the Mediterranean — Egypt, Turkey, Cyprus, Lebanon and Syria, although flavorings and additives vary.

1³/₄ cups (12 oz/350 g) red lentils
2 tablespoons olive oil
1 large onion, finely chopped
2 cloves garlic, pressed (crushed)
1 teaspoon ground cumin
¹/₂ teaspoon ground coriander
8 cups (64 fl oz/2 L) chicken stock
(see page 31)
salt and freshly ground
black pepper
2 tablespoons lemon juice
3¹/₂ oz (100 g) vermicelli pasta,
broken into short lengths
2 tablespoons finely chopped
flat-leaf (Italian) parsley

Place lentils in sieve and pick over to remove extra matter. Rinse under cold running water and drain.

Heat oil in large saucepan. Add onion and cook until transparent, about 10 minutes. Add garlic, cumin and coriander and cook gently 1 to 2 minutes. Stir in lentils and stock and bring to boil. Reduce heat, cover and simmer gently until lentils are soft, about 50 minutes.

Add salt and pepper to taste, lemon juice and pasta. Return to boil, stirring, and boil gently, uncovered, until pasta is tender, about 3 to 4 minutes. Stir in parsley and serve hot.

Fasoulatha Mavromatika

BLACK-EYED BEAN SOUP (GREECE) SERVES 6

Black-eyed beans or peas are native to tropical Africa and Asia, and like chickpeas (garbanzos), fava (broad) beans and lentils, are foods of the Old World. While these others are used widely in the Mediterranean, black-eyed beans are not as popular as they should be. They are sweeter in flavor and cook more quickly than other dried beans. This recipe is a family favorite, and although I have been cooking it for years, my soup never tasted like Mother's. Only recently did my teacher remember to tell me that she added mixed spices to it. The black eye of the beans leaches out into the water causing discoloration. If you wish the soup to have a pleasant tomato color, note the level of the water in the saucepan with the handle of a dry wooden spoon after the beans have been standing for 30 minutes. Pour off the water and replace with fresh water to the level indicated on the spoon handle.

2 cups (14 oz/400 g)
black-eyed beans

8 cups (64 fl oz/2 L) water

1 large onion, finely chopped

15 oz (425 g) can tomatoes,
chopped but undrained

1 tablespoon tomato paste

1 celery stalk, chopped

2 medium carrots, chopped

1/4 teaspoon mixed spices or ground
allspice (pimento)

1 tablespoon chopped
celery leaves

3 tablespoons chopped flat-leaf
(Italian) parsley

1/4 cup (2 fl oz/60 ml) olive oil

1/2 teaspoon sugar

salt and freshly ground
black pepper

To Serve:

extra chopped flat-leaf
(Italian) parsley

crusty bread

Place beans in sieve and pick over to remove extra matter. Rinse under cold running water. Place in large saucepan with 8 cups water and bring slowly to boil. Boil 1 minute. Remove saucepan from heat, cover and let stand until beans are plump, about 30 minutes.

Add onion, tomatoes with their liquid, tomato paste, celery, carrots, spice, celery leaves, parsley, oil and sugar. Cover and simmer gently until beans are tender, about 1 hour. Season with salt and pepper to taste. Pour into soup bowls, sprinkle with parsley and serve hot with bread.

Fasoulatha Mavromatika

AIGO BOULIDO

GARLIC AND SAGE SOUP (FRANCE)   SERVES 4

Garlic has long been regarded as a remedy for many ailments; in combination with sage, its therapeutic properties are claimed to be enhanced. This pick-me-up actually translates as "boiled water" in the patois of Provence, but you have never tasted water like this! For a more substantial dish, poach 4 eggs and place on bread in each bowl before adding soup.

1 head garlic
12 fresh sage leaves
6 cups (48 fl oz/1.5 L) water
salt
2 tablespoons olive oil
freshly ground black pepper
4 thin slices country-style bread
2 cloves garlic, halved
extra virgin olive oil, to serve
4 fresh sage leaves, extra,
to garnish

Separate garlic cloves, and bruise by placing flat of knife on each clove and banging with hand — just enough to split skins (discard these) and break up flesh a little. Wash sage and crumble in fingers to release flavor.

Place garlic, sage, 6 cups water, 2 teaspoons salt, and oil in large saucepan and bring to boil. Cover and simmer 20 minutes. Strain through sieve into bowl; discard sage. Rub garlic through sieve into soup with back of wooden spoon. Return soup to heat, add salt and pepper to taste, and simmer gently while preparing bread.

Dry bread slowly under medium broiler (grill) or in oven at 300°F (150°C/Gas 2) — do not toast. Rub each slice lightly with garlic halves and place in soup bowls. Drizzle a little extra virgin olive oil over each piece. Pour in soup, garnish with sage and serve immediately.

AJO BLANCO CON UVAS MALAGA

GARLIC AND ALMOND SOUP WITH GRAPES (SPAIN)   SERVES 6

A pestle and mortar is traditionally used to make this chilled soup from Malaga; a food processor is easier.

1 cup (5 oz/150 g) whole blanched
almonds
1/2 cup (21/2 oz/75 g) pine nuts
3 cloves garlic
3/4 cup (11/2 oz/45 g) soft white
breadcrumbs
3 cups (24 fl oz/750 ml) iced water
1/4 cup (2 fl oz/60 ml) olive oil
2 to 3 tablespoons sherry vinegar
salt
6 oz (180 g) seedless grapes,
to serve

Grind almonds, pine nuts and garlic in food processor — do not over-process or nuts will become oily. Add breadcrumbs and 1/2 cup iced water and process to fine puree, scraping down sides of bowl occasionally. With motor operating, gradually pour in oil and 2 tablespoons vinegar.

Transfer to bowl and mix in remaining iced water. Add salt and vinegar to taste. Cover and refrigerate until required. Check consistency before serving; if too thick, add a little more iced water.

Serve in soup tureen, large glass bowl or individual bowls, floating peeled grapes on surface.

Passato di Spinaci

PUREED SPINACH SOUP (ITALY)   SERVES 4 TO 6

Italian spinach is stronger in flavor than the variety generally available, often sold as English spinach. In Italy, the spinach is boiled and drained before adding to the stock, but this is not necessay with standard spinach. Use a stainless steel, enamelled cast iron or similar saucepan to make this soup, not aluminum.

1¹/₂ lb (750 g) spinach

2 tablespoons olive oil

1 onion, chopped

¹/₂ celery stalk, chopped

1 small carrot, chopped

5 cups (40 fl oz/1.25 L) chicken stock (see page 31)

salt and freshly ground black pepper

¹/₄ teaspoon ground nutmeg

3 tablespoons grated parmesan cheese

Cut roots from spinach and 1 in (2.5 cm) from ends. Remove any damaged stems and leaves. Wash in several changes of cold water, drain and chop roughly.

Heat oil in large saucepan. Add onion, celery and carrot and cook gently until onion is transparent, about 10 minutes. Add stock and salt and pepper to taste. Cover and simmer 30 minutes. Add spinach and nutmeg and boil gently, uncovered, until spinach is tender, about 10 minutes.

Puree soup in pan with hand-held blender, or in food processor. Return to pan and bring to simmer. Adjust seasoning. Serve in bowls, sprinkled with parmesan.

Cacik

CHILLED YOGURT AND CUCUMBER SOUP (TURKEY)   SERVES 6

Cacık is Turkey's version of the yogurt and cucumber salad prepared in Lebanon, Syria, Cyprus and Greece (see tzatziki on page 49). In Turkey, the mixture is also thinned down and, with a slight variation, presented as a soup. The cucumbers should be small and firm, with under-developed seeds.

2 small green cucumbers, peeled (see page 14)

salt

3 cups (24 fl oz/750 ml) plain (natural) yogurt

2 cloves garlic, pressed (crushed)

2 tablespoons finely chopped fresh mint

1 tablespoon finely chopped fresh dill (optional)

3 tablespoons olive oil

about 1 cup (8 fl oz/250 ml) iced water

freshly ground white pepper

thin cucumber slices, to garnish

mint sprigs, to garnish

Shred cucumber into colander and lightly mix in 1 teaspoon salt. Let stand 20 minutes to drain. Transfer to large bowl and add yogurt, garlic, mint, dill, and olive oil. Cover and refrigerate at least 2 hours.

Just before serving, add iced water until soup is creamy but not too thin — amount depends on thickness of yogurt. Season with salt and pepper to taste. Garnish with cucumber slices and mint.

GAZPACHO

ICED SALAD SOUP (SPAIN)   SERVES 6

Gazpacho was originally taken to Andalusian field workers for their lunch. It has gained an international reputation as a light, refreshing soup, ideal for a hot summer's day. Many versions of gazpacho exist, and even the following recipe is but one version of a particular recipe. When in season, use the long, curved sweet pepper (bull's horn), which are not as fleshy as the bell pepper; this is the type preferred in Spain.

2 lb (1 kg) ripe tomatoes

2 medium-sized sweet long green or bell peppers (capsicums)

2 small green cucumbers or 1 small hot-house cucumber (see page 14)

1 medium purple onion

1 clove garlic, chopped

1 cup (2 oz/60 g) soft white breadcrumbs

2 tablespoons red wine vinegar

1/4 cup (2 fl oz/60 ml) olive oil

1/2 teaspoon ground cumin

salt

about 1/4 teaspoon cayenne pepper

about 3 cups (24 fl oz/750 ml) iced water

tomato juice (optional)

Garlic Croutons:

3 thick slices stale white bread

1/3 cup (3 fl oz/80 ml) olive oil

1 clove garlic, halved

Peel and seed tomatoes. Halve peppers and remove seeds and membranes. Peel cucumbers. Reserve 1 tomato, 1 green pepper, 1 small cucumber or half hot-house cucumber, and half onion.

Roughly chop remaining vegetables and puree in food processor with garlic. Add breadcrumbs, vinegar and oil and process briefly. Add cumin and season to taste with salt and cayenne pepper. Pour into bowl, cover and refrigerate at least 2 hours. Dice reserved vegetables and place in separate bowls. Cover and refrigerate until required.

For garlic croutons: Remove crusts from bread and cut into 1/2 in (1 cm) cubes. Heat oil and garlic in frying pan until hot; remove garlic. Add bread cubes and fry until crisp and golden, stirring often. Drain on paper towels.

To serve, pour soup into large glass or pottery bowl and stir in iced water or combination of water and tomato juice if the tomatoes used were not fully flavored. Garnish with small amount of diced vegetables. Serve with bowls of remaining diced vegetables and garlic croutons.

Gazpacho

Psarosoupa Avgolemono

EGG AND LEMON FISH SOUP (GREECE)   SERVES 6

This soup is one of the best to come from Greek cuisine. The tangy lemon marries well with fish stock, but the soup is equally good if made with chicken stock. Use the basic fish stock recipe, and if the fish heads and backbones contain flesh, remove it, cover and set aside in the refrigerator — it can be added to the soup later if desired. The soup is meant to be lightly thickened, but care must be taken not to allow the egg to separate. A starchy rice is required, such as one used for rice pudding, as it adds a light thickening to the soup. Only the stock can be made ahead. Even the rice must be freshly cooked in the soup just before finishing, otherwise it develops an unpleasant flavor. It is important to stir the cooked soup for several minutes off the heat to prevent it from curdling. The finished soup does not reheat well.

6 cups (48 fl oz/1.5 L) basic fish
stock (see page 31)

1/3 cup (2 1/2 oz/75 g)
medium-grain rice

salt

flaked, cooked fish from fish stock
(optional) (see notes above)

2 eggs, separated

1 egg yolk

juice of 1 lemon

freshly ground white pepper

lemon slices or
shredded lemon peel, to garnish

finely chopped parsley,
to garnish

Bring stock to boil in large saucepan. Add unwashed rice and salt to taste and return to boil. Partly cover and boil until rice is very tender, about 20 minutes — a grain should disintegrate when pressed. Add cooked fish retained from making stock, if desired.

Beat egg whites in bowl until stiff. Beat in yolks, then most of lemon juice. Beat in about 2 cups boiling soup.

Remove saucepan from heat and stir in egg mixture. Taste, add remaining lemon juice if necessary, and good grinding white pepper. Return to low heat and stir to cook egg, about 2 to 3 minutes — the soup will be frothy but only thicken slightly. Remove from heat and keep stirring until soup cools a little, about 2 to 3 minutes. Serve immediately, garnished with lemon and chopped parsley.

Potage Purée de Marrons

CHESTNUT SOUP (FRANCE)   SERVES 6

Chestnut trees thrive in the south of France, particularly in the Ardèche region in the north of Languedoc, which is famous for marrons glacé, made from the finest chestnuts. In winter, chestnut soup is prepared in many a farmhouse kitchen. Two 16 oz (440 g) cans of chestnuts may be used in place of the fresh chestnuts. Drain and add to the saucepan after the vegetables have cooked in the water for 30 minutes.

1¹/₂ lb (750 g) chestnuts

2 leeks

2 tablespoons butter

1 onion, chopped

2 medium carrots, sliced

2 celery stalks, sliced

2 sprigs parsley

4 cups (32 fl oz/1 L) water

salt and freshly ground white pepper

¹/₂ cup (4 fl oz/125 ml) light (single) cream

crusty bread, to serve

Shell and skin chestnuts as directed on page 22; set aside. Cut green tops and roots from leeks, halve lengthwise and wash thoroughly. Slice leeks.

Melt butter in large heavy saucepan. Add onion and cook gently until transparent, about 10 minutes. Add chestnuts, leeks, carrots, celery, parsley sprigs and water. Season with salt and pepper to taste. Cover and simmer until vegetables and chestnuts are tender, about 40 minutes. Discard parsley.

Puree soup in saucepan with hand-held blender, or puree in batches in food processor. Return to pan, add cream and reheat gently. Adjust seasoning and serve hot with warm crusty bread.

Stracciatella alla Romana

EGG AND CHEESE SOUP (ITALY)   SERVES 4

The Italians have interesting nomenclature for many of their recipes including this one. Stracciatella means "little rags" which indicates how the soup should look once cooked; the beaten eggs break up into flakes or fine strands when stirred into the hot broth.

3 large eggs

¹/₄ cup (1¹/₂ oz/50 g) semolina

¹/₄ cup (1 oz/30 g) grated parmesan cheese

1 tablespoon finely chopped flat-leaf (Italian) parsley

pinch of ground nutmeg

4 cups (32 fl oz/1 L) chicken stock (see page 31)

Beat eggs with balloon whisk in large bowl. Beat in semolina, parmesan, parsley, nutmeg and ¹/₄ cup cold stock. Bring remaining stock to boil in saucepan. Pour 1 cup hot stock into egg mixture, whisking constantly. Pour egg mixture into saucepan. Stir constantly with wooden spoon over heat until egg begins to set into fine strands, about 2 to 3 minutes. Serve immediately.

SEAFOOD

In his excellent book, *Mediterranean Seafood*, Alan Davidson identifies almost 200 species of fish, shellfish and other creatures of the deep that are so much a part of the cuisines of the region. The seafood markets of the Mediterranean are indeed a sight to behold, but it is now necessary to bring fish in from outside the region to keep up with demand. Much of the local seafood has equivalents elsewhere, and substitutes are given in these recipes.

It is through Mediterranean cooking that squid, octopus and cuttlefish have found wider acceptance, when not so long ago they were scorned. Crustaceans and shellfish abound, with each area having its particular species of clams, mussels, oysters and scallops. Lobster is a scarcity in the Mediterranean but spiny lobster, popularly known by the French name langouste, is the one you are likely to encounter, and at its best if freshly boiled and served with a proper mayonnaise or a simple dressing of olive oil and lemon juice.

Another creature you are likely to see at Mediterranean fish markets is the very prickly-shelled sea urchin, known also by its French name oursin. It is one of those seafoods "discovered" elsewhere by devotees of Japanese foods; the delicate orange roe is served as a topping for sushi. The urchins' roe are delicious eaten raw, just with a touch of lemon juice. In Mediterranean France, the roe is also included in omelettes, mixed into mayonnaise or added to certain fish soups.

Fish is mostly enjoyed in its simplest form — anointed with fragrant olive oil and fresh herbs, perhaps with a touch of garlic, and adequately salted, before cooking over a glowing charcoal fire. In Mediterranean Spain, cooking seafood "a la plancha" — on a hotplate over a fire — is one of the unforgettable sights, smells and tastes of the region.

Oven-cooked fish dishes also abound; these used to be carried to the town oven for baking, but domestic ovens now do the job. Hearty fish soups and stews are also popular, but dishes such as bouillabaisse are mostly prepared in restaurants rather than in the home. However, the soupe de poissons avec sa rouille is a more likely candidate for the domestic kitchen, more of a meal than a soup, as is the rich and delicious bourride.

The amount of seafood used in the Mediterranean diet may be one of the reasons for the longevity of the locals; but it is also how the seafood is used that accounts for better health.

Mariscada al la Plancha con Salsa Romescu (page 104)

BOURRIDE

FISH SOUP WITH AIOLI (FRANCE)   SERVES 6

Popular all along the Mediterranean coast of France, bourride is claimed by both Languedoc and Provence as their own creation. It is rich but delicious, and makes a substantial meal — two courses in one, really. White-fleshed fish, such as snapper, angler fish, blue-eyed cod and sea bass, are recommended.

3 lb (1.5 kg) thick fish fillets
4 cups (32 fl oz/1 L) rich fish stock (see page 31)
4 egg yolks
1 quantity aioli (see page 36)
12 thick slices baguette (long French bread), toasted

Cut fish into pieces about 3 in (8 cm) long. Heat stock in saucepan until just on simmering point. Add fish and simmer, uncovered, until fish flakes when tested with knife point, about 10 to 15 minutes. Remove fish with slotted spoon to a warm dish, cover with foil and keep warm. Boil stock until reduced by one-third, strain through fine sieve and return to pan over heat.

Beat egg yolks in bowl until light. Beat in 1 cup (8 fl oz/250 ml) aioli. Gradually beat in ladleful of stock. Take pan of stock off heat and pour in aioli mixture, stirring constantly with wooden spoon. Return to medium-low heat and keep stirring until soup thickens a little and just coats back of spoon. Do not boil or egg will curdle. If this happens, remove from heat and beat in a little cold water using balloon whisk.

Place 2 slices of toast in each warm soup bowl, lay piece of fish on top and pour in soup. Serve remaining aioli and fish separately.

bell pepper

Soupe de Poissons Avec Sa Rouille

FISH SOUP WITH ROUILLE (FRANCE)   SERVES 6

Purists insist bouillabaisse can only be cooked with fish found in the Mediterranean. It can be duplicated outside the south of France but a separate list of fish species would need to be devised for the various regions. The following soup-meal is based on an old Provençal recipe called Aigo-Sau, also served with the rouille which is a highlight of bouillabaise. Any white-fleshed fish can be used — try ling, snapper or sea bass. When cooking the fish stock, add the fennel if you like the flavor, but definitely include the orange rind.

2 lb (1 kg) thick white-fleshed fish fillets

3 tablespoons olive oil

1 onion, thinly sliced

2 cloves garlic, pressed (crushed)

4 medium-sized ripe tomatoes, peeled, seeded and chopped

1 lb (500 g) small whole potatoes, peeled and halved

6 cups (48 fl oz/1.5 L) rich fish stock (see page 31)

1 bay leaf, halved

salt and freshly ground black pepper

finely chopped parsley

6 or more thick slices country-style bread, toasted

Rouille:

1/2 cup (1 oz/30 g) soft white breadcrumbs

1/4 teaspoon powdered saffron (optional)

1/4 cup (2 fl oz/60 ml) fish stock

3 cloves garlic, chopped

2 egg yolks

4 teaspoons tomato paste

1 large fresh red chili pepper, seeded and chopped, or 1/4 teaspoon cayenne pepper

3/4 cup (6 fl oz/180 ml) olive oil

salt

Cut fish into 2 in (5 cm) pieces, rinse and pat dry with paper towels.

Warm oil in saucepan. Add onion and cook gently until transparent, about 10 minutes. Add garlic and cook several seconds. Add tomatoes, potatoes, stock, bay leaf, and salt and pepper to taste. Bring to boil, cover, and simmer gently, 15 minutes. Add fish and simmer gently until fish flakes when tested with knife point, about 10 minutes.

For rouille: Soak bread and saffron, if used, in stock. Place in food processor with garlic and process to smooth puree. Add egg yolks, tomato paste and chili pepper or cayenne pepper. While motor is operating, gradually add oil in thin stream to form thick, creamy sauce. Add a little more stock if mixture is too thick. Add salt to taste and extra cayenne if needed — rouille is meant to be spicy. Transfer to bowl.

Pour fish soup into large bowl or soup tureen, sprinkling parsley on top. Spread toast with rouille and place 1 slice in each wide soup bowl. Spoon soup into bowls. Serve with remaining rouille in separate bowl and additional bread or toast, if desired.

Page 90 to 91: A selection of fish and shellfish

Zuppa di Frutti di Mare Caprese

CAPRI SEAFOOD SOUP (ITALY)   SERVES 6

The waters around Capri abound with the fruits of the sea. This soup is one which can contain a combination of seafood, according to what is available.

Ling, snapper, sea bass or hake may be used. Octopus is often added. Prepare a small octopus, about 8 oz (250 g) in weight, according to directions on page 20, leaving it whole. Add to saucepan after onion and garlic has cooked, cover and simmer until tender, about 1 hour — it will cook in its own juices. Remove, cut into small pieces and set aside. Continue cooking the mussels as directed, and return octopus to saucepan after mussels have been removed.

3 tablespoons olive oil

1 onion, thinly sliced

3 cloves garlic, thinly sliced

1/2 cup (4 fl oz/125 ml) dry white wine

1 lb (500 g) mussels, cleaned (see page 20)

4 large ripe tomatoes, peeled, seeded and chopped

2 teaspoons chopped fresh marjoram

6 cups (48 fl oz/1.5 L) basic fish stock (see page 31)

1 bay leaf, halved

salt and freshly ground black pepper

1 1/2 lb (750 g) thick white-fleshed fish fillets

1 lb (500 g) whole uncooked large shrimp (prawns)

12 oysters in shell (optional)

finely chopped flat-leaf (Italian) parsley

crusty bread, to serve

Warm oil in saucepan. Add onion and cook gently until transparent, about 10 minutes. Add garlic and cook several seconds. Add wine and mussels, cover and simmer until mussels open, 4 to 5 minutes, shaking pan occasionally. Remove mussels to bowl and set aside; discard any that have not opened.

Add tomatoes and marjoram to saucepan and simmer, covered, until tomatoes are soft, about 15 minutes. Mash to puree with wooden spoon. Add stock, bay leaf, and salt and pepper to taste and bring to boil.

Cut fish into 2 in (5 cm) pieces, add to soup and simmer gently 10 minutes. Add shrimp and simmer until shrimp turn pink, about 4 minutes.

Scrub, open and remove oysters from shells — leave 2 or 3 oysters in half-shell for garnish, if desired. Remove top shells of mussels and discard. Add mussels and oysters to soup during last 2 minutes when shrimp is cooking.

Pour soup into large bowl or soup tureen, garnish with oysters if desired, sprinkle with parsley and serve with crusty bread.

Insalata di Frutti di Mare

SEAFOOD SALAD (ITALY)   SERVES 6

While this salad of fresh seafood is often served as an antipasto, it makes an excellent lunch on a warm day — especially if eaten outside, and better still, within sight and sound of the sea. If preparing the salad ahead, cover and refrigerate, then bring to room temperature about 1 hour before serving. Options are given to make the seafood selection easier. If it is necessary to omit any of the seafood listed, increase the amounts of those selected. You can use fresh pre-prepared squid rings, or prepare them yourself (see page 20).

2 lb (1 kg) mussels, cleaned (see page 20)

2 lb (1 kg) clams, cleaned (see page 20) (optional)

salt

8 oz (250 g) squid (calamari) rings

8 oz (250 g) shelled fresh sea scallops (optional)

1 lb (500 g) whole cooked jumbo shrimp (large prawns)

crusty bread, to serve

Dressing:

1/2 cup (4 fl oz/125 ml) olive oil

2 to 3 tablespoons lemon juice

2 tablespoons chopped flat-leaf (Italian) parsley

1 teaspoon French mustard

freshly ground black pepper, to taste

Place mussels and clams in large saucepan, cover and cook over medium heat just until they open, about 5 minutes. Remove with slotted spoon and place in bowl, discarding any that are not open. Set aside. Liquid from shellfish in saucepan should be 1 in (2.5 cm) deep; add a little water if necessary to make up quantity.

Bring liquid to gentle simmer, adding salt to taste. Add squid and scallops, cover and simmer over low heat just long enough so they are almost firm, about 1 minute. Do not boil or they will toughen. Drain, transfer to serving dish, and cover with foil.

Peel and devein shrimp and cut into 2 or 3 pieces each. Remove mussels and clams from shells, reserving 6 mussels in half shells. Add shrimp, shelled mussels and clams to squid and scallops.

For dressing: Combine all ingredients in jug; mix well. Pour over seafood. Toss well, garnish with reserved mussels, and serve still slightly warm with crusty bread.

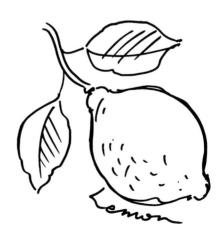

Kalamarakia Tiganita me Skorthalia

FRIED SQUID WITH GARLIC SAUCE (GREECE)   SERVES 6 AS AN APPETIZER

The trick to perfect fried squid is to cook it as briefly as possible, otherwise it ends up tough and chewy. Choose squid with bodies about 5 to 6 in (12 to 15 cm) long. Do not flour all the squid at once, as the flour becomes soggy on standing. This version of garlic sauce uses potato instead of nuts, and is best if used on day of making. The lemon juice and vinegar can be added to the skorthalia earlier to help move the breadcrumb mixture over the food processor blades. Be careful not to overprocess after adding potato or the texture of the sauce may alter and the oil separate.

1¹/2 lb (750 g) fresh squid (calamari), cleaned (see page 20)
¹/2 cup (2 oz/60 g) all-purpose (plain) flour
salt
freshly ground black pepper
vegetable oil, for deep frying
lemon wedges, to serve

Skorthalia:
1 medium potato, about 7 oz (200 g)
6 cloves garlic
salt
¹/2 cup (1 oz/30 g) soft white breadcrumbs
2 tablespoons cold water
1 tablespoon lemon juice
1 tablespoon white wine vinegar
¹/3 cup (3 fl oz/80 ml) olive oil

Clean and cut squid bodies into fairly wide rings, just under ¹/2 in (1 cm) wide; cut fins into strips. Leave tentacles joined together and trim the long feelers. Rinse and drain well in a colander. Set tentacles aside.

Heat oil to 350°F (180°C) in deep fryer. Sift flour with 1 teaspoon salt and a good grinding of black pepper. Place one-third of flour into plastic bag with handful of squid pieces and shake well. Transfer to sieve set over paper and shake off excess flour. Deep fry squid until golden, no more than 3 minutes, stirring often with slotted spoon. Drain on paper towels. Repeat with remaining squid and flour, frying tentacles last.

For skorthalia: Peel and slice potato thickly and boil in water to cover until tender. Drain and let cool. Chop garlic roughly, place in food processor with ¹/2 teaspoon salt, breadcrumbs and water and process until garlic is pulverized. Add lemon juice and vinegar. Add potato and oil and process briefly until light and smooth and adjust salt or lemon juice to taste — consistency should be thick and creamy, stir in a little more water if necessary. Transfer to a bowl and serve immediately, or cover and refrigerate until required.

To serve, pile squid into warm dish and accompany with lemon wedges and skorthalia.

Kalamarakia Tiganita me Skorthalia

CALAMARI RIPIENI AL FORNO

BAKED STUFFED SQUID (ITALY)   SERVES 5 TO 6

The Spaniards call these calamares rellenos and include ham in the stuffing; in Greece and Cyprus, they are kalamaria yemista, with a spicy filling of rice and pine nuts. Select squid with bodies about 4 to 5 in (10 to 12 cm) long. Clean as directed, leaving bodies intact.

2 lb (1 kg) small squid (calamari), cleaned (see page 20)

1/2 cup (4 fl oz/125 ml) olive oil

2 cloves garlic, chopped

2 tablespoons chopped parsley

4 canned anchovy fillets, drained and chopped

1/2 cup (1 oz/30 g) soft breadcrumbs

salt and freshly ground black pepper

1 cup (8 fl oz/250 ml) dry white wine

Simmer squid tentacles in salted water 10 minutes. Drain, chop and place in bowl. Heat 2 tablespoons oil in frying pan. Add garlic and cook gently several seconds. Stir in squid tentacles, parsley, anchovies and breadcrumbs and cook, stirring, 5 minutes. Add salt and pepper to taste, remove from heat and let cool.

Preheat oven to 325–350°F (160–180°C/Gas 3).

Fill squid bodies with stuffing, packing loosely to allow for expansion during cooking. Close top with wooden cocktail sticks or sew with strong thread. Place in single layer in shallow casserole dish. Season lightly with salt and pepper, and drizzle with remaining oil. Pour wine into dish. Bake, uncovered, until squid are tender, about 1 hour, turning occasionally to brown evenly. If necessary, add a little water to dish during cooking to prevent juices scorching. Remove picks or thread and serve hot.

CALAMARES AL JEREZ

SQUID IN SHERRY SAUCE (SPAIN)   SERVES 4

This is a popular way of serving squid in the sherry region of Jerez. I prefer to prepare my own squid (see page 20), but rings bought fresh and ready-prepared are good when simmered in this sauce.

good pinch of saffron threads

1 tablespoon boiling water

2 tablespoons olive oil

1 large onion, chopped

3 cloves garlic, pressed (crushed)

1/4 cup (1 oz/30 g) ground almonds

1/2 cup (4 fl oz/125 ml) dry sherry

2 tablespoon finely chopped parsley

1 lb (500 g) prepared squid (calamari) rings

1/2 cup (4 fl oz/125 ml) water

salt

plain pilaf (see page 37), to serve (optional)

Pound saffron threads in small mortar with pestle. Add boiling water and set aside to steep.

Warm oil in saucepan. Add onion and cook gently until transparent, about 10 minutes. Add garlic and cook 1 minute. Stir in almonds, saffron liquid, sherry, parsley, squid rings, water and salt to taste. Cover and simmer gently until squid is tender, about 45 to 60 minutes, stirring occasionally. Serve with pilaf, if desired.

SOUPIES KRASATO

CUTTLEFISH IN RED WINE (GREECE)   SERVES 6

Cuttlefish are more delicate in flavor than octopus, which is usually prepared in this way. If you find cuttlefish with the ink sac intact, keep 3 to 4 of them and add the ink to the sauce. Unfortunately, the ink sacs rupture easily, and your cuttlefish is more likely to be covered in the ink than contain the sac intact. If cuttlefish is not available, replace with an equal quantity of medium squid (calamari), prepare as directed on page 20. Pasta, boiled rice or plain pilaf (see page 37) are good accompaniments.

3 lb (1.5 kg) cuttlefish, cleaned (see page 20)

4 tablespoons olive oil

1 large onion, chopped

2 cloves garlic, pressed (crushed)

1/2 cup (4 fl oz/125 ml) dry red wine

3 large tomatoes, peeled and chopped

1/2 teaspoon sugar

salt and freshly ground black pepper

2 tablespoons finely chopped flat leaf (Italian) parsley

Cut cuttlefish bodies into thick strips and leave tentacles intact.

Warm oil in deep frying pan. Add onion and gently cook until transparent, about 10 minutes. Add garlic and cuttlefish, and stir over low heat 5 minutes. Add wine, cuttlefish ink if available, tomatoes, sugar, and salt and pepper to taste. Cover and simmer gently over low heat until cuttlefish is tender, about 1 1/2 hours. (Cuttlefish will create its own liquid during cooking, but add a little water during last stages if sauce begins to catch on base of pan.)

Add most of parsley and cook 1 minute. Transfer to warm serving bowl, sprinkle with remaining parsley and serve hot.

GRANSEOLA ALLA VENEZIANA

VENETIAN DRESSED CRAB (ITALY)   SERVES 4

In Venice, the spider crab is simply prepared so that its flavor is not obscured. Other crabs may be used in place of the spider crab — choose ones large enough for individual serves.

4 x 1 lb (500 g) cooked crabs

1/3 cup (3 fl oz/80 ml) olive oil

2 tablespoons lemon juice

salt and freshly ground black pepper

1 tablespoon finely chopped flat-leaf (Italian) parsley

lettuce leaves, to serve

Twist claws and legs from crabs. Cut around underside of each body and remove shell. Rinse body cavity and under-shell where legs were attached. Pick out meat from both sections and place in bowl. Rinse and dry upper shells. Crack legs and claws, remove meat and add to bowl.

Pour olive oil and lemon juice onto crab meat and season with salt and pepper to taste. Add parsley, toss to mix and divide between shells. Cover and refrigerate until required. Serve on bed of lettuce leaves.

OKTAKODI STIFATHO

BRAISED OCTOPUS WITH ONIONS (GREECE)   SERVES 6

One large octopus should be used for this rich stew as the long slow cooking process improves the flavor; however, whole small octopus may be preferred, in which case a shorter cooking time is required. If using small octopus, add the whole onions when adding the tomatoes and simmer only 1 hour. If using a large octopus, simmer for 1 hour before adding the whole onions, then simmer 1 hour more.

2 lb (1 kg) octopus, cleaned (see page 20)

15 oz (425 g) can tomatoes

1 lb (500 g) small whole onions, unpeeled

1/3 cup (3 fl oz/80 ml) olive oil

1 medium onion, chopped

2 cloves garlic, pressed (crushed)

1 bay leaf

1 sprig fresh rosemary

2 whole cloves

2 tablespoons red wine vinegar

1/2 cup (4 fl oz/125 ml) dry red wine

salt and freshly ground black pepper

1 tablespoon finely chopped flat-leaf (Italian) parsley

Place cleaned octopus body and tentacles into saucepan without any liquid. Cover and cook over low heat 20 minutes (octopus creates its own juice and turns pink). Remove octopus, and cut body and tentacles into 1 in (2.5 cm) pieces. Reserve cooking liquid.

Puree tomatoes with their liquid or press through sieve over bowl; set aside. Carefully cut roots and tops from 1 lb (500 g) whole onions and cut cross in root end to prevent middles popping out. Place onions in bowl, cover with boiling water and let stand 2 minutes. Drain, slip off skins and leave onions whole.

Heat half the oil in heavy saucepan. Add whole onions and cook over medium-low heat until just beginning to color, stirring often. Remove and set aside.

Warm remaining oil in saucepan. Add chopped onion and cook gently until transparent, about 10 minutes. Add garlic and cook several seconds. Add prepared octopus and reserved liquid, tomatoes, bay leaf, rosemary, cloves, vinegar, wine, and salt and pepper to taste. Cover and simmer until octopus is tender, about 1 to 2 hours, adding the whole onions at the appropriate time (see introductory note above). Sprinkle with parsley before serving.

Oktakodi Stifatho

Cozze Arrosto

BAKED MUSSELS (ITALY)   SERVES 4 TO 6

If you can obtain large mussels for this easy antipasto or light meal, so much the better.

2 lb (1 kg) large fresh mussels, cleaned (see page 20)

2 oz (60 g) prosciutto crudo, finely chopped

3 tablespoons finely chopped flat-leaf (Italian) parsley

1/2 cup (4 fl oz/125 ml) passata (see page 14)

salt and freshly ground black pepper

1/2 cup (1 oz/30 g) soft white breadcrumbs

1/2 cup (4 fl oz/125 ml) olive oil

Preheat oven to 400–425°F (200–220°C/Gas 6).

Place mussels in large saucepan. Cover and cook over medium heat until mussels open, about 4 to 6 minutes, shaking pan occasionally. Remove mussels from pan, return any that have not opened, cover and cook a little longer. Discard any unopened ones. Remove and discard top shell from each mussel and loosen mussel in shell. If they are small, place two mussels in one shell. Arrange in individual ramekins or in shallow baking dish in single layer.

Mix prosciutto with parsley, passata, and salt and pepper to taste. Spoon mixture evenly over mussels. Toss breadcrumbs with 2 tablespoons of the oil and sprinkle over mussels. Drizzle on remaining oil. Bake on upper shelf in oven until heated through and crumbs are lightly browned, about 6 to 8 minutes. Serve immediately.

Cozze alla Tarantina

MUSSELS TARANTO-STYLE (ITALY)   SERVES 4

Mussels are time-consuming to prepare, and I suggest using this recipe for an intimate dinner for four. The larger the mussels are, the better. Once the mussels are prepared, the cooking time is quite short.

3 cloves garlic

1/3 cup (3 fl oz/80 ml) olive oil

1 large onion, finely chopped

1 cup (8 fl oz/250 ml) dry white wine

2 tablespoons finely chopped flat-leaf (Italian) parsley

freshly ground black pepper

4 thick slices Italian bread

4 lb (2 kg) large fresh mussels, cleaned (see page 20)

finely chopped parsley, to serve

crusty bread, to serve

Peel garlic, leave one clove whole and finely chop remaining cloves. Warm oil in large saucepan. Add onion and cook gently, until very soft and transparent, about 15 minutes, stirring occasionally. Add chopped garlic and cook several seconds. Stir in wine, parsley and pepper to taste, cover and simmer gently 5 minutes.

Meanwhile, toast bread under slow broiler (grill) so it crisps as well as toasts. Halve reserved garlic clove and rub over toast. Keep warm under low heat.

Add mussels to saucepan and cook over high heat until mussels are open, about 6 to 8 minutes, shaking to distribute heat evenly. If any mussels have not opened, cook a little longer. Discard any still not opened.

Place toast in wide soup bowls or pasta plates. Divide mussels amongst bowls. Spoon liquid in pan over mussels, sprinkle with parsley and serve immediately with bread.

Coquilles St Jacques à la Provençale

SCALLOPS PROVENÇAL (FRANCE)   SERVES 4

Scallops need careful cooking otherwise they end up as rubbery discs. Mediterranean scallops are mostly quite small, but the ones you use may be quite large and thick. If they are, slit each in half horizontally so that they cook quickly and evenly. Leave the coral (roe) on the scallops if present. Flour the second batch of scallops just before cooking to prevent stickiness. This dish will serve four as a first course.

1 lb (500 g) shelled fresh sea scallops

1/2 cup (2 1/2 oz/75 g) all-purpose (plain) flour

salt and freshly ground black pepper

2 oz (60 g) butter

2 tablespoons olive oil

2 tablespoons finely chopped French shallots (see page 12) or white onion

2 cloves garlic, pressed (crushed)

1/2 cup (4 fl oz/125 ml) dry white wine

2 tablespoons lemon juice

2 tablespoons finely chopped flat-leaf (Italian) parsley

1/2 cup (1 oz/30 g) soft white breadcrumbs

2 tablespoons butter, melted, extra

Clean any dark veins from scallops and slit each horizontally if large, leaving coral (roe) attached to one half. Place flour with salt and pepper to taste in plastic bag, add half the scallops and shake well to coat. Tip into colander and shake off excess flour onto paper, returning it to bag.

Heat quarter of the butter with half the oil in heavy frying pan until sizzling. Add floured scallops in single layer and cook quickly, turning after 1 minute. Remove to dish. Flour and cook remaining scallops in same amount of butter and oil. Cover and keep warm.

Add remaining butter to pan with shallots and garlic and cook gently over low heat until shallots soften, about 6 minutes. Sprinkle in 1 tablespoon flour, stir well and cook 1 minute. Add wine and lemon juice, stirring constantly until bubbling. Add scallops and parsley, toss to coat with sauce and remove immediately from heat.

Divide scallops between 4 scallop shells or small, shallow ramekins. Toss breadcrumbs with melted extra butter and sprinkle over scallops. Cook briefly under hot broiler (grill) and until breadcrumbs are golden. Serve immediately.

OSTIONES A LA CADITANA

OYSTERS CADIZ-STYLE (SPAIN)   SERVES 4

Fresh oysters are at their best with no more than a squeeze of lemon juice, and perhaps a little freshly ground pepper. However, in Spanish tapas bars, you are likely to be offered this delicious, yet simple, cooked version. Purchase the oysters on the half-shell, freshly opened, or in the shell and open them yourself with an oyster knife. Take care not to over-cook the oysters as they can toughen.

24 fresh oysters in the shell, opened

1 clove garlic, finely chopped

2 teaspoons finely chopped parsley

freshly ground black pepper

1/8 teaspoon cayenne pepper

1/2 cup (1 oz/30 g) dried breadcrumbs

3 tablespoons olive oil

lemon wedges, to serve

Preheat oven to 425–450°F (220–230°C/Gas 7), or heat broiler (grill) to moderately hot.

Place opened oysters in their shells on baking sheet. Combine garlic, parsley, a good grinding of black pepper, cayenne pepper, breadcrumbs and 1 tablespoon oil in bowl. Sprinkle evenly over each oyster. Drizzle with remaining oil.

Bake on top shelf in oven until breadcrumbs are golden brown, about 6 to 8 minutes, or cook under broiler (grill). Serve on individual plates with lemon wedges.

ALMEJAS A LA MARINERA

CLAMS WITH TOMATO AND WINE (SPAIN)   SERVES 4

Choose whatever clams or cockles are available and recommended for brief cooking. In Spain, the carpet-shell clam is preferred, and for a tapa, the tiny wedge-shell clam called coquina is best. This dish will serve four as a light meal or eight as a tapa.

2 lb (1 kg) small fresh clams or cockles, prepared (see page 20)

1/3 cup (3 fl oz/80 ml) olive oil

1 medium onion, finely chopped

2 cloves garlic, pressed (crushed)

1 teaspoon paprika

pinch of cayenne pepper

4 medium-sized ripe tomatoes, peeled and chopped

1/4 cup (2 fl oz/60 ml) dry white wine

salt and freshly ground black pepper

2 tablespoons finely chopped parsley

To Serve:

lemon wedges

crusty bread

Prepare clams or cockles as directed to remove any sand or grit.

Warm oil in large saucepan. Add onion and cook gently until transparent, about 10 minutes. Add garlic and cook several seconds. Add paprika and cayenne pepper and cook gently 1 minute. Add tomatoes, wine, and salt and pepper to taste. Cover and simmer until tomatoes are soft, about 15 minutes.

Add clams or cockles, cover and simmer until opened, about 5 minutes, shaking saucepan occasionally to distribute heat evenly. Discard any clams that have not opened. Pile into deep serving dish or individual small bowls if serving as tapa, or wide soup bowls or pasta plates. Sprinkle with parsley and serve with lemon wedges and crusty bread.

Almejas a la Marinera

Mariscada a la Plancha con Salsa Romescu

GRILLED SHELLFISH WITH ROMESCO SAUCE (SPAIN)   SERVES 6

Cooking "a la plancha" is a method found all along the Spanish Mediterranean seaboard. Fresh fish and shellfish are often only anointed with a garlic-infused oil. In Catalan, the famous romesco sauce is a perfect foil for seafood. If fresh chili peppers are not available, use dried hot chili pepper flakes to taste — about 1 to 2 teaspoons. When cleaning the squid, leave the bodies intact with the skin on.

1 lb (500 g) small squid (calamari) or octopus, cleaned (see page 20)

olive oil

1 clove garlic, finely chopped

1 lb (500 g) large uncooked shrimp (prawns), unpeeled

coarse salt

18 clams or cockles, cleaned (see page 20)

18 large mussels, cleaned (see page 20)

finely chopped parsley, to garnish

Romesco Sauce:

1/3 cup (3 fl oz/80 ml) olive oil

1 medium onion, chopped

2 cloves garlic, pressed (crushed)

3 medium-sized ripe tomatoes, peeled and seeded

1 to 2 long fresh red chili peppers, seeded

1/4 cup (2 fl oz/60 ml) water

1/4 cup (2 fl oz/60 ml) dry white wine

1/2 cup (2 1/2 oz/75 g) whole blanched almonds, toasted

1 canned pimiento
or 1 roasted red pepper (capsicum) (see page 27)

1 tablespoon red wine vinegar

salt and freshly ground black pepper

Place squid bodies and tentacles or octopus in bowl. Add 2 tablespoons oil and garlic, mix well and let stand 20 minutes. Coat shrimp with salt.

For romesco sauce: Heat 1 tablespoon of the oil in saucepan. Add onion and cook gently until soft, about 5 minutes. Add garlic and cook several seconds. Add tomatoes, chili peppers to taste, water and wine. Cover and simmer, 30 minutes. Remove from heat and let cool.

Process almonds in food processor until ground. Add pimiento and tomato mixture and puree. Add remaining olive oil, vinegar, and salt and pepper to taste and process until the mixture has a thick sauce consistency. Transfer to bowl and let cool to room temperature.

Oil a heated barbecue hot plate, add all seafood and cook quickly, turning squid and shrimp, and basting with olive oil. Remove squid and shrimp to large platter as soon as they are cooked, about 3 to 4 minutes — shrimp should be cooked until just pink. When clams or cockles and mussels have opened, remove to platter; discard any that have not opened.

Sprinkle seafood with parsley and serve immediately with romesco sauce.

IMSELI MIXWI

GRILLED GARFISH (MALTA)   SERVES 6

Garfish look wonderful grilled in this way on the barbecue. You do need these fish with their pointed "beaks" for the right effect, but if such fish are not available, use the baste for other fish suitable for the barbecue — it is one used widely throughout the region.

3 lb (1.5 kg) whole garfish
(needle fish)

1 lemon, quartered

1/2 cup (4 fl oz/125 ml) olive oil

juice of 1 lemon

2 cloves garlic, pressed (crushed)

2 tablespoons finely chopped
flat-leaf (Italian) parsley

salt and freshly ground black pepper

lemon wedges, to serve

Scale and clean fish if necessary. Rub cavities with lemon quarters to clean and flavor flesh. Pierce flesh just above tails and insert "beaks" through this to form rings (if you try to pierce flesh with "beaks", they could break).

Beat oil with lemon juice, garlic, parsley, and salt and pepper to taste in bowl. Brush over fish and cook slowly on barbecue grid until cooked through, about 15 minutes, turning frequently and brushing with oil mixture. Serve hot with lemon wedges.

SAMKE MISHWI BI TARATOUR

BARBECUED FISH WITH TAHINI AND PARSLEY SAUCE (LEBANON/SYRIA)   SERVES 6

If sea bream are unavailable, select other fish suitable for cooking whole on the barbecue.

6 x 12 oz (375 g) whole sea bream
(porgy)

3 tablespoons olive oil

juice of 2 lemons

2 cloves garlic, pressed (crushed)
(optional)

salt and freshly ground black pepper

To Serve:

bakdounis bi tahini
(see variation of taratour bi tahini
on page 52)

tabouleh (see page 201) or
other salad of choice

pita bread

Clean and scale fish, rinse well and pat dry with paper towels. Cut 2 to 3 shallow diagonal slashes into each side of fish. Combine olive oil, lemon juice, garlic and salt and pepper to taste in shallow glass or ceramic dish. Add fish, turning to coat. Cover and refrigerate 30 minutes only — do not marinate longer as the lemon juice "cooks" the fish.

Drain fish and reserve marinade. Cook on barbecue over glowing coals until flesh flakes when tested at thickest part with knife point, about 4 to 5 minutes on first side, then 2 to 3 minutes on other side. Brush with marinade during cooking. Lift carefully from barbecue and serve hot with sauce, salad, and bread warmed briefly on barbecue.

SARDALYA SARMASI

SARDINES IN GRAPE VINE LEAVES (TURKEY)   SERVES 4

The leaves of the grape vine are used extensively in Turkey, Cyprus and Greece for wrapping food. They are particularly good wrapped around fish then broiled (grilled) or cooked on the barbecue, and impart a particular fragrance as well as keeping the fish moist. Besides fresh sardines, red mullet (goatfish) can also be prepared in this way. The leaves are removed before eating.

2 lb (1 kg) fresh sardines (about 24)

1/2 cup (4 fl oz/125 ml) olive oil

salt

24 fresh or preserved grape vine leaves

1/2 lemon

freshly ground black pepper

To Serve:

lemon wedges

virgin olive oil

crusty bread

Leave sardines whole or cut off heads as desired. Remove fins from belly. Cut from head, if retained, almost to tail and remove intestines, removing gills as well. Rinse well, drain and pat dry with paper towels.

Place sardines in dish, drizzle with half the oil and sprinkle lightly with salt. Toss lightly to distribute oil, cover and refrigerate at least 30 minutes.

Meanwhile, blanch fresh or preserved grape leaves in boiling water 1 minute. Drain in colander, rinse under cold running water and set aside to drain well.

Place leaf, shiny-side down, on work surface and place sardine across stem end. Squeeze on a little lemon juice and season with pepper. Roll up to top of leaf leaving head exposed if retained. Arrange on rack of broiler (grill) pan. When all rolls are completed, brush all over with olive oil and broil (grill) until leaves begin to scorch, about 3 minutes each side. Alternatively, sardines may be arranged in hinged barbecue grid and cooked on barbecue. Serve hot with lemon wedges, small jug of olive oil and crusty bread.

Sardalya Sarmasi

SARDINE AL FINOCCHIO

BAKED SARDINES WITH FENNEL (ITALY)   SERVES 4

It is important that the sardines be very fresh, otherwise they tend to have a bitter flavor. The fennel seeds help to "sweeten" the fish. This recipe, incidentally, comes from Sardinia.

4 tablespoons olive oil

1 large onion, finely chopped

1/2 cup (4 fl oz/125 ml) dry white wine

4 medium-sized ripe tomatoes, roughly chopped

salt and freshly ground black pepper

1 1/2 lb (750 g) very fresh sardines (about 16)

1 cup (4 oz/125 g) dried breadcrumbs

3 teaspoons fennel seeds, pounded until cracked

Warm 1 tablespoon oil in saucepan. Add onion and cook gently until transparent, about 10 minutes. Add wine, tomatoes, and salt and pepper to taste and bring to boil. Simmer, uncovered, until reduced to a thick sauce, about 15 minutes, stirring occasionally. Meanwhile, clean sardines. Rub off scales with fingers and rinse under running cold water. Cut off heads and slit bodies to tails. Clean insides with fingers. Snip or pinch backbones from tails on inside and pull them away. Rinse thoroughly, then rinse again in bowl of salted water. Close each sardine. Season with pepper and roll in breadcrumbs to coat completely.

Preheat oven to 325–350°F (160–180°C/Gas 3). Puree tomato mixture in food mill or sieve set over bowl. Pour into glass baking dish and arrange sardines in neat rows on sauce. Sprinkle with pounded fennel seeds and drizzle with remaining oil. Bake until golden, about 25 to 30 minutes, adding a little water to sauce if necessary during cooking. Wipe sides of dish and serve at table directly from dish.

SARTANADO

FRIED SEAFOOD PANCAKE (FRANCE)   SERVES 2 TO 6

In Provence, sartan is a frying pan, and this simple method of cooking tiny fish takes its name from the pan. The recipe provides a quick meal for two, or serve it as an informal hors d'oeuvre — each person can pull off a succulent morsel of crispy fried fish.

8 oz (250 g) tiny fresh fish (e.g. whitebait, smelts, anchovies, picarels, herrings or tiny shrimp (prawns), or a combination)

1/2 cup (2 1/2 oz/75 g) all-purpose (plain) flour

salt and freshly ground black pepper

3 tablespoons olive oil

parsley, to garnish

lemon wedges, to serve

Place fish in large sieve and rinse under cold running water, shaking sieve. Drain well. Heat cast iron frying pan, about 9 in (23 cm) in diameter. Place flour in plastic bag and season with salt and pepper. Add fish and shake bag to coat. Tip into colander and shake out excess flour. Add half the oil to heated pan. Add fish and press flat over base with metal spatula so they are close together. Cook over medium-high heat until browned and crisp underneath — the fish should stick together in a round "pancake". Loosen with spatula and invert onto plate. Add remaining oil to pan, slide pancake back into pan and cook other side until browned. Slide onto plate, garnish with parsley and serve hot with lemon.

FRISCIEU DI GIANCHETTI

WHITEBAIT FRITTERS (ITALY)   SERVES 4 TO 6

Italian fritter batter is made with lukewarm water and flour, but soda results in fritters that are light and crisp. Use fresh whitebait, not canned, and look for the tiniest fish available. If they are large, say about 2$^{1}/_{2}$ to 3 in (6 to 8 cm) long, coat with batter and deep-fry as separate fish. These could be served as an antipasto or a main course.

12 oz (375 g) fresh whitebait or smelts

1 cup (5 oz/150 g) all-purpose (plain) flour

1 teaspoon salt

freshly ground black pepper

1 cup (8 fl oz/250 ml) club soda (soda water)

oil, for shallow frying

lemon wedges, to serve

Place whitebait in sieve and rinse well under cold running water. Leave to drain well.

Sift flour with salt and pepper into bowl. Stir in soda, using balloon whisk to prevent lumps forming — consistency should be that of thick cream.

Pour oil into large frying pan until $^{1}/_{4}$ in (5 mm) deep and heat well. Mix whitebait into batter and drop batches of tablespoons of mixture into pan. Shallow fry in batches until crisp and golden, about 2 to 3 minutes, turning once. Drain on crumpled paper towels and serve hot with lemon wedges.

BAKALIARO KROKETES

SALT COD CROQUETTES (GREECE)   SERVES 4

For more information on salt cod, see page 110, and for kasseri cheese, see page 25.

1 lb (500 g) salt cod fillets

1 medium onion, grated

$^{1}/_{2}$ cup (2 oz/60 g) finely grated kasseri or romano cheese

$^{1}/_{4}$ cup (1$^{1}/_{4}$ oz/40 g) all-purpose (plain) flour

2 eggs

freshly ground black pepper

3 cups (24 fl oz/750 ml) light olive or corn (maize) oil

lemon wedges or skorthalia (see page 94), to serve

Place salt cod in bowl in cold water to cover and soak 24 hours, changing water 3 times. Rinse well and place in saucepan with fresh cold water to cover. Bring to boil, boil 2 minutes and let cool. Drain and remove bones and skin. Shred cod finely with fork or process in food processor until finely chopped. Combine cod, onion, cheese, flour, eggs and pepper to taste in bowl. Let stand 30 minutes.

Pour oil into deep saucepan and heat well. Drop heaping teaspoons of cod mixture in batches into hot oil and fry until golden brown and cooked through, about 3 minutes. Remove with slotted spoon and drain on paper towels. Serve hot with lemon wedges or skorthalia.

BRANDADE DE MORUE

PUREE OF SALT COD (FRANCE)   SERVES 6

With the rich harvest of the Mediterranean available, it has always amazed me to see the widespread use of salt cod throughout the northern seaboard and the islands. The cod is not caught in those waters but comes from the north Atlantic. Its popularity stems from the Middle Ages when Roman Catholic and Christian Orthodox religions demanded periods of frequent fasting. The pungent dried slabs of salted fish could withstand long journeys and could be kept for months. It was also cheaper than fresh fish and became the food of the poor.

Once salt cod has soaked sufficiently, it should be cooked — a bit of a problem for meal planning. However, you can boil the cod, let it cool and remove skin and bones once the desalting process is completed, then refrigerate in a covered bowl for 1 or 2 days until required. Warm gently in the microwave oven or in a little of the milk in a covered pan over low heat, then proceed with the processing.

As a serving alternative, the brandade may be piled into individual warmed pots and placed on serving plates with croûtes and olives to serve as a first course.

1 lb (500 g) salt cod fillets
3/4 cup (6 fl oz/180 ml) milk
3/4 cup (6 fl oz/180 ml) olive oil
2 cloves garlic, chopped
2 tablespoons lemon juice
1/4 teaspoon grated nutmeg
freshly ground black pepper

To Serve:
crisp toast or garlic-flavored croûtes
(see page 23)
black olives

Place salt cod in bowl with cold water to cover. Refrigerate 1 to 2 days, changing water 3 to 4 times. To check if saltiness is reduced, taste a tiny piece — if only slightly salty, cod is ready. Drain and place cod in deep saucepan. Add cold water to cover and bring slowly to boiling point. Reduce heat and simmer gently, covered, until cod flakes when tested, about 8 to 10 minutes. Let stand until lukewarm. Drain and remove skin and bones from cod.

Pour milk into saucepan and heat to just below boiling point. Heat oil in another large, heavy saucepan. Process prepared cod with garlic in food processor until finely flaked. While motor is operating, gradually add hot milk and oil alternately — make sure one is well-combined before adding the other. Reserve some milk. Add nutmeg, lemon juice and pepper to taste. If puree is very thick, add reserved milk.

Transfer mixture to saucepan in which oil was heated. Heat through over medium heat, stirring constantly. Pile into shallow dish and surround with crisp toast or croûtes and black olives. Serve hot.

Brandade aux Pommes de Terre (Brandade in Baked Potatoes) Variation: Preheat oven to 350–375°F (180–190°C/Gas 4). Bake 6 large potatoes in their skins until cooked through, about 1 hour. Cut off tops and scoop out most of the flesh, leaving thin shells of skin. Mash potato to fine puree and mix into an equal quantity of brandade mixture. Pile back into potato skins, brush with olive oil and bake 15 minutes. Serve as a light meal.

Brandade de Morue

ALBÓNDIGAS DE ATÚN

TUNA FISHBALLS (SPAIN)   SERVES 4 AS APPETIZER OR 6 AS MAIN

These can be served as tapas or as a main course. The refreshing flavor of white wine and lemon juice complements the tuna. Other fish, such as hake, ling, cod or sea bass may be used instead.

1½ lb (750 g) fresh tuna steaks

4 tablespoons olive oil

1 medium onion, finely chopped

1 cup (2 oz/60 g) soft breadcrumbs

2 tablespoons milk

grated rind of 1 lemon

2 cloves garlic, chopped

2 tablespoons chopped
flat-leaf (Italian) parsley

1 egg

1 teaspoon salt

freshly ground black pepper

all-purpose (plain) flour

Lemon and Wine Sauce:

2 tablespoons butter

1 small onion, finely chopped

1½ tablespoons all-purpose (plain)
flour

½ cup (4 fl oz/125 ml) dry white
wine

1 to 2 tablespoons lemon juice

1 cup (8 fl oz/250 ml) basic fish
stock (see page 31)

1 tablespoon julienned lemon rind
(no pith)

salt and freshly ground
white pepper

Discard skin and any bones from tuna. Chop roughly.

Heat 1 tablespoon oil in small frying pan. Add onion and cook gently until transparent, about 10 minutes. Let cool.

Process tuna, breadcrumbs, milk, lemon rind and garlic in food processor to a coarse paste. Add parsley, egg, and salt and pepper to taste, and process briefly — mixture should have some texture. Transfer to bowl and stir in cooked onion. With moistened hands, shape into walnut-sized balls. Toss in flour to coat.

Heat remaining oil in large frying pan. Add fishballs and cook until golden brown and cooked through, about 6 to 8 minutes, adding more oil to pan if necessary. Drain on paper towels and keep warm.

For lemon and wine sauce: Melt butter in saucepan. Add onion and cook gently until very soft and transparent, about 12 to 15 minutes. Sprinkle in flour, stir and cook gently 2 minutes. Add wine, 1 tablespoon lemon juice and fish stock and stir constantly over medium heat until slightly thickened and bubbling. Add julienned lemon rind and simmer until slightly reduced, about 5 to 6 minutes. Season with salt and pepper to taste and add more lemon juice if necessary.

Serve fishballs with hot sauce.

SALADE NIÇOISE

TUNA, ANCHOVY AND VEGETABLE SALAD (FRANCE)   SERVES 6

The famous Niçoise salad is compromised even in France. I have been served very indifferent versions, the worst (and on more than one occasion) bolstered with boiled rice! Salade Niçoise, and pan bagnat (see page 61), should be a celebration of summer in southern France — simple, refreshing, flavorsome and satisfying. Use brine or oil-packed tuna and if small tomatoes are not available, cut 5 to 6 medium tomatoes into eighths.

12 oil-packed anchovy fillets, drained

8 oz (250 g) can tuna chunks

2 green bell peppers (capsicums)

8 small ripe tomatoes, quartered

1 small cucumber, sliced

4 to 5 red radishes, thinly sliced

1 medium purple onion, thinly sliced

4 hard-cooked (boiled) eggs, quartered

1/2 cup (3 oz/90 g) niçoise or kalamata black olives

crusty French bread, to serve

Dressing:

1/2 cup (4 fl oz/125 ml) extra virgin olive oil

2 tablespoons lemon juice or red wine vinegar

1 small clove garlic, pressed (crushed) (optional)

salt and freshly ground black pepper

8 basil leaves, shredded

Cut anchovy fillets in half lengthwise. Drain and flake tuna. Remove cores, seeds and white membranes from peppers and cut into rings or strips.

Arrange all salad ingredients attractively in wide salad bowl, placing anchovy fillets, tuna and eggs on top. Scatter with olives.

For dressing: Beat all ingredients together in small bowl. Pour evenly over salad — it is not necessary to toss — and serve with crusty bread.

grapes

Carpaccio di Tonno e Pesce Spada

CARPACCIO OF TUNA AND SWORDFISH (ITALY)   SERVES 6

The initial searing of the fish in this recipe is not traditional. It is a method used occasionally in Japanese cuisine, and I prefer it as this ensures any potentially harmful bacteria on the surface is effectively deactivated. If you are sure that the fish is extremely fresh, and has been properly handled, you may decide to dispense with the searing. Purchase fish steaks about 1 in (2.5 cm) thick. Either tuna or swordfish can be used on their own, but the two different colors of the fish make the dish more attractive. If the prepared carpaccio is not to be served immediately, cover with plastic wrap and refrigerate until required — although serve on the same day. An alternative method of serving the carpaccio is to top the fish with chopped black olives and chili peppers and drizzle with olive oil.

4 oz (125 g) thick tuna steak
4 oz (125 g) thick swordfish steak
ice cubes
6 tablespoons extra virgin olive oil
1 small purple onion
6 teaspoon drained capers
1 small fresh hot red chili pepper
1 tablespoon very finely chopped parsley

To Serve:
salt
freshly ground black pepper
lemon wedges
crusty bread or bread rolls

Remove skin from fish if present. Have bowl of cold water containing ice cubes on hand. Heat frying pan over high heat, and when very hot, add 2 teaspoons of the olive oil and swirl around pan. Add 1 fish steak and sear very briefly on each side. Holding steak with tongs, also sear each of the narrow sides. The fish should not be browned, and searing takes barely 30 seconds in all. Remove immediately to bowl of iced water to arrest cooking. Sear remaining fish steak in same way and plunge into bowl.

Remove fish from water, pat dry with paper towels and wrap in freezer wrap. Freeze until just beginning to firm, about 4 to 6 hours.

Meanwhile, cut onion into paper-thin slices and separate into rings. Rinse capers if packed in brine. Halve, seed and remove membrane from chili pepper; chop finely and combine with parsley.

Using sharp knife, cut fish steaks into 1 in x 2 in (2.5 cm x 5 cm) paper-thin slices, with the grain. Finely shred any trimmings from fish. Arrange alternate slices of each fish, overlapping to form a circle, on each of six small chilled serving plates. Mix fish shreds and place a pile in middle of each serve. Scatter onion slices and capers on top. Sprinkle with chili pepper mixture. Drizzle about 1 tablespoon olive oil over each serve. Serve with salt, pepper, lemon wedges and crusty bread or rolls.

Carpaccio di Tonno e Pesce Spada

STUFAT TAT-TUNNAGG

FRESH TUNA CASSEROLE (MALTA)   SERVES 6

Tuna is very popular in Malta, and this simple casserole is a favorite way in which to prepare tuna as it is a complete meal-in-a-dish. Swordfish, albacore or bonito may be used instead.

6 x 4 oz (125 g) tuna steaks
salt and freshly ground black pepper
1 leek
about 4 tablespoons olive oil
1 medium onion, chopped
2 cloves garlic, finely chopped
1½ lb (750 g) potatoes, thinly sliced
1 lb (500 g) ripe tomatoes, peeled and sliced
1 tablespoon capers, drained and rinsed
2 tablespoons chopped black olives
1 teaspoon finely chopped fresh mint
¾ cup (6 fl oz/180 ml) water
finely chopped flat-leaf (Italian) parsley, to garnish

Preheat oven to 350–375°F (180–190°C/Gas 4).

Remove and discard skin from tuna if present. Wipe tuna with damp paper towels. Season lightly with salt and pepper. Trim root and most of green leaves from leek; cut in half lengthwise, wash well and slice finely.

Warm half the oil in frying pan. Add onion and garlic and cook gently until onion is transparent, about 10 minutes. Add leek and cook 5 minutes.

Lightly oil baking dish and place layer of potato slices over base. Top with half the tomatoes, half the onion mixture, and season with salt and pepper. Place fish on top in single layer. Spread with remaining tomatoes and onion mixture and sprinkle with capers, olives and mint. Season lightly with salt and pepper and cover with remaining potatoes. Pour water over and drizzle with remaining oil. Cover dish with lid or foil, shiny-side down, and bake until potatoes are tender, about 45 minutes, removing cover in last 10 minutes to brown. Sprinkle with chopped parsley and serve directly from dish.

THON BI'CHERMOULA

TUNA WITH HERB AND SPICE MARINADE (MOROCCO)   SERVES 4 TO 6

The marinade, chermoula, given in this recipe can be used for lamb, poultry and other seafood, which is then broiled, grilled, barbecued, pan-fried or oven-cooked. This is just one version of many in the Moroccan kitchen — swordfish may also be prepared in this manner. The preserved lemon may be omitted if not available, but it is recommended. For kebabs, use fish steaks cut 1 in (2.5 cm) thick. Trim off skin and cut into cubes. Marinate in chermoula, thread onto skewers, and cook on barbecue, turning and basting often with chermoula.

4 to 6 x 4 oz (125 g) tuna steaks

1/4 preserved lemon, julienned, or lemon slices, to garnish

Chermoula:

1/4 preserved lemon (see page 29)

2 cloves garlic

3 tablespoons chopped fresh coriander leaves (cilantro)

3 tablespoons chopped flat-leaf (Italian) parsley

1/8 teaspoon powdered saffron (optional)

1/2 teaspoon paprika

1/8 to 1/4 teaspoon cayenne pepper

1/2 teaspoon ground cumin

1/2 teaspoon salt

2 tablespoons lemon juice

4 tablespoons olive oil

Remove and discard skin from tuna if present. Rinse tuna, pat dry and place in glass or china dish.

For chermoula: Discard pulp from preserved lemon, rinse peel and pat dry. Process peel with remaining ingredients in food processor until coarse puree.

Pour most of chermoula marinade over tuna, reserving about 6 teaspoons for serving. Turn tuna in marinade to coat, cover and refrigerate at least 2 hours, or overnight.

Drain tuna, leaving thin coating of chermoula, and reserve remaining marinade. Cook under hot broiler (grill), or on barbecue, until just cooked, about 6 to 9 minutes, turning carefully and brushing with marinade during cooking.

Serve hot with a teaspoon of reserved chermoula on each serving. Garnish with julienned preserved lemon peel, or lemon slices.

Psari Savoro

FRIED FISH WITH GARLIC AND ROSEMARY (GREECE)   SERVES 6

This method of cooking fish was a means of preserving it for three to four days without refrigeration. Usually a large quantity of thickened sauce was made, often with tomato added. As the need for such preservation is no longer necessary, the sauce need not be great in quantity, nor thickened. It is a delicious way to cook any type of fish suitable for frying. Whole red mullet (goatfish) and garfish (needle fish) are also popular for such cooking, but any fish suitable for frying can be used. If using whole fish, choose fish of smallish size.

2 lb (1 kg) whole fish or fish fillets
salt
olive oil, for shallow frying
all-purpose (plain) flour
3 cloves garlic, finely sliced
2 teaspoons fresh rosemary leaves
1/2 cup (4 fl oz/125 ml) mild red wine vinegar

Scale and clean fish if necessary. Rinse, pat dry with paper towels and season with salt. If using whole large fish, cut 2 to 3 shallow diagonal slashes on each side. Cover and refrigerate 1 hour if possible.

Coat fish in flour and shake off excess. Pour olive oil in frying pan until 1/4 in (5 mm) deep. Heat well. Add fish and cook quickly until browned and fish flakes when tested with knife point, about 5 minutes each side for whole fish or 2 minutes each side for fillets. Remove to warm serving dish.

Drain and reserve oil from pan, and wipe out pan with paper towels to remove any burnt flour. Return about 2 tablespoons of oil to pan. Add garlic and rosemary, and cook gently until garlic is just lightly browned, pressing rosemary with fork to release flavor. Remove pan from heat. Add vinegar and swirl in pan — take care as it will sizzle. Pour immediately over fish and serve hot.

Psari Savoro

Badem Taratorlu Levrek

POACHED SEA BASS WITH ALMOND SAUCE (TURKEY)   SERVES 6

Fish simply poached becomes something special when served with a creamy garlic sauce called tarator in Turkey or skorthalia in Greece and Cyprus. Almonds are usually used, but hazelnuts, walnuts or pine nuts can replace them. Fish suitable for this dish are sea bass, blue-eyed cod, sole or halibut. A cool salad makes a perfect accompaniment. Any leftover tarator can be covered and stored in the refrigerator for up to a month. Tarator can be used as a dip served with pita bread, or a sauce for fried eggplant (aubergine) slices, boiled young beets (beetroot) or other boiled vegetables.

6 fish fillets or steaks

2 cups (16 fl oz/500 ml) water

salt

1/4 teaspoon black peppercorns

1 tablespoon lemon juice

1 bay leaf

2 sprigs parsley

Tarator:

1 cup (2 oz/60 g) soft white breadcrumbs

1 cup (4 oz/125 g) ground blanched almonds

2 cloves garlic

3 tablespoons lemon juice

4 to 6 tablespoons cold water

1/4 cup (2 fl oz/60 ml) olive oil

salt

paprika, to serve (optional)

Rinse fish and pat dry with paper towels. Pour water in large frying pan with lid to fit. Add salt to taste, peppercorns, lemon juice, bay leaf and parsley, cover and bring to boil. Boil 10 minutes. Add fish and more water if necessary to just cover, reduce heat, cover with lid and simmer until fish flakes when tested with knife point, about 6 to 8 minutes. Let cool in liquid.

For tarator: Process breadcrumbs, almonds, garlic, lemon juice and 4 tablespoons water in food processor until thick and smooth. With motor operating, gradually add oil in thin stream. Add salt to taste and extra water if necessary to make a thick creamy sauce.

To serve, lift fish out of liquid and drain well. Place on individual plates and spoon over tarator to mask fish. Serve with a light dusting of paprika, if desired.

KEGITTA LEVREK

SEA BASS IN PAPER (TURKEY)   SERVES 6

Sea bass is one of the most popular fish in Turkey. It is served here wrapped in a rather basic manner —
not the heart-shaped paper cases of the French en papillote method, but just as effective. Foil is given as
an alternative, but it does not puff up like paper, nor allow some of the steam to escape during the cooking. If using foil, place fish on the shiny side so that the dull side ends up as the outside of the package.
Place cooked packages on warm dinner plates to be opened at the table.

6 x 6 oz (180 g) sea bass fillets
or other firm, white-fleshed
fish fillets

salt and freshly ground black pepper

4 oz (125 g) butter, melted

1 lemon, halved

6 small bay leaves

6 small sprigs fresh thyme

6 small sprigs flat-leaf (Italian)
parsley

4 scallions (spring onions/
green onions), julienned

4 medium tomatoes,
peeled and sliced

Preheat oven to 375–400°F (190–200°C/Gas 5).

Season fish lightly with salt and pepper. Cut 6 sheets parchment (baking paper) or foil large enough to wrap single fish
fillet. Brush middle of each piece with a little melted butter.
Place fish fillet on paper, squeeze a little lemon juice over,
top each with bay leaf, thyme and parsley sprig and some
julienned scallions. Drizzle with more melted butter and
arrange tomato slices on top to cover fish. Season with salt
and pepper and drizzle over more melted butter.

Bring up two sides of wrapping and triple-fold across top.
Twist paper at each end or double-fold foil to seal. Place in
single layer on baking sheet or in shallow oven-proof dish.
If using paper, sprinkle packages with cold water. Bake
25 minutes then serve immediately.

TRIGLIE IN CARTOCCIO

RED MULLET IN PAPER (ITALY)   SERVES 4

Besides the red mullet, mackerel, sea bass or trout are also excellent prepared in this way. The cooking
method is popular throughout Italy, often using an oiled brown paper bag.

4 x 12 oz (375 g) red mullet
(goatfish)

salt

1 lemon, halved

freshly ground black pepper

4 small sprigs fresh rosemary

4 tablespoons olive oil

1 medium onion, finely chopped

1 clove garlic, finely chopped

1 celery stalk, finely chopped

2 tablespoons chopped
flat-leaf (Italian) parsley

Scale and clean fish, leaving heads attached. Rub cavities
with salt. Rinse, drain and wipe dry with paper towels. Cut
2 shallow diagonal slashes on each side of fish. Squeeze
lemon juice into cavities and over skin, and season with salt
and pepper. Place sprig of rosemary in each cavity. Set aside.

Heat 2 tablespoons oil in frying pan. Add onion and cook
gently until transparent, about 10 minutes. Add garlic and
celery and cook gently 10 minutes. Stir in parsley and salt
and pepper to taste.

Preheat oven to 375–400°F (190–200°C/Gas 5). Cut 4 sheets
of parchment (baking paper) large enough to enclose single
fish. Brush with remaining oil and place fish in middle. Divide
onion mixture evenly over fish and squeeze lemon juice on
top. Close parcels and cook as directed in recipe above.

POISSON SAUTÉ SAUCE AUX POIVRONS ROUGES

FRIED FISH WITH RED PEPPER SAUCE (FRANCE)   SERVES 4

Most Mediterranean fish recipes are for stews and soups or oven-baked dishes. Broiled (grilled) or fried fish is usually simply prepared, with olive oil, lemon juice, herbs and garlic used as a marinade or baste. With today's lifestyle, quick-to-prepare fish dishes are desirable; the following is based on Mediterranean flavors, and is French in concept. It needs only boiled new potatoes and a steamed green vegetable such as asparagus as an accompaniment. Fish suitable are sea bass, John Dory, sole or blue-eyed cod. Choose fillets or steaks, allowing 4 oz (125 g) of fish per serve. While not a Mediterranean fish, or even resembling one, fresh salmon fillets or steaks may be used for this recipe.

4 to 8 white-fleshed fish fillets or steaks (cutlets)

1/4 cup (1 oz/30 g) all-purpose (plain) flour

salt and freshly ground black pepper

olive oil, for shallow frying

Sauce aux Poivrons Rouges:

2 canned pimientos or roasted red bell peppers (capsicums) (see page 27)

1 clove garlic, chopped

pinch of cayenne pepper

salt

1/4 cup (2 fl oz/60 ml) dry white wine

1 tablespoon olive oil or aioli (see page 36)

1 tablespoon chopped black olives, to serve

Coat fish in flour seasoned with salt and pepper. Pour oil into large frying pan until 1/4 in (5 mm) deep. Heat well. Add fish in single layer and cook until fish flakes when tested with knife point, about 2 to 4 minutes each side. Keep warm.

For sauce aux poivrons rouges: Puree pimientos or peppers and garlic in food processor. Transfer to small saucepan with cayenne, salt to taste, wine and oil (but not aioli), and simmer gently over low heat, about 3 minutes. If using aioli, stir in just before serving.

To serve, spoon sauce on one side of each warm dinner plate, place fish on top of sauce and sprinkle with olives.

Poisson Sauté Sauce aux Poivrons Rouges

PSARI PLAKI

BAKED FISH (GREECE)   SERVES 6

This baked fish is much like many other fish stews or casseroles of the region, but I have chosen the Greek version for its simplicity. Any kind of firm-fleshed fish suitable for oven-cooking can be used. Choose one whole fish, six serving-sized whole fish or fish steaks or cutlets of the following types: snapper, mackerel, cod, hake, halibut or sea bass, according to the fish available in your area.

3 lb (1.5 kg) fish, whole or portions
juice of 1 lemon
salt
freshly ground black pepper
1/2 cup (4 fl oz/125 ml) olive oil
1 large onion, sliced
2 medium carrots, thinly sliced
1 celery stalk, chopped
1 tablespoon chopped celery leaves
4 large ripe tomatoes,
peeled and chopped
1/2 cup (4 fl oz/125 ml) dry white
wine
1/2 teaspoon sugar

To Serve:
chopped parsley
crusty bread
salad of choice

Scale and clean fish if necessary. Rinse and wipe dry with paper towels. Sprinkle with lemon juice, salt and pepper, and set aside.

Heat oil in large frying pan. Add onion, carrots and celery and cook gently until onion is transparent, about 10 to 12 minutes, stirring often. Add celery leaves, tomatoes, wine and sugar, and simmer covered, 20 minutes.

Preheat oven to 350–375°F (180–190°C/Gas 4).

Spread half the sauce in baking dish. Add fish and top with remaining sauce. Cover with foil or lid and bake 30 minutes. Remove cover and bake until fish flakes when tested with knife point, about 10 minutes.

To serve, sprinkle with parsley and serve directly from dish with crusty bread and salad.

bell pepper

Lenguado en Salsa de Almendras

FLOUNDER WITH ALMOND SAUCE (SPAIN)   SERVES 4

The cooking of Catalan features a special type of sauce mixture called a picada. Its basis is fried bread pounded with nuts, garlic, parsley and sometimes saffron. Usually added to stew-style dishes towards the end of cooking, it adds a special dimension. The following recipe includes a picada as an important element of the dish. If you are unable to purchase flounder fillets, use any white-fleshed fish fillets. A simple green salad makes a good accompaniment.

4 to 8 flounder fillets, depending on size

salt and freshly ground black pepper

4 tablespoons olive oil

1/4 cup (1 1/2 oz/45 g) whole blanched almonds

1/2 cup (1 oz/30 g) soft breadcrumbs

2 cloves garlic, chopped

1 tablespoon chopped parsley

1/8 teaspoon powdered saffron

1/2 cup (4 fl oz/125 ml) dry white wine

1 medium onion, chopped

2 medium-sized ripe tomatoes, peeled and chopped

Remove and discard skin from fish if present. Place fish in oiled shallow oven-proof dish in single layer and season with salt and pepper. Set aside.

Heat 2 tablespoons oil in frying pan. Add almonds and cook over medium heat until barely golden. Add breadcrumbs and garlic and cook until crumbs are golden, stirring often. Place mixture in food processor with parsley and saffron and process to a fine paste, adding a little wine if needed. Transfer to bowl.

Wipe out frying pan to remove any crumbs. Add remaining oil and onion, and cook gently until transparent, about 10 minutes. Add tomatoes and remaining wine, cover and simmer 15 minutes until tomatoes are soft.

Preheat oven to 375–400°F (190–200°C/Gas 5).

Puree tomato mixture in food processor and mix into almond-crumb mixture. Spread over fish and bake until fish flakes when tested with knife point, about 15 minutes. Serve hot.

Dag Afuye

BAKED FISH WITH PINE NUTS (ISRAEL)   SERVES 6

The Israelis have adopted this indigenous recipe into their developing cuisine. Sea bream (porgy), sea bass or snapper are recommended for use, but small fish may also be used.

1 large (about 3 lb/1.5 kg) whole fish

1/2 teaspoon turmeric

salt

1/2 cup (4 fl oz/125 ml) olive oil

1/3 cup (1 1/2 oz/45 g) pine nuts

4 medium onions, sliced

1 hot green chili pepper, seeded and chopped

2 cloves garlic, finely chopped

juice of 1 lemon

3 tablespoons finely chopped flat-leaf (Italian) parsley

2 large ripe tomatoes, peeled, seeded and chopped

freshly ground black pepper

parsley sprigs, to garnish

Scale and clean fish if necessary, leaving head attached. Rinse and wipe dry with paper towels. Cut off fins if desired and cut 3 shallow diagonal slashes in skin on each side. Rub turmeric over fish and sprinkle with salt. Let stand 20 minutes.

Preheat oven to 350–375°F (180–190°C/Gas 4).

Heat 1 tablespoon oil in frying pan. Add pine nuts and cook until golden brown, about 2 minutes, stirring often. Remove with slotted spoon to plate and set aside.

Add remaining oil to pan with onions and cook gently until transparent, about 10 minutes, stirring often. Add chili pepper and garlic, and cook 1 minute. Spread half onion mixture in oven-proof dish large enough to hold fish. Place fish on top, sprinkle with lemon juice and top with remaining onion and parsley. Spread tomatoes evenly over fish and season with salt and pepper.

Bake until fish flakes when tested at thickest part with knife point, about 30 to 60 minutes, depending on size of fish, basting occassionally with pan juices (add a little water only to prevent scorching).

To serve, lift fish onto warm serving platter and spoon onion and tomato mixture on top. Sprinkle with pine nuts and garnish with parsley. Serve hot.

Dag Afuye

Merluza con Espinacas

HAKE WITH SPINACH (SPAIN)   SERVES 4

Acelgas, chard or silverbeet is often used in this dish, but the flavor of spinach is better with fish. Hake is one of the most popular fish in Spanish cuisine; if not available in your region, substitute with another white-fleshed fish (such as cod or ling) that has a large flake when cooked.

1¹/2 lb (750 g) spinach

4 thick hake fillets

3 tablespoons all-purpose (plain) flour

salt and freshly ground black pepper

5 tablespoons olive oil

1 medium onion, finely chopped

2 cloves garlic, finely chopped

2 tablespoons pine nuts

¹/2 cup (4 fl oz/125 ml) dry sherry

2 tablespoons finely chopped parsley

Remove roots from spinach and discard damaged leaves and coarse stems — retain most of the green stems as they are tender. Wash spinach well in several changes of water, drain (but do not dry). Chop coarsely. Place spinach in large saucepan and cook over medium heat until cooked, tossing often. Drain in colander and press with back of wooden spoon to extract moisture. Transfer to board and chop finely.

Preheat oven to 350–375°F (180–190°C/Gas 4).

Coat fish with flour seasoned with salt and pepper to taste. Heat 2 tablespoons oil in frying pan. Add fish and brown quickly on each side. Remove to plate. Wipe out pan with paper towels. Add half remaining oil and onion, cook gently until transparent, about 10 minutes. Add garlic and cook 1 minute. Stir in spinach and transfer to shallow oven-proof dish. Sprinkle with pine nuts and place fish on top. Drizzle over remaining oil and sprinkle with sherry. Bake until fish flakes when tested with knife point, about 15 to 20 minutes. Sprinkle with parsley and serve hot directly from dish.

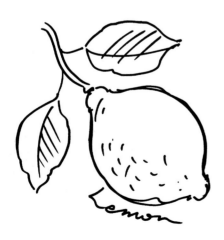

Daurade au Fenouil

BREAM WITH FENNEL (FRANCE)   SERVES 4

Fish has a special affinity to fennel, whether it be the seeds, the green stalks and feathery leaves or the dry fennel stalks for adding to the fire when cooking fish on the barbecue. It is surprising how easy it is to find fennel growing in the wild; I gather mine at a local park where it flourishes in a tract of wasteland. If fresh fennel is not available, sprinkle a few fennel seeds in the cavity and 1 teaspoon fennel seeds over the onion and garlic.

The daurade (gilt-head bream), popular in the South of France for this particular dish, can be substituted with sea bream (porgy) or sea bass outside the region. If using a large fish, choose one about 2½ lb (1.25 kg) in weight with head. For single-serve fish, each whole fish should weigh about 10 to 12 oz (300 to 350 g).

1 large or 4 small gilt-head or sea bream

salt and freshly ground black pepper

4 to 5 tablespoons olive oil

6 green fennel stalks with feathery sprigs attached

4 to 6 sprigs fresh thyme

1 medium white onion, thinly sliced

2 cloves garlic, finely sliced

2 lemons

1 cup (8 fl oz/250 ml) dry white wine

Preheat oven to 375–400°F (190–200°C/Gas 5).

Scale and clean fish if necessary, leaving head attached. Clean cavity by rubbing with salt. Rinse and wipe dry with paper towels. Cut 3 to 4 shallow diagonal slashes into fish on each side and season inside and out with salt and pepper. Brush cavity with a little of the oil and insert feathery sprigs of fennel from stalks together with thyme sprigs, reserving 2 sprigs of thyme.

Lightly oil shallow oven-proof dish large enough to hold fish in single layer. Spread onion slices over base and sprinkle with garlic. Cut fennel stalks to fit into dish and place on top of onion with reserved thyme sprigs. Place prepared fish on top, brush with a little more oil, turn over and brush other side with oil.

Thinly slice lemons, discarding ends and removing any seeds. Overlap lemon slices on top of fish, pour wine into dish and drizzle remaining oil over top of all ingredients. Bake until fish flakes when tested with knife point, about 25 minutes for small fish, 35 minutes for large fish. Baste towards end of cooking with pan juices. Remove fish to warm platter. Strain pan juices and pour over fish.

MEAT AND POULTRY

Meat is regarded as a very special food in the Mediterranean as the land is not conducive to grazing large herds, especially cattle. Sheep, however, can cope with less than lush pastures and goats thrive on almost anything. Because goat meat is not readily available outside the region, no recipes have been given in this chapter, but good quality kid can be used as a substitute in most lamb dishes.

Pork is a popular meat in Spain, southern France and Italy, and to a lesser extent in Greece (although Greek Cypriots are very fond of pork and use it frequently). More beef is available these days, and in Italy and France, veal is highly esteemed. Lamb reigns supreme in North African countries, in the Levant and Greece. Variety meats (offal) are considered delicacies, especially lamb and veal liver, kidneys, brains and sweetbreads, tripe and oxtail.

Poultry is universally popular — mostly free-range and not marketed as it is outside the region. In North Africa, they are particularly fond of chicken and use a great deal of it. I have used portions rather than whole chicken in many recipes as commercially produced chickens have more fat than the free-range ones and chicken portions are usually leaner. Ease in preparation, of course, has been a deciding factor in choosing chicken dishes for this book.

Pigeons are specially bred in North Africa, especially in Egypt, and in Morocco for the famous bisteeya, but I have used chicken breasts for this recipe. The hunting of rabbits, pigeons, quail, partridge, pheasant, wild duck and other game birds is an age-old tradition to add more meat to the pot. However, the French raise ducks and geese to perfection, also producing excellent goose and duck liver, fois gras, in the north of Languedoc. Any visitor to France cannot help but be impressed by the vast range of charcuterie available to locals, who usually buy it prepared in preference to making it at home. Because French charcuterie is so widely manufactured and readily available in international markets, only a simple chicken liver pâté has been given in the recipes.

Preserved meats and sausages are important to Mediterranean cooking, especially for adding to dishes with other foods or serving as appetizers. Italy has its range of salamis, mortadella, prosciutto and fresh sausages. Spain has an impressive array of pork products, including chorizo, blood sausage and the cured and air-dried pork, jamon serrano. Greece, Turkey and Cyprus use a spiced, air-dried beef, their version of pastrami. Cypriot Greeks make a pork sausage. I have only used those prepared meats that are readily available, but have given a recipe for merguez, Tunisia's spicy lamb sausage, for the adventurous.

Poulet à Quarante Gousses d'Ail (page 132)

POULET À QUARANTE GOUSSES D'AIL

CHICKEN WITH 40 CLOVES OF GARLIC (FRANCE)   SERVES 4

While this recipe is attributed to the Dauphine region bordering Provence to the north, it is also popular in Provence. However, cooks in Dauphine insist that Provençal garlic be used. The aroma of this dish is heavenly; with the garlic cloves cooked in their paper-shrouds, their flavor is mellowed. Traditionally a flour paste is used to seal the casserole dish around the lid, but foil works just as well. For the best effect, uncover the chicken at the table so the full aroma is enjoyed. A tossed green salad is a simple yet perfect accompaniment.

3 lb (1.5 kg) roasting chicken
salt and freshly ground black pepper
6 sprigs fresh thyme
3 sprigs fresh rosemary
2 small bay leaves
1/4 cup (2 fl oz/60 ml) olive oil
40 large cloves garlic, unpeeled
thick slices of baguette
(long French bread)

Preheat oven to 350–375°F (180–190°C/Gas 4).

Clean chicken cavity if necessary, rinse and dry well with paper towels and season inside and out with salt and pepper. Place 3 sprigs thyme, 1 sprig rosemary and 1 bay leaf in cavity.

Heat oil in large frying pan. Add chicken and cook until lightly colored all over, about 3 minutes each side. Place in deep casserole dish just large enough to hold chicken. Place 2 to 3 cloves of garlic in chicken cavity, and place remainder around chicken. Pour over oil from frying pan and place remaining herb sprigs and bay leaf on top of chicken. Cover dish tightly, sealing well with a strip of foil around rim, scrunching it to form a tight seal. Bake 1 3/4 hours — do not remove cover during cooking.

Remove dish from oven and let stand, covered, 10 minutes before serving. Meanwhile toast bread under broiler (grill) and place in serving basket.

Carve chicken, or cut into pieces, and serve with garlic cloves and toasted bread. The garlic is squeezed out of its skin onto the toast or chicken.

DJEJ MAHSHE BIL SEKSU

CHICKEN STUFFED WITH COUSCOUS, ALMONDS AND RAISINS (MOROCCO)   SERVES 4

In Morocco, a whole chicken was usually steamed over boiling water, as domestic ovens were unknown when the Moroccan cuisine was developing. Oven-cooking is now becoming more common, and it does improve the flavor of this delicious dish. The following method is a combination of roasting and steaming, which gives succulent, moist chicken full of flavor. Normally the stuffing makes use of leftover couscous from a previous meal; if you do have couscous left over, use 1¹/₂ cups (8 oz/250 g) cooked couscous, omitting the boiling water-salt-butter mixture used in the stuffing ingredients. To check if the chicken is cooked, push a leg towards the breast — the chicken is cooked when the leg moves easily.

3¹/₂ lb (1.75 kg) roasting chicken
salt and freshly ground black pepper
paprika
1 cup (8 fl oz/250 ml) water
2 tablespoons butter, softened

Couscous Stuffing:
¹/₃ cup (1¹/₂ oz/45 g) raisins
¹/₂ cup (4 fl oz/125 ml) water
¹/₂ teaspoon salt
2 oz (60 g) butter
¹/₂ cup (3¹/₂ oz/100 g) couscous
¹/₂ cup (2¹/₂ oz/75 g) whole
blanched almonds
¹/₂ teaspoon sugar
¹/₂ teaspoon ground cinnamon
¹/₄ teaspoon paprika
freshly ground black pepper

Clean chicken cavity if necessary, rinse and dry with paper towels, and season cavity with salt.

For couscous stuffing: Barely cover raisins with boiling water in small bowl. Let stand until plump, about 10 minutes. Combine ¹/₂ cup water, salt and half the butter in saucepan, bring to boil and remove from heat. Stir in couscous, cover and let stand, until water is absorbed, about 10 minutes. Melt remaining butter in frying pan. Add almonds and cook until golden brown, about 2 minutes. Add almonds and butter to couscous with sugar, cinnamon, paprika, pepper to taste, and drained raisins. Mix thoroughly and lightly with a fork.

Preheat oven to 350–375°F (180–190°C/Gas 4).

Pack chicken cavity loosely with couscous stuffing, close opening with poultry skewers and tie legs together with string. Tuck wing tips under body and secure neck skin with a poultry skewer. Season with salt, pepper and paprika. Place breast-side up in roasting pan and pour in water. Spread softened butter over chicken and bake 2 hours, basting often.

Transfer chicken to warm platter, cover with foil and let stand in warm place 10 minutes. Pour pan juices over chicken, if desired. Serve with couscous stuffing.

Kotopoulo Me Bamyes

CHICKEN WITH OKRA (GREECE)   SERVES 4

Okra, native to tropical Africa, features in North African cuisine and is also used in Greece, Cyprus and the Levant. It is often added to meat and poultry stews or cooked in a tomato sauce rather than simply boiled or steamed. Many cooks thread prepared okra with a needle and strong cotton, passing the needle through the conical stems, and tying into a "necklace". Added to the stew, it is then lifted out with the handle of a wooden spoon if the stew needs to be stirred, or when it is time to serve. When serving with chicken, the okra "necklace" is draped over or around chicken, and the thread is snipped and pulled out. The presoaking of okra reduces its viscosity.

1 lb (500 g) okra

salt

1/2 cup (4 fl oz/125 ml) distilled white vinegar

2 x 1 1/2 lb (750 g) young chickens (poussins)

2 tablespoons olive oil

2 tablespoons butter

1 onion, finely chopped

1 clove garlic, pressed (crushed)

15 oz (425 g) can tomatoes, chopped but undrained

1 tablespoon tomato paste

1 teaspoon sugar

1/2 cup (4 fl oz/125 ml) dry white wine

1 bay leaf

freshly ground black pepper

finely chopped parsley, to serve

Trim stalk tips from okra, and trim carefully around conical tops of stalks to remove fibrous layer, taking care not to cut into pods. Dissolve 1 teaspoon salt in vinegar in large bowl. Add okra and turn in mixture using your hands. Let stand 30 minutes. Drain in colander and rinse well.

Halve chickens, rinse and dry with paper towels. Heat oil and butter in large wide saucepan. Add chicken halves and cook until browned all over, about 3 minutes each side. Remove chicken to a plate.

Reduce heat, add onion to pan and cook gently until transparent, about 5 minutes. Add garlic and cook several seconds. Add tomatoes with their liquid, tomato paste, sugar, wine, bay leaf, and salt and pepper to taste. Return chicken to pan, turn in sauce, cover and simmer gently 20 minutes.

Place okra carefully on top of chicken — it should not be covered with sauce. Cover and simmer until okra and chicken are tender, about 20 minutes. Remove okra with slotted spoon to warm dish. Lift chicken onto serving platter, pour sauce over and arrange okra around chicken. Sprinkle with chopped parsley before serving.

Kotopoulo Me Bamyes

Djej Makalli

CHICKEN WITH PRESERVED LEMON AND OLIVES (MOROCCO)   SERVES 6

This would have to be one of the best-known Moroccan recipes. Usually a whole chicken is jointed, but boneless, skinless chicken breasts are recommended in this recipe. Chicken livers are often added to give body to the sauce — the following recipe uses much less liquid than usual, so they are excluded. If you do not have preserved lemons, you can use the grated rind of 1 lemon in cooking, and finish with blanched julienne strips of lemon rind — not the same, although the dish still tastes good. While this dish is often served on its own as a separate course in Morocco, it is excellent served with a plain rice pilaf (see page 37).

3 cloves garlic, pressed (crushed)

1/2 teaspoon ground ginger

1/2 teaspoon ground cumin

1/4 teaspoon freshly ground black pepper

1/8 teaspoon cayenne pepper

1/2 teaspoon ground turmeric

pinch of powdered saffron (optional)

2 tablespoons olive oil

6 single (half) chicken breast fillets

1 large onion, finely chopped

3/4 cup (6 fl oz/180 ml) chicken stock (see page 31)

3 tablespoons chopped fresh coriander leaves (cilantro)

3 tablespoons chopped flat-leaf (Italian) parsley

salt

1 preserved lemon (see page 29)

18 kalamata olives

1 to 2 tablespoons lemon juice

Combine garlic, spices and 1 teaspoon oil in large dish. Add chicken, rub with spice paste, cover and refrigerate 2 to 3 hours, or overnight.

Heat remaining oil in large frying pan with lid to fit. Add onion and cook gently until transparent, about 10 minutes. Increase heat, add chicken and cook, turning, until chicken becomes white, about 5 minutes. Add stock to marinating dish and stir well to mix with any remaining marinade. Add stock mixture to chicken with herbs and salt to taste. Reduce heat, cover and simmer gently 20 minutes.

Meanwhile, remove pulp from preserved lemon and discard. Rinse the peel and cut into julienne strips. Place olives in small saucepan, cover with water, bring to boil, then drain. Repeat twice until there is no trace of bitterness. Add lemon peel strips and olives to chicken, cover and simmer until cooked through, about 10 minutes. Add lemon juice to taste and adjust seasoning.

POLLO TONNATO

CHICKEN WITH TUNA SAUCE (ITALY)   SERVES 6

Vitello tonnato is a wonderful summer dish, but with veal being rather expensive, it is usually reserved for special occasions. I use chicken breasts and serve it more frequently. It is even more delicious than the veal version. Freeze the remaining chicken stock for later use in other recipes requiring light stock.

3 cups (24 fl oz/750 ml) water

1 cup (8 fl oz/250 ml) dry white wine

1 onion, chopped

1 carrot, sliced

1 celery stalk, sliced

2 sprigs flat-leaf (Italian) parsley

2 bay leaves

1 teaspoon salt

1/4 teaspoon whole black peppercorns

6 single (half) chicken breasts, on the bone with skin

watercress, to garnish

Tuna Sauce:

6 oz (180 g) can tuna in oil, drained

6 canned anchovy fillets, drained

2 egg yolks

1/2 teaspoon dry mustard (mustard powder)

3 teaspoons drained capers

1 tablespoon lemon juice

3/4 cup (6 fl oz/180 ml) olive oil

Combine water and wine in large saucepan. Add vegetables, parsley, bay leaves, salt and peppercorns and bring to boil. Add chicken, cover and simmer very gently until chicken is tender, about 50 minutes. Let chicken cool in this stock.

Remove chicken from stock, reserving stock. Carefully separate chicken meat from bones in one piece. Place chicken in dish, cover and set aside. Skim fat from stock and strain stock through sieve lined with cheesecloth (muslin). Store stock in separate container in refrigerator while making tuna sauce.

For tuna sauce: Place tuna, anchovy fillets, egg yolks, mustard, 1 teaspoon capers and lemon juice in food processor or blender. Process until smooth. While motor is operating, very gradually pour in oil in thin stream. Transfer sauce to bowl. Add 2 to 4 tablespoons chicken stock gradually to sauce to give thin cream consistency. Adjust seasoning with salt and pepper.

Spread half the tuna sauce over chicken. Cover with plastic wrap and refrigerate several hours or overnight. Just before serving, spread on a little more tuna sauce. Sprinkle with remaining capers and garnish with watercress. Serve remaining tuna sauce separately.

Page 138 to 139: Djej Mahshe Bil Seksu (page 133), Boeuf en Daube à la Provençale (page 142) and Gigot d'Agneau à la Provençale (page 158)

OFF TAPUZIM

ORANGE CHICKEN (ISRAEL)   SERVES 6

Israel's citrus fruits are considered amongst the best of the Mediterranean, and are used extensively in their developing cuisine. This recipe uses a vegetable margarine as dairy foods cannot be combined with any type of meat, nor eaten at the same meal, according to kashrut (dietary laws). For the best flavor, use orange blossom honey if available. Use a swivel peeler to remove thin strips of citrus rinds with as little pith as possible, then julienne.

3¹/2 lb (1.75 kg) roasting chicken, jointed

grated rind of 2 oranges

grated rind of 1 lemon

1¹/2 teaspoons salt

1 teaspoon dry mustard (mustard powder)

3 tablespoons honey

2 oz (60 g) vegetable margarine, melted

1 cup (8 fl oz/250 ml) fresh orange juice

2 tablespoons lemon juice

3 teaspoons cornstarch (cornflour)

1 tablespoon water

julienned orange and lemon rind, to garnish

extra honey

Dry chicken pieces with paper towels. Combine grated rind, salt, mustard and honey. Spread mixture over chicken, cover and let stand in cool place 30 minutes.

Preheat oven to 325–350°F (160–180°C/Gas 3).

Pour a little margarine into shallow baking dish and add chicken, skin-side up, in single layer. Pour combined orange and lemon juices over chicken, then spoon over remaining margarine. Bake 45 minutes. Turn chicken over and bake 30 minutes more. Turn skin-side up again and bake until cooked through and skin is browned, about 15 minutes. Baste occasionally during cooking.

Remove chicken to serving platter and keep warm. Strain juices from baking dish into small saucepan and skim off excess fat. Combine cornstarch and water, add to saucepan and bring to boil, stirring constantly. Simmer gently over very low heat. Boil julienned rind in water in separate saucepan 5 minutes. Drain and toss with a little honey. Pour sauce over chicken and garnish with julienned rind.

OFF SUM-SUM

SESAME FRIED CHICKEN (ISRAEL)   SERVES 6

Sesame seeds are an ancient food used extensively in eastern Mediterranean and North African countries. This is definitely an Israeli recipe with the sesame seed coating imparting a delightful, nutty flavor. Take care the seeds are not burnt in the initial browning.

6 single (half) skinless chicken breast fillets

1/2 cup (2 1/2 oz/75 g) sesame seeds

1/2 cup (2 1/2 oz/75 g) all-purpose (plain) flour

1 teaspoon salt

freshly ground black pepper

1 teaspoon paprika

1 large egg

3 tablespoons water

oil, for shallow frying

Trim any fat from chicken pieces and dry with paper towels. Combine sesame seeds, flour, salt and pepper in a dish. Coat chicken pieces lightly in mixture, shaking off excess. Beat egg and water in shallow bowl. Dip chicken into egg mixture to coat, then coat again with sesame seed mixture. Place chicken on tray, cover and refrigerate 30 minutes if time permits.

Preheat oven to 325–350°F (160–180°C/Gas 3).

Pour oil into frying pan until 1/4 in (5 mm) deep and heat over medium heat. Add chicken and shallow fry until light golden brown, about 2 minutes each side — do not cook chicken through or coating will burn.

Arrange chicken in single layer in baking dish and bake until cooked through, about 25 minutes. Serve hot.

FILET DE BOEUF AU TAPENADE

POACHED BEEF FILLET WITH TAPENADE (FRANCE)   SERVES 6 TO 8

A perfect meal for warm, sunny days, served with crusty bread and a salad platter of Belgian endive (witloof), romaine (cos) lettuce, tiny radishes, bell pepper (capsicum), celery, scallions (spring onions/green onions), tomato and cucumber sticks. Use canned or packaged stock, broth or consommé (you may have to dilute it, so follow directions on the can), or use home-made stock; do not use stock powder or cubes.

2 lb (1 kg) piece beef tenderloin (fillet)

3 cups (24 fl oz/750 ml) beef stock (see page 31)

freshly ground black pepper

1 quantity tapenade (see page 48)

capers, chives and black olives, to garnish

Trim silver skin and fat from beef, taking care not to separate muscles. Tie at intervals with kitchen string. Pour stock in saucepan just large enough to hold beef and add pepper to taste. Bring to boil, add beef and boil gently 3 minutes. Reduce heat to a bare simmer, cover and cook very gently on low heat 30 minutes (liquid should barely tremble — do not allow to boil). Remove from heat and let stand 5 minutes. Remove beef from liquid, wrap in foil and let stand until cool. Strain stock and store in a jar in refrigerator for use in other recipes. Slice beef thinly and arrange slices on platter. Spoon tapenade over beef and garnish with capers, chives and olives. Serve immediately or cover with plastic wrap and refrigerate, bring to room temperature before serving.

Boeuf en Daube à la Provençale

DAUBE OF BEEF PROVENÇAL (FRANCE)   SERVES 6

A daube takes its name from the daubière, a pot-bellied casserole with a small opening, designed to retain moisture during cooking. Many daubes appear in the cooking of Provence, using the meat or game available in the various areas. They are traditionally served with boiled pasta although boiled potatoes can also be served as an accompaniment. The cooking must be slow to bring the meat to melting tenderness. Boneless beef chuck steak is ideal for this daube but other stewing beef can be used. Dried orange peel is preferred but a piece of fresh rind, removed in a wide strip with a swivel peeler, can be used instead. Serve hot straight from the casserole dish.

3 lb (1.5 kg) lean stewing beef

1 large onion, sliced

2 medium carrots, cut in chunks

bouquet garni
(2 sprigs each thyme and parsley
and 1 bay leaf, tied together)

1 cup (8 fl oz/250 ml) red wine

2 tablespoons brandy

3 tablespoons olive oil

4 oz (125 g) lean bacon, diced

1 large onion, extra,
cut into thick wedges

2 cloves garlic, pressed (crushed)

1/2 cup (4 fl oz/125 ml) water

strip of orange rind

salt and freshly ground black pepper

1/2 cup (2 1/2 oz/75 g) black olives,
pitted

finely chopped parsley,
to serve (optional)

Trim beef if necessary and cut into 1 in (2.5 cm) cubes. Combine beef, sliced onion, carrots, bouquet garni, wine and brandy in plastic container with lid. Seal and shake to distribute marinade. Refrigerate 6 hours or overnight, shaking container occasionally. Lift beef and flavoring ingredients from marinade liquid and place in large casserole dish. Reserve marinade liquid.

Preheat oven to 325–350°F (160–1870°C/Gas 3).

Heat oil in frying pan. Add bacon and cook until lightly browned. Add onion wedges and cook until tinged with brown flecks, about 10 minutes. Add garlic and cook several seconds. Add reserved marinade, water, orange rind, and salt and pepper to taste. Bring to boil and pour over beef in casserole dish. Cover and bake until beef is tender, about 2 hours — check after 1 hour that beef is just covered with liquid and add water if necessary. Adjust seasoning and sprinkle with olives and parsley before serving.

Boeuf en Daube à la Provençale

Kefta Kebab

GROUND MEAT KEBABS (MOROCCO, TUNISIA, ALGERIA)   SERVES 6

This is street food in the Maghreb, served in bread with an extra sprinkling of salt and cumin, but I like to add salad vegetables. Purchase meat that is not too lean. If you are using long skewers, have two portions of meat mixture on each skewer. Use one portion on short skewers. To cook the kebabs, remove the grid from the barbecue if possible and place skewers so that the ends rest on the sides of the barbecue. A Habachi barbecue is ideal for cooking these. Otherwise, place skewers on barbecue grid so that meat lies between the grid bars.

2 lb (1 kg) finely ground (minced) lamb or beef

4 tablespoons chopped parsley

2 tablespoons chopped fresh coriander leaves (cilantro)

1 small onion, chopped

1 1/2 teaspoons salt

freshly ground black pepper

1/2 teaspoon ground allspice

1/8 teaspoon cayenne pepper

1 teaspoon ground cumin

1 teaspoon paprika

olive oil

pita or other flat bread, warmed, to serve

Place meat, parsley, coriander, onion, salt, pepper to taste, and spices in bowl. Pass through meat grinder (mincer) twice using the fine screen, or process in four batches in food processor. Knead to a smooth paste by hand if grinder is used; if processed, knead to blend flavors evenly. Cover bowl and refrigerate 30 minutes.

With moistened hands, take generous tablespoons of kebab paste and mold into 4 in (10 cm) long finger shapes around flat, sword-like skewers. As skewers are prepared, place across baking dish with ends of skewers resting on each side. Cover and refrigerate 1 hour if time permits.

Brush kebabs lightly with oil and barbecue until cooked through, about 2 to 3 minutes, turning frequently.

To serve, slide kebabs off skewers and serve with warm bread.

grapes

PULPETTUN

MEAT LOAF (MALTA)   SERVES 6

A tasty meat loaf, reflecting the Italian influence in Malta's cuisine.

1 large onion, grated

1½ cups (3 oz/90 g)
soft breadcrumbs

½ cup (4 fl oz/125 ml) red wine

3 tablespoons chopped parsley

2 eggs, beaten

2 tablespoons grated romano cheese

1½ teaspoons salt

freshly ground black pepper

2 lb (1 kg) finely ground
(minced) beef

3 hard-cooked (boiled) eggs, shelled

2 tablespoons olive oil

2 tablespoons tomato paste

¾ cup (6 fl oz/180 ml) hot water

1 clove garlic, pressed (crushed)

½ teaspoon sugar

Preheat oven to 325–350°F (160–180°C/Gas 3).

Combine onion, breadcrumbs, half the wine, parsley, beaten eggs, cheese, and salt and pepper in large bowl. Add beef and mix well, then knead well with hand.

Dampen a board with water and place beef mixture on it. Shape into thick loaf, press a little to flatten and place whole eggs along middle. Bring beef mixture up over eggs and shape into roll. Use moistened hands to smooth roll.

Pour oil into baking dish and carefully lift beef roll into dish. Brush all over with oil. Bake 20 minutes.

Meanwhile, combine remaining wine, tomato paste, hot water, garlic, sugar, and salt and pepper to taste in jug and pour over roll. Bake until cooked through, about 40 minutes, basting occasionally — add a little water to dish if sauce begins to scorch. Lift roll onto platter, slice and serve with sauce from dish.

ALBONDIGAS

FRIED MEATBALLS (SPAIN)   SERVES 4 TO 6

Pork is traditionally used for these meatballs, but veal or beef can be used instead, or in combination. You can also make mini balls — fry them and serve as a tapa with aioli (see page 36) rather than in salsa.

1 lb (500 g) finely ground
(minced) pork

8 oz (250 g) finely ground
(minced) veal or beef

3 oz (90g) cooked ham,
finely chopped

1 medium onion, grated

1 clove garlic, pressed (crushed)

3 tablespoons chopped parsley

½ cup (1 oz/30 g) soft breadcrumbs

2 eggs

salt and freshly ground black pepper

all-purpose (plain) flour

olive or sunflower oil, for frying

1 quantity salsa de tomate
(see page 33)

Combine ground meat, ham, onion, garlic, parsley, breadcrumbs and eggs in bowl, adding salt and pepper to taste. Let stand 10 minutes, then mix again, using hands. With moistened hands, shape into large walnut-sized balls, place on tray, cover and refrigerate 30 minutes.

Pour oil into frying pan until ½ in (1 cm) deep and heat over medium-high heat. Coat meatballs in flour and shallow fry in batches until golden brown and cooked through, about 5 minutes, turning frequently. Drain on paper towels.

Heat salsa de tomate in saucepan. Add meatballs and heat through before serving.

KEFTETHES

FRIED MEAT PATTIES (GREECE)   SERVES 6

Kofta, ground meat dishes, abound in the Middle East and North Africa. This is a Greek version, with herbs and lemon adding flavor rather than the spices popular elsewhere. They are made fairly large for main courses and accompanied by vegetables of choice. The same mixture can be shaped into small balls to serve as a mezethaki for 12 to 15 people — either by themselves or with plain (natural) yogurt mixed with chopped fresh mint and pressed (crushed) garlic, as pictured. The keftethakia variation can be made ahead, refrigerated, then reheated in a 350°F (180°C/Gas 4) oven for 10 to 15 minutes. For both versions, coat with flour in batches before frying to avoid stickiness.

1 large onion, roughly chopped

1/2 cup (1 oz/30 g) chopped flat-leaf (Italian) parsley, packed

2 teaspoons chopped fresh mint

4 to 5 slices (about 3 oz/90 g) crustless stale white bread

2 eggs

3 tablespoons lemon juice

1 1/2 teaspoons salt

freshly ground black pepper

2 lb (1 kg) finely ground (minced) beef or lamb

1/2 cup (2 1/2 oz/75 g) all-purpose (plain) flour

oil, for shallow frying

1 1/2 cups (12 fl oz/375 ml) saltsa domata (see page 32), to serve (optional)

Place onion, parsley and mint in food processor and process until finely chopped. Soak bread in water and squeeze dry. Add bread to onion mixture with eggs, lemon juice, salt and generous grinding of pepper. Process to thick puree. Add one-quarter of the meat and process just enough to combine. Add mixture to remaining meat in large bowl, and mix thoroughly with hands. Cover and let stand 10 minutes, or refrigerate up to 1 hour.

With moistened hands, shape mixture into apricot-sized balls and place on tray. Place flour in deep dish.

Pour enough oil into large frying pan to cover base and heat over medium-high heat. Coat about 15 meatballs in flour, flatten into patties about 1/2 in (1 cm) thick and shallow fry until browned and cooked through, about 3 minutes each side. Remove patties and drain on paper towels. Repeat with remaining mixture. Serve hot either plain or with saltsa domata, if desired.

Keftethakia (Cocktail Meatball) Variation: Shape mixture into small walnut-sized balls, coat with flour and deep fry in batches until cooked through, about 3 minutes. Drain on paper towels.

Keftethakia

Moussaka me Aginares

MEAT AND ARTICHOKE PIE (GREECE)   SERVES 6 TO 8

Moussaka is one of the best known Greek dishes. Although it is usually made with eggplant (aubergine), other vegetables can be used alone or in combination, such as zucchini (courgettes) and potatoes. In Greece, artichokes are plentiful and usually inexpensive, and when in season, this version of moussaka is relished. To enjoy the authentic version, you would need about 20 globe artichokes, stripped down to the heart, boiled and sliced. As this would be time consuming to prepare, and also very expensive in most regions, canned or frozen artichoke hearts make a more than acceptable substitute. Moussaka can also be layered in individual dishes and baked for about 30 minutes.

2 tablespoons olive oil

1 large onion, chopped

2 cloves garlic, finely chopped

2 lb (1 kg) lean ground (minced) beef or lamb

2 x 15 oz (425 g) cans tomatoes, chopped but undrained

2 tablespoons tomato paste

1/2 teaspoon ground cinnamon

2 tablespoons chopped parsley

2 teaspoons sugar

salt and freshly ground black pepper

4 to 5 x 14 oz (400 g) cans artichoke hearts or 9 oz (280 g) boxes frozen artichokes, thawed

2 tablespoons dried breadcrumbs

Bechamel Sauce:

3 oz (90 g) butter

1/2 cup (2 1/2 oz/75 g) all-purpose (plain) flour

3 cups (24 fl oz/750 ml) milk

1/4 teaspoon grated nutmeg

salt and freshly ground pepper

3 tablespoons grated kefalotiri or parmesan cheese

2 eggs, beaten

Warm oil in large frying pan. Add onion and cook gently until transparent, about 10 minutes. Add garlic and cook several seconds. Increase heat, add meat and cook until meat loses its red color, stirring often to break up lumps. Add tomatoes and their liquid, tomato paste, cinnamon, parsley, sugar and salt and pepper to taste. Reduce heat, cover and simmer 20 minutes. If still too liquid, uncover and cook over medium heat until only a little moisture remains.

Drain canned artichokes and cut lengthwise into 3 to 4 slices. (Frozen artichokes are usually already sliced.) Grease a large oven-proof dish, at least 2 in (5 cm) deep, and dust with dried breadcrumbs. Layer half the artichoke slices on base. Top with meat mixture and finish with remaining artichokes. Preheat oven to 350–375°F (180–190°C/Gas 4).

For bechamel sauce: Melt butter in heavy saucepan. Stir in flour and cook 2 to 3 minutes without allowing it to color. Remove pan from heat and pour in milk all at once, stirring constantly. Return to heat and stir until thickened. Boil gently 1 minute. Remove from heat and add nutmeg, salt and pepper to taste, and 1 tablespoon grated cheese. Let cool slightly and stir in eggs. Pour over artichokes and sprinkle with remaining cheese.

Bake 45 minutes or until top is golden brown and puffed. Let stand 10 minutes. Cut into squares to serve.

Melitzanes Moussaka (Eggplant Moussaka) Variation: Substitute 2 lb (1 kg) oval eggplant (aubergine) for artichokes. Cut into 1/4 in (5 mm) slices, sprinkle with salt and let stand in colander 30 minutes. Rinse briefly, dry with cloth and brush with olive oil. Place on baking sheet and cook under hot broiler (grill) until lightly browned on each side. Use three layers of eggplant and two layers of meat sauce when preparing dish and finish as above.

Lasagne al Forno

BAKED LASAGNE WITH MEAT SAUCE (ITALY)   SERVES 6

Many versions of baked lasagne appear in Italian cuisine, and the purist would only use fresh pasta. Pasta manufacturers, even in Italy, have taken the pain out of this dish by producing instant lasagne. It saves a lot of the time and effort involved in boiling the standard lasagne sheets two or three at a time to prevent them sticking together. Of course, cooked fresh pasta can be used instead (see page 30).

2 tablespoons olive oil

1 large onion, finely chopped

1 clove garlic, finely chopped

12 oz (375 g) lean ground (minced) beef

12 oz (375 g) lean ground (minced) pork

4 oz (125 g) small mushrooms, sliced

15 oz (425 g) can tomatoes

3 tablespoons tomato paste

1/4 cup (2 fl oz/60 ml) water

1/4 cup (2 fl oz/60 ml) dry white wine

1 tablespoon chopped fresh basil

2 tablespoons chopped flat-leaf (Italian) parsley

1 teaspoon sugar

salt and freshly ground black pepper

Besciamella (White Sauce):

2 oz (60 g) butter

1/3 cup (1 1/2 oz/50 g) all-purpose (plain) flour

2 1/2 cups (20 fl oz/625 ml) milk

1/4 teaspoon grated nutmeg

salt and freshly ground white pepper

To Assemble:

8 oz (250 g) instant lasagne sheets

1 cup (4 oz/125 g) shredded mozzarella cheese

1/3 cup (1 1/2 oz/50 g) grated parmesan cheese

Heat oil in saucepan. Add onion and cook gently until transparent, about 10 minutes. Add garlic and cook several seconds. Add ground meat, increase heat and cook until meat changes color, stirring often to break up lumps. Add mushrooms and cook about 3 minutes. Puree tomatoes with their liquid and add to saucepan with tomato paste, water, wine, herbs, sugar, and salt and pepper to taste. Cover and simmer gently 30 minutes. Finished sauce should be quite liquid.

For besciamella: Heat butter in heavy saucepan until frothing, but do not allow to brown. Stir in flour with wooden spoon and cook 2 minutes over low heat. Remove saucepan from heat. Add milk all at once, stir well, return to medium heat and cook until thickened and bubbling, stirring constantly. If sauce becomes lumpy, stir briskly with balloon whisk. Add nutmeg and salt and pepper to taste. Place plastic wrap directly on surface to prevent skin forming and set aside.

Preheat oven to 325–350°F (160–180°C/Gas 3).

To assemble: Spread several tablespoons of meat sauce over base of greased 7 in x 12 in (18 cm x 30 cm) rectangular oven-proof dish. Add layer of lasagne sheets and cover with half the meat sauce. Drizzle over 1/2 cup besciamella. Sprinkle with one-third of the cheeses.

Add second layer lasagne sheets, top with remaining meat sauce, another 1/2 cup besciamella and half the remaining cheeses. Top with lasagne sheets. Spread remaining besciamella over top and sprinkle with remaining cheeses.

Bake until lasagne is tender and top is golden brown, about 30 to 40 minutes. Let stand 5 minutes before cutting into squares to serve.

Seksu Bil Lahm

COUSCOUS WITH LAMB AND VEGETABLES (MOROCCO)   SERVES 6

Couscous, as served in Morocco (and Algeria and Tunisia), is presented at the end of a banquet to ensure that guests do not depart hungry; in the home, it is a popular Friday lunch, using leftover meat pieces and bones, and vegetables on hand. Usually the meat content is just enough to add extra flavor to the copious broth, but if required for a main course, the amount of meat can be increased. Lamb, chicken and fish are usually prepared for couscous, with beef seldom used, but it can substitute in the following recipe. Moroccons often add saffron, but as its delicate flavor would be masked by other ingredients, it can be omitted; harissa is a "must" in Tunisia, although it is also used in Morocco.

2 lb (1 kg) boneless lamb leg meat, cubed

2 tablespoons olive oil

3 medium onions, quartered

2 cloves garlic, pressed (crushed)

3 in (8 cm) cinnamon stick

1/2 teaspoon turmeric

3 tablespoons chopped flat-leaf (Italian) parsley

3 tablespoons chopped fresh coriander leaves (cilantro)

1 lb (500 g) ripe tomatoes, peeled and chopped

2 tablespoons tomato paste

3 cups (24 fl oz/750 ml) water

salt and freshly ground pepper

4 medium carrots, peeled and quartered lengthwise

4 small white turnips, peeled and quartered

15 oz (425 g) can chickpeas (garbanzos), drained

1 quantity couscous (see page 37)

1 cup (4 oz/125 g) shelled fresh or frozen broad beans (optional)

1 lb (500 g) zucchini (courgettes), trimmed and quartered lengthwise

1/2 quantity harissa (see page 33), to serve (optional)

Trim excess fat from lamb. Warm oil in large saucepan. Add onions, garlic, cinnamon and turmeric and cook gently 5 minutes. Increase heat, add lamb, and cook, stirring often, until lamb is sealed, about 5 minutes. Add herbs, tomatoes, tomato paste, water, and salt and pepper to taste. Reduce heat, cover and simmer 45 minutes. Add carrots, turnips and chickpeas, cover and simmer 30 minutes.

Soak couscous as directed in recipe on page 37, separating grains with fork.

Add broad beans and zucchini to saucepan, increase heat and bring to boil. Place couscous in prepared steamer and place on top of saucepan, sealing edges of steamer with foil as described. Cook, uncovered, 20 minutes, stirring couscous occasionally with fork.

Turn couscous onto heated platter, and pour over melted butter. Toss lightly and mound into peak. Garnish with some lamb and vegetables from saucepan, if desired. Place remaining lamb and vegetables (discarding cinnamon) into deep serving dish, adding broth from saucepan. If serving with harissa, mix harissa with 3/4 cup (6 fl oz/180 ml) of broth in small bowl.

Seksu Bil Lahm

CASSOULET

CASSEROLE OF LAMB AND BEANS (FRANCE)   SERVES 6

This is a simplified version of the famous Languedoc bean casserole, which can vary greatly from town to town. To make an authentic cassoulet, you will need to have certain ingredients on hand, such as preserved goose or duck, sausages of the region, salt pork, and mutton. This recipe uses readily available ingredients, and while the natives of Languedoc may not approve, your guests will. If you can obtain them, brown 1 lb (500 g) Toulouse sausages in the pan after the lamb is browned and add to the casserole with the lamb. These are traditionally used in a cassoulet, and may be available at gourmet delicatessens. Alternatively, substitute other fresh pork and garlic sausages. Serve cassoulet with a simple tossed green salad.

2 cups (14 oz/400 g) dried
navy (haricot) beans

2 lbs (1 kg) boneless lamb
or mutton, cubed

4 oz (125 g) streaky bacon pieces
or slices

1 tablespoon butter or oil

2 large onions, chopped

3 cloves garlic, pressed (crushed)

2 tablespoons tomato paste

15 oz (425 g) can tomatoes,
chopped but undrained

bouquet garni
(2 sprigs each thyme, marjoram,
parsley; 1 celery stalk with leaves
and 1 bay leaf, tied together)

2 teaspoons salt

freshly ground black pepper

chopped parsley, to garnish

Wash beans well; place in large bowl and add three times their volume of cold water. Soak overnight in a cool place. Drain, place in saucepan and cover with cold water. Bring to boil, cover and simmer gently 1 hour. Drain and reserve 2 cups (16 fl oz/500 ml) of cooking liquid.

Preheat oven to 325–350°F (160–180°C/Gas 3).

Cook bacon in frying pan until fat melts and bacon browns. Remove bacon to deep casserole dish, leaving fat in pan. Add butter or oil to pan and brown meat. Remove to casserole dish. Add onion and garlic to pan and cook gently until onion is soft, about 10 minutes. Transfer to casserole dish with tomato paste, tomatoes with their liquid, reserved bean liquid, bouquet garni, salt and pepper to taste. Stir in beans. Cover tightly and bake until meat is tender, about 2 1/2 hours, stirring every 30 minutes. Discard bouquet garni, sprinkle with parsley and serve from dish at table.

SALSICCE E FAGIOLI

SAUSAGES WITH BEANS (ITALY)   SERVES 6

This substantial dish from Tuscany is popular as a warming wintertime meal. Well spiced Italian coarse pork sausages are available at Italian markets and gourmet delicatessens.

2 cups (14 oz/400 g) cannellini or great northern beans

1 bay leaf

1 small onion, quartered

1 small carrot, quartered

4 cloves garlic, peeled

salt

1½ lb (750 g) fresh spicy Italian pork sausages

3 tablespoons olive oil

2 tablespoons tomato paste

½ teaspoon sugar

freshly ground black pepper

crusty bread, to serve

Place beans in sieve and pick over to remove extra matter. Rinse under cold running water. Place in large bowl with three times their volume of cold water and soak overnight in a cool place. Drain.

Place beans in saucepan with cold water to cover and bring to boil. Add bay leaf, onion, carrot and 2 garlic cloves. Cover and boil gently until tender, about 1 to 1½ hours, adding salt to taste after 1 hour. Discard bay leaf, onion and carrot. Drain beans, reserving ½ cup (4 fl oz/125 ml) cooking liquid.

Prick sausages well. Place in frying pan, cover with water and bring slowly to the boil. When almost boiling, pour off water. Return pan to heat, add oil and fry sausages gently until browned and cooked through. Remove to warm platter and keep warm.

Finely chop remaining garlic, add to oil in pan and cook several seconds. Stir in tomato paste and cook several seconds then add reserved bean liquid. Stir in sugar, and salt and pepper to taste and bring to boil. Add beans, cover, and simmer gently 10 minutes. Place sausages on beans, cover, and simmer 5 minutes. Pile beans onto platter, place sausages on top and serve with crusty bread.

bell pepper

Tagine Lahm Bil Beleh

LAMB TAGINE WITH DATES (MOROCCO)   SERVES 6

Fresh dates feature in this dish; the dried dates are added to extend the flavor and thicken the sauce. You can serve it with couscous (see page 37), although in Morocco, a tagine is served on its own.

2 lb (1 kg) boneless lamb leg or shoulder meat

2 tablespoons butter

1 large white onion, finely chopped

1¹⁄₂ cups (12 fl oz/375 ml) water

1 teaspoon ground ginger

1 teaspoon ground cinnamon

¹⁄₃ cup (2 oz/60 g) chopped dried pitted dates

salt and freshly ground black pepper

2 tablespoons honey

2 tablespoons lime juice

12 fresh dates

1 tablespoon butter, extra

¹⁄₄ cup (1 oz/30 g) whole blanched almonds

fresh lime or preserved lemon (see page 29), to garnish

Trim excess fat from lamb and cut into 1 in (2.5 cm) cubes. Melt butter in a heavy saucepan. Add onion and cook gently until transparent, about 10 minutes. Increase heat, add lamb and cook until sealed, stirring often. Add water, spices and chopped dried dates and season with salt and pepper to taste. Cover and simmer over low heat until lamb is tender, about 1¹⁄₂ hours. Stir in honey and lime juice and adjust seasoning if necessary. Place whole fresh dates on top, cover and simmer 5 minutes.

Melt extra butter in frying pan. Add almonds and cook until golden; remove to plate.

To serve, transfer lamb tagine to serving dish, arranging fresh dates on top. Sprinkle with almonds and garnish with fresh lime slices or strips of preserved lemon peel.

Quotban

LAMB KEBABS (MOROCCO)   SERVES 6

There are many versions of kebabs in the Maghreb, some combine lamb with kidney or liver, a few use lamb only. In Morocco, they add small cubes of lamb tail fat between the lamb cubes; beef suet is often given as a substitute as lambs outside the region are of other breeds. Serve kebabs in warm bread with salads, pickles and olives served separately.

2 lb (1 kg) boneless lamb leg meat

¹⁄₂ cup (4 fl oz/125 ml) fresh lemon juice

4 tablespoons olive oil

2 teaspoons shredded fresh ginger root

3 cloves garlic, pressed (crushed)

¹⁄₂ teaspoon ground allspice

¹⁄₄ teaspoon cayenne pepper

freshly ground black pepper

salt

Trim excess fat from lamb and cut into ³⁄₄ in (2 cm) cubes. Combine lamb, lemon juice, oil, ginger root, garlic, allspice, cayenne and pepper in bowl. Stir well, cover and refrigerate 2 hours at least or overnight, stirring occasionally.

Thread lamb onto skewers and cook over glowing coals on barbecue, basting frequently with marinade. Cook to pink stage, or well done if preferred — do not overcook or lamb will toughen. Season with salt after cooking, if desired. Serve hot.

Tagine Lahm Bil Beleh

Navarin d'Agneau

NAVARIN OF LAMB (FRANCE)   SERVES 4 TO 6

While navarin is prepared in other regions of France, it is also popular with southern French cooks, particularly in Provence.

2 tablespoons butter or oil

2 lb (1 kg) boneless lamb leg meat, cubed

1 medium onion, chopped

2 cloves garlic, finely chopped

2 tablespoons all-purpose (plain) flour

1 cup (8 fl oz/250 ml) chicken stock (see page 31)

2 tablespoons tomato paste

1/2 cup (4 fl oz/125 ml) dry white wine

1 teaspoon sugar

1 1/2 teaspoons salt

freshly ground black pepper

bouquet garni
(2 sprigs each thyme and parsley and 1 bay leaf, tied together)

6 to 8 small, whole onions

3 small turnips, peeled and quartered

12 baby carrots, scraped

1 cup (4 oz/125 g) fresh shelled peas

1 tablespoon finely chopped parsley

crusty bread, to serve

Preheat oven to 300–325°F (150–160°C/Gas 2).

Heat butter or oil in heavy frying pan over medium-high heat and brown lamb in batches. Transfer lamb to casserole dish as it browns. Add chopped onion and garlic to pan and cook gently over low heat until onion is soft, about 10 minutes. Stir in flour and cook until lightly colored. Add stock and wine, stirring until sauce thickens and bubbles. Stir in tomato paste, sugar, salt and pepper. Pour over lamb and add bouquet garni. Cover and bake 1 1/2 hours.

Peel whole onions and cut a cross in root ends. Add onions, turnips and carrots to casserole dish, cover and bake until lamb is tender, about 1 hour, adding peas after 30 minutes. Discard bouquet garni and sprinkle with parsley. Serve from casserole dish with crusty bread.

MERGUEZ

SPICY LAMB SAUSAGES (TUNISIA)   MAKES ABOUT 3 LB (1.5 KG) SAUSAGES

These spicy sausages of Tunisia have found fame abroad. Also used in Morocco and Algeria, with a lighter touch of the fiery Tunisian harissa, French-Algerians took them to France, and they are now made by butchers there as well as in other countries. The sausages are broiled (grilled), fried or used in egg dishes. A food processor makes short work of the blending, but the recipe is still rather lengthy. Don't try to reduce the salt — it is important in the binding process of the meat where the salt reacts with the myosin in the meat to create a natural binder — and use pure cooking salt, not table salt. Sausage fillers are available as attachments for some food processors and meat grinders. Special hand-held sausage fillers are also available. Purchase either fresh or dry collagen sausage casings from the butcher. Dry casings come already "shirred" into a cylinder shape. For the amount of lamb required, purchase a leg over 4 lb (2 kg) in weight; a boned forequarter should provide sufficient meat. Store sausages loosely covered in refrigerator 1 day before cooking for flavors to develop.

3 lb (1.5 kg) boneless lamb leg or forequarter meat

3 teaspoons salt

1 teaspoon freshly ground black pepper

2 to 3 teaspoons harissa (see page 33)

2 teaspoons ground fennel seeds

2 teaspoons ground coriander

2 tablespoons paprika

2 teaspoons ground cumin

1 teaspoon ground allspice

4 cloves garlic, finely chopped

1 cup (8 fl oz/250 ml) iced water

thin sausage casings

Trim any fine skin and thick gristle from lamb, but leave a good proportion of fat. Cut into 3/4 in (2 cm) cubes; check weight. If lamb is not very cold after preparation, cover and refrigerate at least 2 hours in coldest part of refrigerator.

Place lamb in large bowl, sprinkle with salt and mix well. Process in six batches in food processor with steel blade until finely ground (minced). Transfer to wide dish. Mix in pepper, harissa to taste, spices and chopped garlic. Process again in six batches to mix flavorings evenly into meat, adding 2 to 3 tablespoons iced water to each batch. Transfer to large bowl and mix well with hand.

If sausage casings are fresh, rinse salt from casings and soak in warm water 30 minutes. Run cold water through each length of casing to check for holes. Fit about 3 ft (1 m) of fresh casing onto nozzle of sausage filler or large funnel. If using dry casings, cut off 3 in (8 cm) length of shirred casing.

Pass lamb mixture through sausage filler or push through funnel with end of wooden spoon. When mixture appears at end of nozzle, stop and pull casing over end of nozzle. Tie casing, then continue with filling. Let sausage curl into dish. When casing is filled, leave open end unfilled and untied, and fill more casings as necessary.

Stretch sausage along work surface and press half-way point with finger. Twist at this point 3 times. Even out sausage between twist and tied end, mark half-way point and twist again, and continue to twist at half-way points until required sausage lengths are formed. Twist in the same manner towards untied end, smoothing out sausage after each twist. Tie off end.

Use within 2 days, or store properly wrapped in the freezer.

Agnello Forno al Rosmarino

ROAST LAMB WITH ROSEMARY (ITALY)   SERVES 4

This is a more modern approach to lamb cooking than is actually practiced in Italy, but the essence of the recipe is the same. Traditionally a leg of lamb is used, but lamb racks take much less time to cook, and are much easier to serve. Reduce cooking time if medium-rare is desired, but lamb tastes best if pink. Time depends on size. Serve racks as they are on each plate, or slice into chops between the rib bones.

4 racks of lamb (3 to 4 ribs each), depending on size of racks

2 oz (60 g) pancetta or streaky bacon

3 sprigs fresh rosemary

3 cloves garlic

salt and freshly ground black pepper

3 tablespoons olive oil

fresh rosemary sprigs, to garnish

Preheat oven to 350–375°F (180–190°C/Gas 4).

Trim excess fat from lamb racks if necessary. Make incisions into the outer surface of each rack. Cut pancetta into short strips, pull leaves from 1 sprig rosemary, and cut 2 cloves garlic into slivers. Insert piece of pancetta, few leaves of rosemary and sliver of garlic into each incision. Season lamb with salt and pepper, and brush all over with a little olive oil.

Place remaining rosemary sprigs and garlic clove into base of roasting pan and pour in remaining oil. Place lamb racks over rosemary, meat-side up. Roast until lamb is tender and pink inside, about 40 to 50 minutes, basting occasionally with oil in pan. Remove lamb to serving platter, cover loosely with foil, and let stand 5 minutes before serving. Serve garnished with fresh rosemary.

Gigot d'Agneau à la Provençale

ROAST LAMB PROVENÇAL (FRANCE)   SERVES 6 TO 8

4 lb (2 kg) leg of lamb

salt and freshly ground black pepper

3 lb (1.5 kg) medium potatoes

4 to 6 cloves garlic, chopped

1 cup (8 fl oz/250 ml) chicken stock, (see page 31)

2 tablespoons olive oil

2 tablespoons finely chopped parsley

Wipe lamb with damp paper towels. Season with salt and pepper. Cover and bring to room temperature.

Preheat oven to 400–425°F (200–220°C/Gas 6). Peel potatoes and cut into 1/2 in (1 cm) slices. Place in oiled roasting pan, overlapping slices. Season with salt and pepper, and sprinkle with garlic. Place lamb leg in middle of potatoes and pour stock around potatoes. Brush lamb and potatoes with olive oil. Roast 30 minutes. Reduce to 350–375°F (180–190°C/Gas 4) and roast until lamb is tender and pink inside, about 1 hour, or longer for well-done lamb. Turn lamb twice during cooking and baste with pan juices occasionally — if juices dry out, add a little water to pan. Remove lamb to platter and let stand 15 minutes in warm place before carving, keeping potatoes hot in warm oven. Sprinkle potatoes with parsley and serve with carved lamb moistened with pan juices.

Agnello Forno al Rosmarino

Avya Yahnisi

LAMB AND QUINCE STEW (TURKEY)   SERVES 6

In the Middle East and North Africa, quinces are a popular addition to meat stews, where their refreshing tartness and fragrance is appreciated. Their use goes back to Persian influence in these regions. To make pomegranate juice, put fresh pomegranate seeds, a handful at a time, into a doubled piece of cheesecloth (muslin) and squeeze juice into a bowl using your hands. Alternatively, dibs roman (pomegranate syrup) is available at Middle Eastern markets; use 4 teaspoons of syrup mixed with water to make 1 cup. Only add the tomato paste if you have used water and not the pomegranate syrup or juice.

2 lb (1 kg) boned lamb shoulder
1 tablespoon sunflower oil
1 large onion, chopped
1 cup (8 fl oz/250 ml) water mixed with 1 tablespoon tomato paste, or 1 cup pomegranate juice
3 in (8 cm) cinnamon stick
1/2 teaspoon ground allspice
salt and freshly ground black pepper
2 quinces, peeled, cored and halved
2 tablespoons butter
1/2 teaspoon ground cinnamon
pinch of ground cloves
3 tablespoons sugar
2 tablespoons lemon juice
plain pilaf (see page 37), to serve

Trim excess fat from lamb and cut into 1 in (2.5 cm) cubes. Heat oil in heavy-based saucepan or Dutch oven and brown lamb in batches over high heat, removing to plate when browned. Reduce heat, add onion to pan and cook gently until softened, about 5 minutes. Add water and tomato paste mixture (or pomegranate juice). Stir well to lift browned juices. Return lamb to pan and add cinnamon stick, allspice, and salt and pepper to taste. Cover and simmer 1 hour.

Cut each quince half into quarters. Melt butter in frying pan, add quinces and cook over medium heat several minutes, turning pieces. Sprinkle with ground cinnamon, cloves and sugar and place on top of lamb in pan. Add half the lemon juice, cover and simmer until lamb is tender, about 30 minutes, gently shake pan occasionally. Add more lemon juice to taste and adjust seasoning if necessary. Serve hot with pilaf.

Lomo a la Naranja

LOIN OF PORK WITH ORANGE (SPAIN)   SERVES 6

Sherry, the classic Spanish wine, and sweet, juicy oranges combine to counter the richness of pork. Originally, the loin was cooked in a large pot as stove-top cooking was usual. Make sure the rind (skin) is removed from the pork — ask the butcher to remove it and trim the fat to a thin layer before rolling and tying the loin. Serve the pork with boiled new potatoes and steamed green vegetables.

3 lb (1.5 kg) boneless pork loin roast, rolled and tied

salt and freshly ground black pepper

2 tablespoons light olive oil

1 medium onion, sliced

2 medium carrots, sliced

1 cup (8 fl oz/250 ml) chicken stock, (see page 31)

2 sweet oranges

2 teaspoons cornstarch (cornflour)

3 tablespoons fino or other dry sherry

Preheat oven to 350–375°F (180–190°C/Gas 4).

Season pork with salt and pepper. Pour oil into roasting pan, add pork and brush with oil. Place onion and carrots around pork and season with salt and pepper. Roast until cooked — juices should run clear when pierced with skewer — about 1¹/₂ to 2 hours (time depends on thickness of pork). Add stock to pan after 20 minutes, and replenish with water during latter stage of cooking to keep vegetables moist. Turn pork during roasting to brown evenly.

While pork is cooking, cut julienne strips of rind from 1 orange, then completely peel both oranges, removing pith and all traces of membrane. Working over a bowl, segment oranges into bowl, discarding seeds, and squeezing juice out of any remaining membrane. Cover julienned rind with water in small saucepan and boil 5 minutes. Drain and add to orange segments.

When pork is cooked, remove to serving platter, cover with foil and let stand in warm place. Skim excess fat from roasting pan contents and puree contents in blender, food mill or food processor. Pour into small pan and stir in combined cornstarch and sherry. Heat, stirring constantly, until slightly thickened and boiling gently. Add orange peel, segments and juice, and heat gently 5 minutes.

To serve, carve pork into thin slices and spoon over orange sauce.

CHULETAS DE CERDO CON CIRUELA PASA

PORK CHOPS WITH PRUNES (SPAIN)   SERVES 6

The cooking of the Catalan region features many meat and game recipes cooked with fruit. This is one of the least complicated of such recipes. Prunes do not require pre-soaking unless very dry, in which case cover with the water and soak overnight, adding the wine, cinnamon stick and sugar when cooking. The chops should be well-trimmed with only a thin layer of fat, and cut about 3/4 in (2 cm) thick.

6 pork loin chops
freshly ground black pepper
8 oz (250 g) pitted prunes
1/2 cup (4 fl oz/125 ml) dry red wine
1 cup (8 fl oz/250 ml) water
1 cinnamon stick
2 teaspoons sugar
1 tablespoon olive oil
salt
2 teaspoons cornstarch (cornflour)

Season pork chops with pepper and set aside.

Place prunes in saucepan with wine, water, cinnamon stick and sugar. Cover and bring slowly to a simmer. Simmer gently 20 minutes until plump. Set aside.

Heat large frying pan, add oil and tilt pan for oil to just cover surface. Add chops and fry over medium heat until just cooked through, about 6 minutes each side — do not overcook. Remove chops to warm platter and season lightly with salt. Drain fat from pan.

Remove cinnamon stick from prunes and discard. Strain liquid into frying pan. Mix cornstarch with a little water to form paste and add to pan. Stir over heat until sauce is thickened and bubbling. Add prunes and heat thoroughly. Pour over chops and serve immediately.

Chuletas de Cerdo con Ciruela Pasa

Scallope di Maiale al Marsala

PORK ESCALOPES WITH MARSALA (ITALY)   SERVES 4

This quick-to-prepare recipe comes from Sicily, hence "scallope" instead of the usual "scallopine".

1½ lb (750 g) whole pork tenderloin (fillet)

freshly ground black pepper

2 tablespoons olive oil

2 tablespoons butter

3 teaspoons all-purpose (plain) flour

½ cup (4 fl oz/125 ml) sweet marsala wine

½ cup (4 fl oz/125 ml) chicken stock, see page (31)

salt

Cut pork into 1¼ in (3 cm) thick slices; tapered tail end can be thicker as this will be treated differently. Cut each slice almost in half across grain and open out. Cut tail end with grain almost through, and open out. Gently flatten escalopes with smooth side of meat mallet, taking care not to tear. Season with pepper.

Heat large frying pan over high heat. Add half the oil and half the butter and immediately add layer of escalopes. Cook over high heat until just cooked, about 1 minute each side. Remove to plate. Add remaining oil and cook remaining escalopes, removing when cooked. Reduce heat, add remaining butter and sprinkle in flour. Remove from heat and stir with fork, adding marsala and stock. Return to medium-low heat and stir until sauce thickens and bubbles. Add salt to taste. Return pork to pan, and turn to glaze and heat through; do not allow sauce to boil. Serve immediately.

Conejo a la Cazadora

RABBIT HUNTER-STYLE (SPAIN)   SERVES 6

Just one of the many ways in which rabbit is prepared in Spain, where it is highly esteemed. Serve it with boiled potatoes. If you have a wild rabbit, I suggest it be given the vinegar treatment (see page 165).

3 lb (1.5 kg) rabbit, disjointed

3 tablespoons olive oil

1 large onion, chopped

1 clove garlic, pressed (crushed)

4 oz (125 g) piece jamon serrano or prosciutto crudo, diced

2 tablespoons brandy

4 oz (125 g) small mushrooms

15 oz (425 g) can tomatoes, pureed

¾ cup (6 fl oz/180 ml) dry red wine

1 bay leaf

2 sprigs fresh thyme

2 sprigs fresh parsley

salt and freshly ground black pepper

chopped parsley, to garnish

Rinse rabbit thoroughly, paying particular attention to neck area. Dry well with paper towels. Heat 1 tablespoon oil in heavy-based flameproof casserole dish or Dutch oven and brown rabbit pieces all over. Remove to plate.

Add remaining oil and onion to pan and cook gently over low heat until transparent, about 10 minutes. Add garlic and jamon serrano and cook 2 to 3 minutes. Return rabbit to casserole dish. Pour over brandy, ignite and shake pan until flames die down. Add mushrooms and cook 5 minutes, stirring occasionally. Add tomatoes, wine, herbs tied in bunch, and salt and pepper to taste. Cover and simmer until rabbit is tender, about 1 to 1½ hours (time depends on age of rabbit). Remove lid during last stage of cooking to reduce sauce if necessary; it should be quite thick. Transfer to serving dish and sprinkle with parsley before serving.

KOUNELOPITA KEFALONIKI

CEPHALONIAN RABBIT PIE (GREECE)   SERVES 6 TO 8

The island of Cephalonia is famous for its pies, with feta cheese often included for extra flavor. Adding a little rice to pies is the Greek method of taking up excess juices to prevent the pastry becoming soggy. If you prefer, you can use a shortcrust pastry instead of the fillo horiatiko (oil pastry); double the recipe given for the base of pissaladière (see page 238).

3 lb (1.5 kg) rabbit, jointed

1/2 cup (4 fl oz/125 ml) distilled white vinegar

3/4 cup (6 fl oz/180 ml) dry red wine

1 tablespoon red wine vinegar

1 teaspoon dried rigani or marjoram

2 bay leaves

2 teaspoons chopped fresh rosemary

3 cloves garlic

3 tablespoons olive oil

freshly ground black pepper

1 large onion, chopped

15 oz (425 g) can tomatoes, chopped but undrained

salt

1/4 cup (1 1/2 oz/50 g) rice

3 tablespoons chopped parsley

4 oz (125 g) feta cheese, diced

1 quantity fillo horiatiko (see page 232)

milk, for glazing

Place rabbit in bowl with white vinegar and add water to cover. Let stand 2 hours, rinse and pat dry. Place rabbit in clean bowl with red wine, wine vinegar, herbs, 1 chopped clove garlic, 1 tablespoon olive oil and a good grinding of black pepper. Mix well, cover and refrigerate several hours or overnight, turning pieces occasionally. Lift rabbit from marinade and drain well, reserving marinade.

Heat 2 tablespoons olive oil in large deep saucepan and brown rabbit all over in batches, transferring to dish when browned. Add onion and cook gently until softened, about 6 to 8 minutes. Finely chop remaining garlic, add to pan and cook several seconds. Add marinade, tomatoes with their liquid and salt to taste. Cover and simmer gently until very tender with meat almost falling from bones, about 1 to 1 1/2 hours (time depends on age of rabbit).

Remove rabbit to plate. Boil liquid in pan until reduced by half. Discard bay leaves. Separate rabbit meat from bones, cut in thick strips and return to pan. Stir in rice and parsley and simmer to partly cook rice, about 5 to 6 minutes.

Preheat oven to 350–375°F (180–190°C/Gas 4).

Divide pastry into two, with one piece larger than the other. Roll out larger piece to fit 10 in x 12 in (25 cm x 30 cm) baking dish. Line dish with pastry and spread rabbit filling evenly over base. Scatter diced feta evenly on top. Roll out remaining pastry and place on top. Press edges together to seal. Brush top with milk and cut a number of small slits in pastry. Bake until golden brown, about 45 minutes. Let stand 10 minutes before cutting into squares to serve.

PEBRONATA

BRAISED VEAL WITH RED PEPPERS (FRANCE)   SERVES 6

This is based on a Corsican recipe for pebronata, a red pepper sauce used in Corsica with grilled meats. In Provence, the sauce is cooked with veal. Serve with creamy mashed potatoes and steamed green vegetables.

3 tablespoons olive oil

2 lb (1 kg) stewing veal, cubed

1 onion, chopped

3 cloves garlic, finely chopped

4 juniper berries, crushed

2 tablespoons all-purpose (plain) flour

1 cup (8 fl oz/250 ml) dry white wine

15 oz (425 g) can tomatoes, chopped but undrained

2 sprigs fresh thyme

1 bay leaf

salt and freshly ground pepper

2 large red bell peppers (capsicums), cut into strips

2 tablespoons chopped parsley

Preheat oven to 325–350°F (160–180°C/Gas 3).

Heat half the oil in heavy-based flameproof casserole dish or Dutch oven. Brown veal in batches over high heat, removing to plate when browned. Reduce heat, add remaining oil and onion and cook gently until transparent, about 10 minutes. Add garlic and juniper berries and cook several seconds. Sprinkle in flour, stir well and cook gently 1 to 2 minutes. Add wine and tomatoes with their liquid, and stir over medium heat until thickened. Return veal to dish. Add thyme, bay leaf, and salt and pepper to taste. Cover and bake 45 minutes. Add bell pepper strips and parsley and bake until veal is tender, about 45 minutes more. Remove thyme sprigs and bay leaf before serving.

FRITTURA PICCATA

ESCALOPES OF VEAL IN LEMON SAUCE (ITALY)   SERVES 4

Escalopes of veal (scallopine) can be any tender part of the veal cut into thin steaks, usually from the loin or leg of veal. They should be cooked quickly and served immediately after cooking.

8 veal escalopes (thin leg steaks)

4 oz (125 g) piece prosciutto crudo, 1/4 in (5 mm) thick

1/4 cup (about 1 oz/30 g) all-purpose (plain) flour

salt and freshly ground black pepper

2 tablespoons extra light olive oil

3 tablespoons butter

2 tablespoons finely chopped flat-leaf (Italian) parsley

juice of 1 lemon

1/4 cup (2 fl oz/60 ml) chicken stock, (see page 31)

If necessary, gently pound escalopes with flat side of meat mallet until very thin. Cut prosciutto into strips. Combine flour with salt and pepper to taste in shallow bowl. Coat escalopes with seasoned flour, shaking off excess. Heat oil and 2 tablespoons butter in large frying pan, and when very hot, add escalopes and cook quickly until browned and just cooked through, about 1 minute each side. Remove to warm serving plate and keep warm. Add prosciutto to pan and cook quickly, stirring, until it turns pink. Spoon over veal. Add remaining butter to pan with 1 teaspoon seasoned flour and stir over heat several seconds. Add parsley, lemon juice and stock, stir well and bring to boil. Boil several seconds and pour over veal and prosciutto. Serve immediately.

Frittura Piccata

OSSI BUCHI

BRAISED VEAL SHIN (ITALY)   SERVES 6

Although this dish is from Lombardy, the following version is redolent with Mediterranean flavors. The marrow is the highlight of this meal. There is a special tool for removing the marrow but a fondue fork does just as well — provide one at each place setting.

3 to 4 lb (1.5 to 2 kg) veal shin, cut in 2 in (5 cm) pieces

all-purpose (plain) flour

salt and freshly ground black pepper

2 tablespoons olive oil

2 tablespoons butter

1 large onion, finely chopped

2 cloves garlic, pressed (crushed)

15 oz (425 g) can tomatoes, chopped but undrained

2 tablespoons tomato paste

1/2 cup (4 fl oz/125 ml) dry white wine

1 teaspoon sugar

thinly peeled strip lemon rind

1 tablespoon chopped fresh marjoram

3 tablespoons chopped flat-leaf (Italian) parsley

grated rind of 1 lemon

risotto alla Milanese (see page 224), to serve

Tie kitchen string around veal pieces, if desired, to keep them intact. Combine flour with salt and pepper to taste. Coat veal in seasoned flour. Heat oil and butter in large, heavy-based saucepan and brown veal all over. Remove to dish when browned. Reduce heat, add onion and cook gently until soft, about 10 minutes. Add garlic and cook several seconds. Add tomatoes with their liquid, tomato paste, wine and sugar. Add lemon rind strip, marjoram and half the parsley. Return veal to pan, placing pieces upright so marrow does not fall out of bones. Cover and simmer gently until veal is tender, about 2 hours. Add a little stock to pan after 1 hour if necessary — juices from veal will add to liquid content.

Remove veal pieces to serving dish and discard strings. Adjust seasoning of sauce and pour over veal. Mix remaining parsley with grated lemon rind to make gremolata, and sprinkle on top. Serve with risotto.

CANARD AUX NAVETS

DUCK WITH TURNIPS (FRANCE)   SERVES 4

A dish for winter, when turnips are at their best — crisp and sweet. Choose small white turnips and never substitute the yellow-fleshed rutabaga, also known as swede. The recipe is from Languedoc, and is also prepared in Provence.

4 lb (2 kg) duck

salt and freshly ground black pepper

1 tablespoon light olive oil

1 1/2 tablespoons all-purpose (plain) flour

1/2 cup (4 fl oz/125 ml) dry white wine

1 cup (8 fl oz/250 ml) chicken stock, (see page 31)

bouquet garni (2 sprigs each thyme and parsley and 1 bay leaf, tied together)

8 baby onions, peeled

6 small white turnips, peeled and quartered

2 teaspoons sugar

2 tablespoons muscat wine

1 tablespoon finely chopped parsley

Preheat oven to 375–400°F (190–200°C/Gas 5).

Season cavity of duck with salt and pepper. Tuck wings underneath and secure neck skin with poultry skewer. Prick skin all over with fine skewer. Heat oil in heavy-based flameproof casserole dish or Dutch oven, add duck and brown all over until fat is released. Remove duck to plate, drain and reserve all but 2 tablespoons fat from casserole dish. Sprinkle flour into casserole dish and cook, stirring often, until golden brown. Stir in white wine and stock, and stir until sauce bubbles. Add bouquet garni and salt and pepper to taste. Return duck to casserole dish, cover and bake 40 minutes.

Heat 2 tablespoons reserved duck fat in large frying pan. Add onions and cook over medium-high heat until lightly browned. Remove with slotted spoon. Add turnips and cook, sprinkling with sugar to caramelize. Place turnips and onions around duck in casserole dish, spooning sauce over them. Cover and bake 20 minutes. Remove lid and bake uncovered until duck is tender, about 15 minutes.

Remove duck to warm serving platter. Lift out turnips and onions with slotted spoon and arrange around duck. Discard bouquet garni. Cover duck with tent of foil and keep warm.

Skim fat from sauce. Place casserole dish on stove-top and bring sauce to boil over medium heat. Adjust seasoning and stir in muscat wine. Strain into sauceboat and serve with duck. Sprinkle parsley over vegetables before serving.

QUAGLIE IN SALMI

BRAISED QUAILS (ITALY)   SERVES 4

Wrapping the quail in prosciutto crudo keeps the breast meat moist as well as adding flavor. There is no need to cover the whole quail with the prosciutto, as long as the breast is covered. Woodcock, pheasant and pigeon are also prepared in this way — buy them with giblets or purchase chicken livers separately for this recipe.

8 quails

salt and freshly ground black pepper

6 oz (180 g) paper-thin slices prosciutto crudo

1/3 cup (3 fl oz/80 ml) olive oil

4 fresh sage leaves

1/3 cup (3 fl oz/80 ml) dry white wine

1/3 cup (3 fl oz/80 ml) sweet marsala

2 canned anchovy fillets, drained

milk

1 tablespoon drained capers

4 oz (125 g) chicken livers or giblets from quails

8 slices country-style bread

sage sprigs, to garnish

Clean quail and pat dry with paper towels. Season cavities with salt and pepper. Tie legs together so quails keep their shape. Season outside of quails with pepper and wrap in prosciutto, pressing on firmly. Tie with cotton if desired.

Heat all but 2 tablespoons olive oil with sage in heavy-based flameproof casserole dish or Dutch oven. Add quails and brown all over on medium-high heat. Reduce heat and add wine and marsala. Cover and simmer gently until quail are tender when pierced with a fork, about 20 to 25 minutes, basting occasionally during cooking with juices in casserole dish and adding a little wine if juices reduce excessively.

Preheat oven to 375–400°F (190–200°C/Gas 5).

Transfer casserole dish to oven and bake uncovered until quails are lightly browned, about 5 minutes.

Meanwhile, soak anchovy fillets in milk 10 minutes. Rinse, pat dry with paper towels, and chop finely. Rinse capers well and chop finely. Clean chicken livers or quail giblets and chop finely. Toast bread slices.

Heat remaining oil in frying pan. Add anchovies, capers and livers or giblets and cook, mashing well with fork to make paste. Season to taste with pepper. Spread paste onto toast and keep warm in low oven. Remove quails from casserole dish, discard cotton, and arrange on warm platter. Pour juices from casserole dish around quails, and arrange toast on sides of platter — don't allow it to sit in juices. Garnish with sage sprigs and serve immediately.

Quaglie in Salmi

RABO DE TORO

OXTAIL STEW (SPAIN)   SERVES 4 TO 6

One would expect oxtail to feature in Spanish cooking; although the recipe is attributed to Andalusia, it is prepared in many other regions. Long, slow cooking is required to tenderize the meat and bring out its flavor. I like to cook oxtail the day before required, refrigerate it, then lift off the fat before reheating. Not only is the fat content reduced, but the flavor is so much better. This being the case, don't waste good olive oil for the browning — other oils, especially sunflower, are used in Spain. Choose one with a bland, unobtrusive flavor. Traditionally this stew is cooked on top of the stove, and you can do this if you wish. However, the slow, encompassing heat of the oven cooks the oxtail more evenly. Boiled green beans and potatoes make good accompaniments.

3 tablespoons cooking oil

1 large onion, chopped

2 cloves garlic, finely chopped

2 medium carrots, thickly sliced

1 celery stalk, chopped

4 lb (2 kg) oxtail,
cut in 2 in (5 cm) pieces

salt and freshly ground black pepper

all-purpose (plain) flour

15 oz (425 g) can tomatoes

1/2 cup (4 fl oz/125 ml)
dry white wine

1 cup (8 fl oz/250 ml) beef stock

1 teaspoon paprika

2 tablespoons chopped flat-leaf
(Italian) parsley

1 bay leaf

2 sprigs fresh thyme

Heat 1 tablespoon oil in large frying pan. Add onion and cook gently 5 minutes. Add garlic, carrot and celery and cook 10 minutes, stirring often. Transfer to large casserole dish.

Preheat oven to 300–325°F (150–160°C/Gas 2).

Season oxtail pieces with salt and pepper, and coat with flour. Heat remaining oil in frying pan and brown oxtail in batches, transferring to casserole dish.

Puree tomatoes with their liquid and add to frying pan with wine, stock, paprika and herbs. Bring to boil, stirring well to mix any browned juices in pan. Pour over oxtail, cover and bake until oxtail is very tender, about 2 1/2 to 3 hours — check after 1 hour, and if liquid does not just cover oxtail, add a little stock or water. Skim off surface fat and remove bay leaf and thyme sprigs before serving or reheating.

TRIPPA ALLA TREVISANA

TRIPE IN TOMATO SAUCE (ITALY)   SERVES 6

Tripe is coming back into favor, and this recipe from the Veneto is a simple, yet tasty way in which to prepare it. Try an accompaniment of risotto con gli asparagi (see page 222) or risotto Milanese (see page 224). Even though tripe is purchased already dressed — washed and partly pre-cooked — it does benefit from a brief blanching before cooking. To test for tenderness, take out a strip of tripe and pull with fingers; if it breaks apart easily, it is ready. Begin testing tripe after 1 hour of cooking, as over-cooked tripe disintegrates.

2 lb (1 kg) honeycomb tripe

3 tablespoons olive oil

2 medium onions, chopped

2 cloves garlic, finely chopped

3 tablespoons chopped flat-leaf (Italian) parsley

1/2 cup (4 fl oz/125 ml) dry white wine

15 oz (425 g) can tomatoes, chopped but undrained

salt and freshly ground black pepper

extra chopped parsley, to garnish

Rinse tripe well. Place in large saucepan, cover with cold water and bring to boil. Drain, rinse and pat dry with paper towels. Cut into strips about 3 in x 1/2 in (8 cm x 1 cm).

Warm oil in heavy-based saucepan. Add onions and cook gently until transparent, about 10 minutes. Add garlic and cook several seconds. Add tripe, parsley and wine, stir well and simmer 2 minutes. Add tomatoes with their liquid and salt and pepper to taste. Cover and simmer gently over low heat until tripe is tender, about 1 1/2 to 2 hours, adding a little water if sauce looks too dry and testing tripe occasionally after 1 hour of cooking. Transfer to warm serving dish and sprinkle with parsley before serving.

SIKOTAKI AFELIA

FRIED LIVER WITH CORIANDER (CYPRUS)   SERVES 4

The Cypriots are very fond of coriander seeds, and use them in a range of dishes called afelia. The main ingredient may be pork, new potatoes, mushrooms or liver, and it must contain red wine and definitely contain freshly crushed coriander seeds. Take care when cooking the liver as it can toughen very easily. Corn (maize) oil is widely used in Cypriot cooking, particularly when frying, but olive oil is also used. Serve with boiled new potatoes and steamed green vegetables.

1 lb (500 g) lamb or calf liver

all-purpose (plain) flour

salt and freshly ground black pepper

4 tablespoons corn (maize) oil or olive oil

1/4 cup (2 fl oz/60 ml) dry red wine

2 tablespoons red wine vinegar

2 to 3 teaspoons crushed coriander seeds

Cut liver into 1/2 in (1 cm) slices, removing any skin or tubes if present. Divide each slice into two or three manageable pieces. Combine flour with salt and pepper to taste and coat liver with flour just before cooking.

Heat oil in frying pan over medium-high heat. Add liver and cook until browned but still a little pink in middle, about 1 minute each side. Remove to plate.

Add wine and vinegar to pan and bring to boil. Return liver to pan and sprinkle with coriander. Toss over heat just long enough to warm liver. Serve immediately.

VEGETABLES, PASTA AND GRAINS

It is the vegetables of the Mediterranean that give the cuisines their color, their excitement, their vibrancy. Yet vegetables are not esteemed as highly as one would expect. Together with dried beans and other legumes, they were a means of existence in the agricultural societies, a product of their labors, extending often meager supplies of meat or fish. Through necessity, a very valuable aspect of the regional diet has evolved. Nutritionists believe that the high intake of vegetable foods in Mediterranean diets is beneficial in that, as well as vitamins, minerals and fiber, they contribute a large number of different antioxidants. These antioxidants, also found in olive oil and red wine, are under close scrutiny, and are being identified as an important factor in maintaining good health.

With this need to depend heavily on plant foods, a rich and varied cuisine has developed around them — fritters, pies, cooling salads and colorful vegetable stews and casseroles redolent with herbs. And in most, there is the fragrant olive oil to give them their essential character. The simplest way, however, of introducing Mediterranean cuisine into your kitchen, is to serve boiled or steamed green vegetables dressed only with a dribble of olive oil, and perhaps a squeeze of lemon juice. Forget the dabs of butter or margarine, or rich sauces. Not only will you find they taste good, your health will benefit.

With regard to pasta, no other food has had such a meteoric rise in popularity. Where once pasta, like bread, was avoided because we thought it fattening, we have heeded the health professionals and now include more of such foods in our diet.

Italy is the acknowledged home of pasta, making well over 100 different types of dried and fresh, home-made varieties. Disregard the Marco Polo story, as there is evidence that the Etruscans made pasta, and the ancient Romans also used it. Many Italian pasta shapes are used widely in the region, especially spaghetti, macaroni, vermicelli, cannelloni and ravioli.

Couscous is the "pasta" of the Maghreb, and is also used in Egypt, Malta and Sicily. Polenta (cornmeal) was welcomed into Italy when brought from the New World, and it became an important food item of the poor, especially in the colder regions. Burghul (steamed cracked wheat) is the grain of the Levant, its preparation going back to ancient times. Rice was introduced by the Arabs, and has been an important grain in the region ever since. From its use in paellas and other rice dishes in Spain, through the creamy risottos of Italy, to the pilafs of Greece, Cyprus and Turkey, rice has been given a Mediterranean identity far removed from its role in Asian cuisines.

Marak dar Marhzin (page 189)

RATATOUILLE

VEGETABLE CASSEROLE (FRANCE)   SERVES 6

Similar vegetable braises and casseroles, too numerous to mention, are prepared in most other countries of the Mediterranean region. Usually ratatouille is braised on the stove-top, with many Provençal cooks preferring to fry the eggplant, zucchini and peppers separately to prevent the whole becoming an unrecognisable mass. Oven-cooking overcomes this problem, and saves preparation time. If ratatouille is not to be eaten on the day of cooking, cover and refrigerate, then bring to room temperature or reheat as required — do not leave overnight at room temperature.

1 lb (500 g) small oval eggplants (aubergines)

salt

4 zucchini (courgettes)

2 green bell peppers (capsicums)

1 red bell pepper (capsicum)

6 medium-sized ripe tomatoes, peeled (see page 13)

1/2 cup (4 fl oz/125 ml) olive oil

2 tablespoons chopped parsley

1 tablespoon chopped fresh basil leaves

1 teaspoon chopped fresh marjoram or oregano

2 large onions, sliced

2 cloves garlic, finely chopped

freshly ground black pepper

Cut eggplants into slices, about 3/4 in (2 cm) thick. Layer in colander, sprinkling liberally with salt. Let stand 30 minutes. Trim zucchini and cut into chunks. Halve peppers lengthwise, discard seeds and membranes and cut into wide strips. Cut tomatoes into quarters.

Rinse eggplant and dry with cloth. Heat about 2 tablespoons oil in large frying pan until very hot. Quickly fry half the eggplant slices, just until lightly browned. Remove to large oven dish, about 2 in (5 cm) deep. Add a little more oil to pan and fry remaining eggplant. Add to dish with prepared vegetables and sprinkle with herbs.

Preheat oven to 325–350°F (160–180°C/Gas 3).

Heat remaining oil in pan. Add onion and cook over low heat until transparent, about 10 minutes. Add garlic and cook several seconds. Spread onion, garlic and oil over vegetables and season with salt and pepper. Cover with foil (dull side up) and cook in oven 40 minutes. Remove foil and cook 10 minutes more or until vegetables are tender.

Clean sides of dish and serve hot directly from dish, or let cool to room temperature. Serve with warm crusty bread.

Briami me Feta

VEGETABLE CASSEROLE WITH FETA (GREECE)   SERVES 6

Briami is the Greek version of the French ratatouille (see page 176), just two of the many Mediterranean casseroles that contain the vegetables associated with the region. With feta cheese and potatoes, the dish serves as a complete meal, but can be used as an accompaniment to simply cooked chicken and meats.

1 lb (500 g) eggplants (aubergines)

salt

1 lb (500 g) zucchini (courgettes)

1 lb (500 g) potatoes

1 green bell pepper (capsicum)

1 red bell pepper (capsicum)

2 cloves garlic, pressed (crushed)

15 oz (425 g) can tomatoes, chopped but undrained

2 tablespoons tomato paste

1 teaspoon sugar

freshly ground black pepper

2 large onions, sliced

2 tablespoons chopped parsley

1 tablespoon chopped fresh dill

1/2 cup (4 fl oz/125 ml) olive oil

8 oz (250 g) feta cheese, thinly sliced

crusty bread, to serve

Preheat oven to 325–350°F (160–180°C/Gas 3).

Cut eggplants into 3/4 in (2 cm) slices, sprinkle liberally with salt and let stand in colander 30 minutes. Rinse and squeeze slices dry in a cloth. Wash and slice zucchini diagonally into thick chunks. Peel potatoes and slice a little thinner than eggplant. Seed bell peppers; cut into rings. Combine garlic, tomatoes with their liquid, tomato paste and sugar in bowl.

Lightly oil large oven dish. Arrange eggplant, zucchini, potatoes, and bell peppers in alternating layers, seasoning with salt and pepper to taste, and covering each layer with onion rings, tomato mixture and sprinkling of herbs. Repeat layers until vegetables are used, finishing with tomato mixture and herbs. Pour oil over top, cover with foil and bake until vegetables are tender, about 1 1/2 hours.

Remove cover and place feta on top. Bake, uncovered, until feta softens and melts a little, about 15 minutes.

Serve hot or warm with crusty bread.

bell pepper

Patatas con Chorizo

POTATOES WITH CHORIZO SAUSAGE (SPAIN)   SERVES 4 TO 8

Potatoes were introduced into Spain from the New World in the 16th century, and have featured in their cooking ever since. It took a while before other countries adopted the potato, regarding it with much suspicion, but the Spaniards, having seen the natives of South America consuming them with no ill-effect, adopted them wholeheartedly into their cuisine. This recipe is just one of many enjoyed throughout Spain, and can be served as a light meal, accompaniment, or tapa dish. Choose potatoes about the size of a large apricot and peel them if desired. If serving as a tapa, use larger potatoes, peel and cut into 3/4 in (2 cm) cubes. Reduce cooking time to 15 to 20 minutes.

2 lb (1 kg) small white-skinned potatoes

1 smoked chorizo sausage

2 to 3 slices bacon, about 3 oz (90 g)

2 tablespoons olive oil

1 clove garlic, pressed (crushed)

pinch of cayenne pepper

1/2 teaspoon paprika

salt

1 tablespoon finely chopped parsley

If leaving potatoes unpeeled, wash well and dry in clean cloth. Cut chorizo into 1/4 in (5 mm) thick slices. Remove rind from bacon and cut bacon into small squares.

Heat oil in large frying pan with lid to fit. Add chorizo and bacon and cook, stirring often, until lightly browned and fat is melted. Add garlic, cayenne pepper and paprika, stir well and cook several seconds. Add potatoes and stir to coat with oil. Reduce heat to low, cover and cook until potatoes are tender, about 30 minutes, stirring occasionally. Season with salt to taste and transfer to warm serving bowl. Sprinkle with parsley and serve immediately.

Patate alle Olive e Acciugata

POTATOES WITH OLIVES AND ANCHOVIES (ITALY)   SERVES 6

In Abruzia and Molise, they give the humble potato a hearty lift with anchovies, olives and capers of the region, and olive oil. These are excellent served alongside barbecued meats and fish.

2 lb (1 kg) medium potatoes

3 tablespoons olive oil

6 canned anchovy fillets, drained and chopped

8 black olives, pitted and chopped

1 tablespoon capers, drained, rinsed and chopped

salt and freshly ground black pepper

2 tablespoons chopped flat-leaf (Italian) parsley

Peel and cut each potato into 6 wedges. Dry well in clean cloth.

Place large, heavy frying pan with lid to fit over medium-high heat and heat well. Add oil and potatoes and cook 2 to 3 minutes to heat through, shaking pan to prevent potatoes sticking. Scatter anchovies, olives and capers over potatoes, and season with salt and pepper to taste. Cover pan, reduce heat to medium-low and cook until potatoes are tender, about 25 to 30 minutes, turning with metal spatula halfway through cooking. Sprinkle with parsley and serve hot.

Patatas con Chorizo

PARMIGIANA DI MELANZANE

EGGPLANT WITH CHEESE (ITALY)   SERVES 4 TO 6

Broiling (grilling) the eggplant in this dish should appeal to those who like olive oil but are concerned about the amount that eggplant absorbs when fried. Serve as a light meal or, at room temperature, as an appetizer.

3 lb (1.5 kg) large eggplants (aubergines)

salt

1/4 cup (2 fl oz/60 ml) olive oil

2 cups (16 fl oz/500 ml) sugo di pomodoro (see page 32)

1/2 cup (2 oz/60 g) grated parmesan cheese

2 cups (8 oz/250 g) shredded mozzarella cheese

1 tablespoon chopped fresh basil (optional)

crusty bread, to serve

Cut eggplants lengthwise into 1/2 in (1 cm) slices. Place in colander, sprinkling each layer with salt, and let stand 30 minutes. Rinse briefly and dry slices in clean cloth. Brush baking sheet with oil. Arrange eggplant in single layer, brush with oil and cook under hot broiler (grill) until browned on each side. Set aside and cook remaining eggplant slices.

Preheat oven to 350–375°F (180–190°C/Gas 4). Brush wide, shallow casserole dish with oil and arrange eggplant in single layer. Cover with a thin layer of sugo di pomodoro, sprinkle with some parmesan and mozzarella. Repeat layers, finishing with thick layer sugo di pomodoro and generous sprinkling of mozzarella, then parmesan. Sprinkle with basil, if desired. Bake until bubbling and cheese is browned, about 25 to 30 minutes. Serve hot or warm with crusty bread.

MELITZANES HARAKTES

STUFFED EGGPLANT (GREECE)   SERVES 4 TO 6

The resemblance of these to the Turkish imam bayildi is more than coincidental. While the Turkish name is still used by Greeks, my mother referred to them by haraktes meaning "slit" or "nicked". Long slender purple eggplants of even, medium size are necessary for this dish; they do not require salting. Serve as a light meal, or as an accompaniment to broiled, grilled or roasted chicken or lamb.

3 lb (1.5 kg) long (Japanese) eggplants (aubergines)

3/4 cup (6 fl oz/180 ml) olive oil

3 medium onions, halved and thinly sliced lengthwise

3 to 4 cloves garlic, cut into slivers

2 tablespoons finely chopped flat-leaf (Italian) parsley

1 tablespoon chopped celery leaves

3 large ripe tomatoes, peeled and chopped

2 oz (60 g) kasseri or pecorino cheese, finely diced

1/2 teaspoon sugar

salt and freshly ground black pepper

crusty bread, to serve

Wash and remove eggplant stems. Dry and cut 4 deep lengthwise slits evenly around each eggplant. Heat 1/2 cup oil in large frying pan. Add eggplants and cook gently on all sides until beginning to soften. Remove to plate and let cool. Add onions to pan and cook gently until transparent, about 10 minutes. Add garlic and cook several seconds. Transfer to bowl and mix in parsley, celery leaves, tomatoes, cheese, sugar, and salt and pepper to taste.

Preheat oven to 350–375°F (180–190°C/Gas 4). Stuff onion mixture into each slit in eggplants. Place filled eggplants in single layer in casserole dish and spread any remaining onion mixture on top. Pour over 1/4 cup oil. Cover with lid or foil, shiny-side down, and bake 35 minutes. Remove cover and bake 10 minutes more. Serve hot or at room temperature with crusty bread

MELITZANES PAPOUTSAKIA

STUFFED EGGPLANTS (GREECE)   SERVES 4 TO 8

Papoutsakia means "little shoes", which aptly describes this popular eggplant dish. Serve it as a first course or as a main course with a simple green salad. Medium zucchini (courgettes) can also be prepared in the same way.

4 x 8 oz (250 g) eggplants
(aubergines)

salt

oil, for shallow frying

2 tablespoons olive oil

1 large onion, finely chopped

2 cloves garlic, finely sliced

1 lb (500 g) ground (minced)
beef or lamb

2 medium-sized ripe tomatoes,
peeled and chopped

2 tablespoons chopped
flat-leaf (Italian) parsley

pinch each cinnamon and nutmeg

1/2 teaspoon sugar

salt and freshly ground black pepper

3 large tomatoes, sliced

grated kefalotiri cheese or
parmesan cheese

1 cup (8 fl oz/250 ml) water

chopped parsley, to garnish

Halve eggplants lengthwise. Cut around flesh 1/4 in (5 mm) in from skin, then make 4 deep cuts across and into flesh, taking care not to pierce skin. Sprinkle cut surfaces with salt and let stand 30 minutes.

Pat eggplants dry with paper towels. Pour oil into large frying pan until 1/4 in (5 mm) deep and heat well. Add eggplant and shallow fry 2 minutes on skin side, 5 minutes on flesh side. Let cool, scoop out flesh carefully, leaving thin shell. Chop flesh and set aside. Place eggplant shells in single layer in baking dish.

Warm 2 tablespoons oil in saucepan. Add onion and garlic and cook gently until onion is transparent, about 10 minutes. Increase heat. Add meat, stir well and cook until meat begins to brown, about 10 minutes. Add chopped tomatoes, parsley, spices, sugar, and salt and pepper to taste. Cover and simmer gently 20 minutes. Add reserved eggplant flesh and simmer 10 minutes.

Preheat oven to 325–350°F (170–180°C/Gas 3).

Fill eggplant shells with meat mixture. Place 3 to 4 tomato slices on top of each and sprinkle with cheese. Pour water into base of dish and bake, uncovered, until cooked through and cheese is melted, about 40 minutes. Sprinkle with parsley. Serve hot.

Mnazlit Batinjan

CHICKPEA AND EGGPLANT STEW (LEBANON, SYRIA)   SERVES 6

This combination of chickpeas and eggplant provides a complete meal. It is one of the recipes used during times of fasting which makes it an ideal vegetarian meal.

1¹/2 cups (11 oz/315 g) dried chickpeas (garbanzos)

1¹/2 lb (750 g) oval eggplants (aubergines)

salt

¹/3 cup (3 fl oz/80 ml) olive oil

1 large onion, chopped

2 cloves garlic, pressed (crushed)

15 oz (425 g) can tomatoes, chopped but undrained

2 tablespoons chopped flat-leaf (Italian) parsley

freshly ground black pepper

pita bread, to serve

Place chickpeas in sieve and pick over to remove extra matter. Rinse under cold running water and drain. Place in bowl with three times their volume of cold water and soak overnight in refrigerator.

Drain chickpeas and place in saucepan with water to cover. Bring to boil, cover and simmer until tender, about 1¹/2 to 2 hours. Drain, reserving about 1 cup cooking liquid, and return chickpeas to saucepan.

Meanwhile, cut eggplants crosswise into ³/4 in (2 cm) thick slices. Cut each slice into quarters. Layer in colander, sprinkling salt over each layer and let stand 30 minutes. Rinse under cold running water, drain and dry in clean cloth.

Heat 1 tablespoon oil in frying pan. Add onion and cook gently until transparent, about 10 minutes. Add garlic and cook several seconds. Add mixture to chickpeas. Heat remaining oil in frying pan. Add eggplant and cook, stirring gently with wooden spoon, until pieces are lightly browned but not completely cooked, about 5 minutes. Place on top of chickpeas and pour over combined tomatoes with their liquid, 1 tablespoon parsley, and salt and pepper to taste. Cover and simmer gently, without stirring, until eggplant is cooked but still intact, about 20 minutes.

Mix eggplant gently through chickpeas, and if mixture looks too dry, add a little reserved chickpea liquid. Pile onto warm serving dish and sprinkle with remaining parsley. Serve hot or at room temperature with pita bread.

Mnazlit Batinjan

182

CAPONATA

SWEET-SOUR EGGPLANT SALAD (ITALY)   SERVES 6

In Sicily, each cook seems to have her own version of caponata. There is one version, caponata di scampi e molluschi, so complex that it would take a week just to assemble the ingredients! The following is much simpler, but it is important that a good quality vinegar be used, and added with caution to achieve a balance of the sweet and sour flavors.

2 lb (1 kg) oval eggplants (aubergines)
salt
3/4 cup (6 fl oz/180 ml) olive oil
2 celery stalks, chopped
2 medium onions, sliced
3 tablespoons tomato paste
1/2 cup (4 fl oz/125 ml) water
10 green olives, pitted and chopped
2 tablespoons drained capers, rinsed
4 teaspoons sugar
freshly ground black pepper
3 to 5 tablespoons red wine vinegar
3 tablespoons pine nuts, toasted

Cut unpeeled eggplants into 3/4 in (2 cm) cubes. Layer in colander, sprinkling with salt and let stand 30 minutes. Shake well to remove any remaining moisture and dry well in clean cloth. Heating 2 tablespoons oil at a time in frying pan, cook eggplant cubes in batches until browned and cooked through, about 10 minutes, tossing often. Remove to dish lined with paper towels to drain.

Heat remaining oil in frying pan. Add celery and cook quickly until lightly browned but still crisp. Remove to bowl with slotted spoon. Reduce heat, add onions and cook gently until soft, about 6 to 8 minutes.

Dissolve tomato paste in water and add to frying pan with celery, olives, capers, sugar, and pepper to taste. Bring to boil and simmer 10 minutes. Add 3 tablespoons vinegar and cook until fumes dissipate. Stir in eggplant and pine nuts. Add more vinegar to taste if needed. Transfer to bowl and serve warm or at room temperature.

BROCCOLI ALLA SICILIANA

BROCCOLI WITH ANCHOVIES (ITALY)   SERVES 5 TO 6

In Sicily, green cauliflower is used for this easy vegetable dish. It is available outside Italy, and if you find it, use two heads in place of the broccoli. Beet (beetroot) leaves, chard (silverbeet) and turnip greens can also be finished with the anchovy and breadcrumb dressing.

1 1/2 lb (750 g) broccoli
4 tablespoons olive oil
1/2 cup (1 oz/30 g) soft breadcrumbs
4 cloves garlic, finely chopped
2 tablespoons mashed drained canned anchovy fillets
2 tablespoons lemon juice

Wash broccoli and separate into florets, leaving as much stem as possible. Cook in boiling, salted water, uncovered, until just tender, about 6 to 8 minutes.

Meanwhile, heat oil in frying pan. Add breadcrumbs and cook over fairly high heat until crisp and golden, stirring often. Add garlic and anchovies and cook 2 to 3 minutes, mashing anchovies so they dissolve into oil.

Drain broccoli and transfer to warm serving dish. Sprinkle with lemon juice and then breadcrumb mixture, scraping crumbs from pan using spatula. Serve immediately.

Prassa me Avgolemono

LEEKS WITH EGG AND LEMON SAUCE (GREECE)   SERVES 6

The delicate egg and lemon sauce of Greek cooking marries well with many vegetables and is an ideal alternative to butter-rich hollandaise. Globe artichokes, broccoli, asparagus and celery may also be served with the sauce; boil until just tender in lightly salted water to cover, drain and serve with the sauce. Only use dill with artichokes. Serve as a first course or as a vegetable accompaniment.

6 to 8 leeks
salt
1 cup (8 fl oz/250 ml) water
1 sprig fresh dill
1 tablespoon olive oil
1 tablespoon chopped fresh dill

Saltsa Avgolemono:

1¹/2 cups (12 fl oz/375 ml) chicken stock (see page 31)
3 teaspoons cornstarch (cornflour)
3 eggs, separated
juice of 1 lemon
salt and freshly ground white pepper

Cut most of green tops from leeks, leaving a short section of light green. Trim roots carefully so that leeks can remain intact. Slit each leek lengthwise and carefully wash between layers. Place leeks in large deep frying pan or sauté pan with lid to fit. Add ¹/2 teaspoon salt, water, dill sprig and oil. Bring to boil, partly cover and simmer 10 minutes. Remove lid and simmer until tender, about 10 minutes. Remove leeks carefully to serving dish and keep warm. Discard dill.

For saltsa avgolemono: Bring stock to boil in saucepan. Combine cornstarch with a little cold water and gradually stir into simmering stock to thicken slightly. Simmer gently.

Beat egg whites in bowl until stiff. Beat in egg yolks and most of the lemon juice. Gradually beat in hot stock and return to saucepan. Add salt and pepper to taste and more lemon juice if needed to give tangy flavor. Return to low heat and stir 2 minutes to cook egg — do not allow to boil.

Pour sauce over leeks, sprinkle with dill and serve hot.

Carote al Marsala

GLAZED MARSALA CARROTS (ITALY)   SERVES 6

This Sicilian way with carrots is particularly good. It makes excellent use of Sicily's own marsala — use the sweet one for this recipe.

1¹/2 lb (750 g) medium carrots
2 tablespoons olive oil
¹/4 cup (2 fl oz/60 ml) water
thinly peeled strip of lemon rind
salt and freshly ground black pepper
¹/4 cup (2 fl oz/60 ml) sweet marsala

Peel carrots and cut into ¹/4 in (5 mm) slices. Heat oil in heavy saucepan. Add carrots and cook over medium heat 3 to 4 minutes, stirring occasionally. Reduce heat and add water, lemon rind, and salt and pepper to taste. Cover tightly and simmer gently until carrots are tender, about 12 to 15 minutes.

Remove lid and increase heat to evaporate any moisture. Add marsala and cook a few minutes more until carrots are glazed and very little liquid remains, stirring occasionally. Remove lemon rind and serve carrots hot.

Oignons à la Monegasque

SWEET AND SOUR ONIONS WITH RAISINS (MONACO)   SERVES 6

While the home-cooking of Monaco follows that of Provence, this dish is a specialty of the principality. Serve as an accompaniment to plainly cooked meat. The onions' cooking time depends on their size.

1¹/₂ lb (750 g) small pickling (pearl) onions

3 tablespoons olive oil

2 tablespoons tomato paste

1 cup (8 fl oz/250 ml) water

2 tablespoons red wine vinegar

1 tablespoon sugar

bouquet garni (sprig each thyme and parsley, bay leaf and leafy celery top, tied together)

4 tablespoons raisins

salt and freshly ground black pepper

Using sharp knife, trim tops from onions and trim roots carefully, without cutting into onion layers. Place in bowl, cover with boiling water and let stand 10 minutes. Drain, slip off skins and cut cross in root end of each onion to prevent middles popping out. Heat oil in heavy saucepan. Add onions and cook gently, stirring, 5 minutes. Add remaining ingredients, cover and simmer over low heat 30 minutes, stirring occasionally. Remove lid and simmer until liquid is reduced to thick sauce and onions are tender when pierced with fine skewer, about 15 to 30 minutes, stirring occasionally to prevent sticking. If necessary, add more vinegar or sugar to give pleasing sweet-sour flavor. Let cool to room temperature. Remove bouquet garni before serving.

Tian de Courgettes et Blettes

GRATIN OF ZUCCHINI AND GREENS (FRANCE)   SERVES 6

A tian is both a Provençal glazed earthenware gratin dish and any vegetables cooked in one. Blette is chard but 1¹/₂ lb (750 g) spinach may be used instead. Serve as a light meal or as an accompaniment.

1¹/₂ lb (750 g) zucchini (courgettes)

salt

8 to 10 chard (silverbeet) leaves

3 tablespoons olive oil

2 medium onions, sliced

1 clove garlic, finely chopped

¹/₄ cup (2 oz/60 g) medium-grain rice

³/₄ cup (6 fl oz/180 ml) water

3 eggs, beaten

2 tablespoons finely chopped parsley

2 oz (60 g) gruyère cheese, shredded

2 tablespoons grated parmesan cheese

freshly ground black pepper

¹/₂ cup (1 oz/30 g) soft white breadcrumbs

Trim stems and round ends from zucchini and slice thinly. Layer in colander, sprinkle each layer with salt, and let stand 30 minutes. Rinse then pat dry. Remove white stems from chard and wash leaves well. Shred fairly finely and set aside.

Preheat oven to 350–375°F (180–190°C/Gas 4). Heat half the oil in large saucepan. Add onions and cook gently until transparent, about 10 minutes, stirring occasionally. Add garlic and cook several seconds. Add rice and water and bring to boil. Cover and simmer gently until water is absorbed, about 6 to 8 minutes. Add zucchini and chard, cover and simmer 10 minutes, stirring occasionally. Remove from heat and let cool slightly. Add eggs and toss well. Add parsley, half the cheeses, and salt and pepper to taste and mix well. Transfer to greased shallow baking or gratin dish and spread evenly. Sprinkle with breadcrumbs and remaining cheeses, and drizzle with remaining oil. Bake until golden brown, about 30 to 35 minutes. Serve hot from dish.

Oignons a la Monegasque

186

COSTE DI BIETE SALTATE

SAUTEED CHARD STEMS (ITALY)   SERVES 6

Chard leaves are often used alone in recipes (see pages 186 and 220). However, the stems can be boiled and, in Greek cooking, dressed with olive and lemon juice, or finished as a gratin with bechamel sauce and cheese in French and Italian cooking. Serve this recipe as an accompaniment to meat or poultry.

1 lb (500 g) chard (silverbeet) stems
salt
1/4 cup (2 fl oz/60 ml) olive oil
2 cloves garlic, finely chopped
2 tablespoons chopped parsley
freshly ground black pepper
fresh lemon juice (optional)

Wash stems well, cut off discolored ends and carefully pull off strings, as you would celery, so that stem itself is not pulled away. Slice wide stems in half lengthwise and cut stems into 3 in (8 cm) lengths. Bring large stainless steel or enamelled saucepan of water to boil, add salt to taste and stems. Boil until just tender 8 to 10 minutes, stirring occasionally to keep stems submerged, otherwise they discolor. Drain in colander and run cold water over to arrest cooking.

Just before serving, place olive oil in large frying pan over medium heat. Add garlic and cook until just beginning to brown lightly. Add drained stems and parsley and heat through, stirring often. Season with pepper to taste and add a good squeeze of lemon juice if desired. Serve immediately.

FRITTATA DI ZUCCHINE

ZUCCHINI OMELETTE (ITALY)   SERVES 4

Rather than turning it in the frying pan, this is an easy way to cook a frittata — Italy's omelette.

2 tablespoons olive oil
2 onions, sliced
4 zucchini (courgettes), thinly sliced
6 eggs
1/3 cup (3 fl oz/80 ml) cold water
1 tablespoon chopped fresh basil
or parsley
1/4 teaspoon grated nutmeg
salt and freshly ground black pepper
4 tablespoons grated parmesan
cheese
shaved parmesan cheese, to garnish
fresh basil or parsley sprigs,
to garnish

Warm 1 1/2 tablespoons oil in large frying pan. Add onions and cook gently until beginning to soften, about 5 minutes. Add zucchini and cook over medium heat until zucchini are soft and lightly colored, about 10 minutes, stirring often. Let stand 10 minutes to cool. Beat eggs lightly with fork in bowl. Beat in water, basil or parsley, nutmeg, and salt and pepper to taste. Add zucchini mixture and 3 tablespoons parmesan and stir thoroughly.

Heat remaining oil in 8 in (20 cm) frying pan over medium heat. Add egg mixture and spread vegetables evenly with spatula. Reduce heat to low and cook gently until lightly golden underneath and set around edge, with top still runny, about 15 minutes. Sprinkle with remaining grated parmesan.

Wrap handle of pan in foil if not heat-proof and place pan under hot broiler (grill) until frittata is puffed and golden brown on top, about 2 to 3 minutes. Loosen with spatula and slide onto serving dish. Garnish with shaved parmesan and herbs. Serve hot, or cold as picnic food, cut into wedges.

Marak dar Marhzin

PUMPKIN STEW (MOROCCO)   SERVES 4 TO 6

A marak is a vegetable version of tagine, usually served as a separate course. The following recipe combines pumpkin with root vegetables and can be served with couscous as suggested, or with boiled brown rice for a modern vegetarian dish. You can add 15 oz (425 g) can chickpeas (drained and rinsed) with the pumpkin to give the stew more substance, if you wish.

3 tablespoons butter or oil

2 large onions, finely chopped

2 cloves garlic, finely chopped

1 teaspoon turmeric

1 teaspoon ground ginger

1 teaspoon ground cinnamon

2 medium carrots, sliced

2 small white turnips, peeled and quartered (optional)

3 cups (24 fl oz/750 ml) water

1 lb (500 g) butternut pumpkin (squash), peeled and cubed

1 lb (500 g) sweet potato, peeled and cubed

1 teaspoon harissa (see page 33)

1/3 cup (1 1/2 oz/45 g) raisins

3 teaspoons honey

salt and freshly ground black pepper

fresh coriander leaves (cilantro), to garnish

couscous (see page 37), cooked, to serve

lime wedges, to serve

Melt butter in large heavy saucepan. Add onion and cook gently 10 minutes. Add garlic and spices and cook 2 minutes, stirring occasionally. Add carrots, turnips and water and bring to boil. Cover and simmer 10 minutes. Add pumpkin, sweet potato, harissa, raisins, honey and salt and pepper to taste. Cover and simmer 20 minutes more or until vegetables are tender.

Transfer to warm bowl and garnish with coriander leaves. Alternatively, pile hot cooked couscous onto warm platter, make a hollow in middle and spoon in pumpkin mixture.

Serve with lime wedges in a separate bowl, to be squeezed on according to individual taste.

Pages 190 to 191: Ratatouille (page 176), Slata Mechouia (page 206) and Insalata di Finnochio (page 205)

Spinaci alla Romana

SPINACH WITH RAISINS AND PINE NUTS (ITALY)   SERVES 6

This method of preparing spinach and other greens such as beet (beetroot) leaves, chard (silverbeet) and turnip greens, is also known in Catalan cooking. The addition, before the garlic, of chopped onion softened in oil is popular. This recipe is also known in Southern France, minus the raisins.

3 tablespoons raisins
2 lb (1 kg) spinach
2 tablespoons olive oil
2 tablespoons pine nuts
2 tablespoons butter
1 clove garlic, thinly sliced
salt and freshly ground
black pepper

Cover raisins with warm water in bowl and soak 15 minutes.

Cut off roots and about 1 1/2 in (4 cm) of stems from spinach and discard damaged leaves. Wash spinach thoroughly and drain but do not dry. Place in large saucepan, cover and cook over medium heat until wilted, tossing occasionally to distribute heat. Transfer to colander and press with back of wooden spoon to remove excess moisture.

Heat half the oil in large frying pan. Add pine nuts and cook until golden, about 3 minutes, stirring often. Remove with slotted spoon and set aside. Heat remaining oil and butter in pan. Add garlic and cook gently until lightly golden. Add spinach, drained raisins, and salt and pepper to taste. Cook gently until well heated, about 10 minutes, stirring occasionally. Add pine nuts and toss. Serve hot.

Judias Verdes con Jamón

GREEN BEANS WITH HAM (SPAIN)   SERVES 6

While this dish would be served as a separate course at a Spanish meal, it is an excellent accompaniment to main courses, especially meat and poultry stews, casseroles and roasts.

12 oz (375 g) fresh young
green beans, preferably stringless
4 oz (125 g) cooked ham,
sliced 1/4 in (5 mm) thick
2 tablespoons olive oil
1 small onion, finely chopped
2 cloves garlic, finely chopped
freshly ground black pepper

Top and tail beans, stringing only if necessary. Rinse and add to saucepan of boiling, salted water. Return to boil and boil, uncovered, 4 minutes. Drain in colander and rinse under cold running water. Drain well. Cut ham slices into 1/4 in (5 mm) wide strips.

Warm oil in large frying pan. Add onion and cook gently until transparent, about 10 minutes. Add garlic and cook 1 minute. Add ham strips, beans, and pepper to taste. Toss well, cover and cook over low heat until beans are just tender but still crisp, about 6 to 8 minutes. Serve hot.

Guisantes a la Espanola (Green Peas with Ham) Variation: Substitute 2 cups (10 oz/300 g) shelled fresh or frozen peas for beans. Do not blanch; add to pan with ham strips and add 3 to 4 tablespoons water and 1 teaspoon sugar. Cook until tender, and stir in a little chopped fresh mint, if desired.

MARAK MATISHA BIL MELOKHIAS

BRAISED OKRA WITH TOMATOES (MOROCCO)   SERVES 6

I like okra, providing its viscous sap has been reduced. While this recipe comes from Morocco, and is popular in other North African countries, the okra preparation before cooking is Greek, as this reduces the viscosity and prevents the okra from splitting. Serve as part of a Moroccan meal or as a separate dish, with couscous if desired.

1 lb (500 g) fresh okra

1/2 cup (4 fl oz/125 ml) distilled white vinegar

3 tablespoons olive oil

1 large onion, sliced

2 cloves garlic, chopped

2 x 15 oz (425 g) cans tomatoes, chopped but undrained

2 tablespoons chopped parsley

1 teaspoon paprika

salt and freshly ground black pepper

extra chopped parsley, to serve

Wash okra and trim stalks but do not remove cone-shaped tops. Place in bowl, pour over vinegar and turn with hand to coat. Let stand 20 minutes. Drain, rinse well and dry gently with clean cloth.

Heat oil in saucepan. Add onion and garlic and cook gently until onion is transparent, about 10 minutes. Add tomatoes with their liquid, parsley, paprika, and salt and pepper to taste. Simmer over medium-low heat until thick, about 20 minutes, stirring occasionally.

Add okra, cover and simmer gently over low heat until okra is tender, about 20 to 25 minutes. Transfer carefully to serving dish and sprinkle with extra chopped parsley. Serve hot or at room temperature.

FENOUIL BRAISÉ

BRAISED FENNEL (FRANCE)   SERVES 6

While fennel is very much a part of Italian cuisine, most of the recipes using it come from the north. Provence had adopted and adapted many Italian dishes, the following recipe among them.

6 fennel bulbs

bouquet garni
(2 sprigs each parsley and thyme, 1 bay leaf, tied together)

2 tablespoons olive oil

salt and freshly ground black pepper

2 tablespoons grated parmesan cheese

Preheat oven to 350–375°F (180–190°C/Gas 4). Cut leafy tops and stems from fennel bulbs and keep leaf sprigs for garnish. Remove outside leaves of bulbs and trim bases. Bring large saucepan of salted water to boil. Add bouquet garni and whole fennel bulbs and return to boil. Boil until fennel are just cooked but still firm, about 10 to 15 minutes. Drain in colander, discard bouquet garni and let stand 10 minutes. Cut each bulb in half lengthwise and place, cut-side down, onto layers of paper towels to drain thoroughly. Place fennel cut-side down in lightly-oiled baking dish. Drizzle with olive oil and season with salt and pepper. Sprinkle with parmesan and bake until heated through and lightly browned, about 15 minutes. Snip some fennel leaves over fennel bulbs to garnish and serve hot from dish.

CHAKCHOUKA

PEPPERS WITH TOMATOES AND EGGS (TUNISIA)   SERVES 4

This is but one version of chakchouka prepared in the Maghreb. Eggs are an important ingredient in the cooking of this region as they are an inexpensive meat substitute. In Tunisia, the spicy merguez sausage (see page 157) often features in this dish but spicy Italian sausage can be substituted — prick 4 Italian sausages and fry them gently in an oiled frying pan until cooked through, cut into thick slices and add with the tomatoes. The amount of eggs you add to the vegetables depends on whether you are cooking a light snack or a main course.

2 green bell peppers (capsicums)

1 red bell pepper (capsicum)

1/3 cup (3 fl oz/80 ml) olive oil

2 cloves garlic, finely chopped

3 medium-sized ripe tomatoes, peeled and chopped

1 teaspoon harissa (see page 33), or 1/4 teaspoon cayenne pepper with 1/2 teaspoon ground cumin

3 tablespoons chopped flat-leaf (Italian) parsley

salt

4 to 8 eggs

paprika

crusty bread, to serve

Halve bell peppers, remove cores, seeds and membrane and cut into long strips just under 1/2 in (1 cm) wide. Heat oil in large frying pan. Add bell pepper strips and cook over medium heat 5 minutes, stirring often. Add garlic and cook several seconds. Add tomatoes, harissa (or cayenne pepper and cumin mixture), parsley, and salt to taste. Cover and simmer until vegetables are tender, about 15 minutes. Remove lid, and make 4 to 8 hollows in vegetables. Break number of eggs required into hollows, cover and simmer until eggs are cooked as desired. Sprinkle lightly with paprika and serve hot with crusty bread.

Chakchouka

Mahshi Flayfli bil Hummus

PEPPERS STUFFED WITH CHICKPEAS (LEBANON)   SERVES 6

Stuffed vegetables and cabbage leaves are popular in the Levant; this is a meatless version, ideal for vegetarians. Served with crusty bread and a salad of your choice, it provides a filling, flavorsome meal.

12 medium-sized
green bell peppers (capsicums)

Chickpea and Rice Stuffing:

1/4 cup (2 fl oz/60 ml) olive oil

6 scallions (spring onions/green onions), chopped

1 cup (7 oz/210 g) long-grain rice

15 oz (425 g) can chickpeas (garbanzos), drained

4 tablespoons chopped flat-leaf (Italian) parsley

2 medium tomatoes, peeled and chopped

1/2 teaspoon ground allspice

salt and freshly ground black pepper

Tomato Sauce:

2 tablespoons olive oil

1 medium onion, grated

1 clove garlic, pressed (crushed)

1 cup (8 fl oz/250 ml) water

3 tablespoons tomato paste

1 teaspoon sugar

salt and freshly ground black pepper

2 tablespoons finely chopped flat-leaf (Italian) parsley

Cut tops from bell peppers, trim and reserve. Discard seeds and white membrane. Add peppers to saucepan of boiling salted water and boil 5 minutes. Remove and invert to drain on layers of paper towels.

For chickpea and rice stuffing: Heat oil in frying pan. Add scallions and cook gently 2 to 3 minutes. Remove from heat, add remaining stuffing ingredients and season to taste with salt and pepper.

Stand bell peppers upright in an oiled baking dish and fill loosely with prepared stuffing. Replace tops of peppers.

Preheat oven to 325–350°F (170–180°C/Gas 3).

For tomato sauce: Warm oil in small saucepan. Add onion and garlic and cook gently 5 minutes. Stir in remaining sauce ingredients and bring to boil.

Pour tomato sauce over bell peppers, cover with lid or foil and bake 45 minutes. Remove cover and bake 15 minutes, basting peppers with sauce if necessary to keep them moist. Serve hot.

PEPERONATA

PEPPER AND TOMATO STEW (ITALY)   SERVES 6

Traditionally, the peppers would be skinned for this dish. However, this is time-consuming and the dish will taste just as good if the peppers are unskinned. This makes an excellent antipasto served at room temperature, or it can be served as an accompaniment to main meals. Choose heavy, fleshy bell peppers.

4 bell peppers (capsicums),
red, green and yellow if possible

3 large ripe tomatoes,
peeled and seeded

4 tablespoons olive oil

2 medium onions, sliced

2 cloves garlic, finely chopped

salt and freshly ground black pepper

2 tablespoons finely chopped
flat-leaf (Italian) parsley

Discard core, seeds and membrane from bell peppers and cut lengthwise into thick strips. Chop tomatoes roughly.

Heat oil in large frying pan with lid to fit. Add onions and cook gently until transparent, about 10 minutes, stirring often. Add garlic and cook several seconds. Add pepper strips, tomatoes, and salt and pepper to taste. Toss well, and simmer, covered, until peppers are tender, about 20 minutes. Sprinkle with parsley. Serve hot or at room temperature.

Fagiolini alla Peperonata (Green Beans, Peppers and Tomato Stew) Variation: This Sicilian version uses 1 red and 1 yellow bell pepper (or 2 red ones) in place of the 4 bell peppers above. Top and tail 8 oz (250 g) young green beans and add to pan with bell pepper strips, which should be cut to the same width as beans. Add 1 tablespoon chopped fresh oregano in place of parsley.

ASPARIGI IN SALSO UOVO

ASPARAGUS WITH EGG SAUCE (ITALY)   SERVES 6 AS AN APPETIZER

Choose slender green spears, not the large white ones, to enjoy asparagus as prepared in the Veneto.

4 hard-cooked (boiled) eggs

1 tablespoon white wine vinegar

2 teaspoons lemon juice

1/2 cup (4 fl oz/125 ml) extra virgin
olive oil

salt and freshly ground black pepper

11/2 lb (750 g) green asparagus
spears

1 teaspoon sugar

Cook eggs as directed in recipe page 58. When cold, shell and chop roughly. Process in food processor bowl with vinegar and lemon juice to thick puree. With motor operating, gradually add oil to form creamy sauce. Add salt and pepper to taste and more juice if necessary. Pour into a jug.

Snap off woody ends from asparagus and trim ends neatly with knife. Remove lower leaf scales with paring knife — if asparagus is young and fresh, this is not necessary.

Place wire rack in base of deep, 10 in (25 cm) frying or sauté pan with lid to fit, or a large electric frying pan. Add water to just come level with rack, add salt to taste and sugar, and bring to boil. Spread asparagus across rack, cover and steam until crisp-tender, about 8 minutes. Remove with egg lifter to flat dish lined with paper towels. Transfer immediately to heated platter or six plates. Pour stream of egg sauce along center of spears. Serve immediately.

FUL MEDAMIS

SIMMERED FUL BEANS (EGYPT)   SERVES 6

Ful, ful medamis, faba, tic, Egyptian brown beans — these are the various names used for this most ancient of beans, popular in Egypt for centuries, perhaps from the time of the Pharaohs. The beans look like small, rounded fava (broad) beans and can be found in Middle Eastern and Greek markets; fava beans cannot be substituted as their flavor is too strong.

Long, slow cooking is required; indeed in Egypt, where ful medamis is the national dish, purveyors simmer their beans overnight so that they are ready for the early morning customers. The lemon juice and olive oil are added to taste, and the beans are eaten with accompaniments of choice.

2 cups (13 oz/400 g)
ful medamis beans

6 cups (48 fl oz/1.5 L) water

1/4 cup (1 1/2 oz/45 g) red lentils

salt

3 cloves garlic, pressed (crushed)

1/2 teaspoon ground cumin

To Serve:

finely chopped flat-leaf (Italian)
parsley

lemon wedges

freshly ground black pepper

1 quantity taratour bi tahini
(see page 52) (optional)

romaine (cos) lettuce leaves

sliced tomato and cucumber

6 hard-cooked (boiled) eggs
(optional)

pita bread

olive oil

Place beans in sieve and pick over to remove any extra matter. Rinse under cold running water. Place in bowl with 6 cups water, cover and soak overnight in refrigerator.

Transfer beans and their soaking water to large saucepan. Place lentils in sieve and pick over to remove any extra matter. Rinse under cold running water and add to saucepan with beans. Bring slowly to boil, cover and simmer over very low heat until beans are very tender, about 5 to 6 hours — do not stir while cooking or beans will stick to saucepan. Stir in salt to taste, garlic and cumin.

To serve, spoon hot beans into wide soup bowls or pasta plates and sprinkle with parsley. Serve with lemon wedges, black pepper, taratour bi tahini, lettuce, tomato, cucumber, eggs and bread placed in bowls and dishes, with a small jug of olive oil.

Ful Medamis Meze (Pureed Ful Beans Appetizer) Variation: Puree 2 cups cooked ful beans with their liquid. Let cool and add olive oil and lemon juice to taste. Swirl into shallow dish, drizzle with a little olive oil and sprinkle with parsley. Serve with pita bread.

Ful Medamis

AGINARES ME KOUKIA

ARTICHOKES WITH FAVA BEANS (GREECE)   SERVES 4 TO 6

When fava (broad) beans are in season in Greece, this is one way in which they are enjoyed. It is important to select young beans — if the shelled beans are black where they attach to the pod, they are too old, but can be used if the black spots are carefully removed with a paring knife. The stems of the artichokes are edible and can be included. Use the top 4 in (10 cm) of each stem, peeling off fibrous layer down to the white core. Halve and add to the bowl with the rest of the artichokes.

1 lemon, halved

6 globe artichokes

1/3 cup (3 fl oz/80 ml) olive oil

8 scallions (spring onions/
green onions), thinly sliced

3 cups (24 fl oz/750 ml) water

2 teaspoons sugar

4 tablespoons chopped fresh dill

1/4 cup (2 fl oz/60 ml)
fresh lemon juice

2 teaspoons salt

freshly ground black pepper

3 cups (12 oz/375 g) shelled fresh,
young fava (broad) beans

5 teaspoons cornstarch (cornflour)

extra chopped dill, to garnish

crusty bread, to serve

Add juice of half lemon to bowl of cold water. Cut stems off artichokes close to base. Discard 2 to 4 layers of outer leaves, depending on age of artichokes (remove less if young). Trim carefully around base where leaves were removed. Cut about 1 in (2.5 cm) from top of each artichoke, if desired. As you prepare artichokes, rub cut surfaces immediately with remaining lemon half. Cut each artichoke into quarters, remove choke and prickly leaves with spoon and discard. Drop artichokes into the bowl of water.

Heat oil in large saucepan. Add scallions and cook gently until soft, about 2 minutes. Add water, sugar, dill, lemon juice, salt, pepper to taste, prepared artichokes and fava beans. Bring to boil, cover and simmer until a leaf can be pulled off easily from artichokes and beans are tender, about 30 to 40 minutes.

Combine cornstarch with a little cold water in bowl and stir in cupful of cooking liquid. Gradually pour cornstarch mixture into saucepan, tilting saucepan back and forth to distribute it. Heat until slightly thickened and boil gently 2 minutes.

Remove artichokes with slotted spoon and arrange on serving platter. Pour over sauce and fava beans and sprinkle with extra dill. Serve warm or at room temperature with crusty bread.

FRITTEDDA

ARTICHOKES WITH FAVA BEANS AND PEAS (ITALY)   SERVES 6

This combination of fava (broad) beans and peas from Sicily is quite different from the Greek recipe (see page 200) and illustrates how flavorings can transform similar ingredients.

6 young globe artichokes

1 lemon

1/2 cup (4 fl oz/125 ml) olive oil

6 scallions (spring onions/
green onions), chopped

1 1/2 cups (12 fl oz/375 ml) water

1/4 teaspoon grated nutmeg

salt and freshly ground black pepper

2 lb (1 kg) fresh, young fava (broad)
beans, shelled

1 lb (500 g) green peas, shelled

2 teaspoons sugar

1 teaspoon chopped fresh mint

1 teaspoon white wine vinegar

Prepare artichokes as directed in recipe on page 200 and set aside in bowl of lemon water.

Warm oil in large saucepan. Add scallions, and cook gently 3 minutes. Drain artichokes, add to pan and cook gently 5 minutes, stirring often. Add water, nutmeg, and salt and pepper to taste, cover and simmer 20 minutes. Add beans and peas and simmer, covered, until vegetables are tender, about 20 minutes. Stir in sugar, mint and vinegar and simmer, uncovered, 5 minutes. Adjust seasoning. Serve hot or at room temperature.

TABOULEH

BURGHUL AND PARSLEY SALAD (LEBANON)   SERVES 6

The burghul (bulghur) should share the limelight in this salad with the parsley. Many cooks, however, prefer the emphasis on parsley, which must be flat-leaf (Italian). Chop fairly finely on a board, not in a food processor as it bruises the leaves. This quantity will serve six as a salad or twelve as an appetizer. Before tomatoes are added, the salad can be stored, covered, in the refrigerator for up to two days.

3/4 cup (4 oz/125 g) fine burghul
(steamed, cracked wheat)

6 scallions (spring onions/
green onions)

3 cups (6 oz/180 g) chopped flat-leaf
(Italian) parsley

3 tablespoons finely chopped
fresh mint

1/4 cup (2 fl oz/60 ml)
fresh lemon juice

1 1/2 teaspoons salt

freshly ground black pepper

2 large, firm ripe tomatoes,
peeled, seeded and diced

1/3 cup (3 fl oz/80 ml) olive oil

romaine (cos) lettuce leaves,
to serve (optional)

Place burghul in fine sieve, rinse under cold running water and tip into large bowl. Cover and let stand 20 minutes to swell and soften. Chop scallions finely, including tender parts of green leaves. Add to softened burghul and mix with wooden spoon, pressing mixture well to release flavor of scallions into burghul. Add parsley and mint and toss lightly. Beat lemon juice, salt and pepper to taste in jug, pour over salad and toss well.

Two hours before serving, add tomatoes and oil to salad. Toss lightly, cover and refrigerate until required. Spoon into lettuce leaf-lined serving dish, if desired.

Insalata di Borlotti e Radicchio

BORLOTTI BEAN AND RED CHICORY SALAD (ITALY)   SERVES 6

The speckled, fresh borlotti or cranberry beans are available in summer. Dried, they go by the same names; both fresh and dried are used in Italian cooking. When cooking fresh beans, I have found that they remain intact if the pan is not covered. If fresh beans are not available, soak 1 cup (6½ oz/200 g) dried beans in cold water overnight, drain, cover with fresh water and boil until tender, about 1½ hours — do not add salt during cooking. Drain and use as for the fresh beans. Or you can use 2 x 15 oz (425 g) cans borlotti beans, heated in their liquid, drained and rinsed briefly under hot water.

2 lb (1 kg) fresh borlotti (cranberry) beans in shell or 1 lb (500 g) shelled

salt

2 heads radicchio (red chicory)

½ cup (4 fl oz/125 ml) extra virgin olive oil

2 tablespoons red wine vinegar

freshly ground black pepper

Shell beans and place in saucepan with cold water to cover generously. Bring slowly to boil and boil gently until tender, about 15 to 20 minutes. Drain and add about ¾ teaspoon salt, toss and let stand until warm.

Wash and dry radicchio leaves in salad spinner or by wrapping in clean cloth. Reserve a few larger outer leaves and shred remaining leaves into ¼ in (5 mm) wide strips. Combine warm beans with radicchio strips.

Beat oil with vinegar, and salt and pepper to taste in jug. Pour over beans and radicchio and toss well. Line shallow serving dish with reserved radicchio leaves, pile salad on top and serve immediately.

Insalata Caprese

CAPRI SALAD OF TOMATO AND MOZZARELLA (ITALY)   SERVES 6

This is one of the most popular antipasti dishes, probably because of its simplicity. Choosing the right tomatoes is essential; if you can find them, select vine-ripened tomatoes, even though they are usually more expensive (see page 13 for more detail). Bocconcini is also preferable — it is fresh mozzarella in small balls, almost white and moist, and may also be known as buffalo mozzarella. Whichever form of cheese you choose, it should be traditional, i.e. round in shape, not in a rectangular block. Have the cheese well-chilled so it is easier to slice. At the stage where the tomato and cheese have been layered on a platter, the salad may be covered with plastic wrap and refrigerated for several hours. Bring to room temperature before finishing off, as this is when tomatoes taste their best.

5 medium-sized ripe tomatoes

8 oz (250 g) bocconcini cheese or small mozzarella cheese

3 tablespoons shredded fresh basil leaves

2 to 3 tablespoons extra virgin olive oil

salt and freshly ground black pepper

fresh basil sprigs, to garnish

Cut tomatoes into ¼ in (5 mm) slices, discarding ends. Cut cheese into slices of similar thickness.

Arrange alternate slices of tomato and cheese, beginning around edge of serving platter, then fill middle. Just before serving, sprinkle over basil and drizzle with oil. Season lightly with salt and grind over pepper. Garnish with fresh basil sprigs and serve at room temperature

Insalata di Borlotti e Radicchio

SHALADA BORTOKAL BIL JAZAR

ORANGE SALAD WITH CARROT (MOROCCO)   SERVES 6

Moroccan orange salads are refreshing and palate-cleansing. They go well with meat and poultry dishes, although in Morocco salads are served as an appetizer and left on the table to be picked at during the remainder of the meal.

3 sweet oranges
2 medium carrots, shredded
orange juice
2 tablespoons lemon juice
3 teaspoons superfine (caster) sugar
2 tablespoons olive oil
salt and freshly ground black pepper
fresh coriander leaves (cilantro) or flat-leaf (Italian) parsley, to garnish
1 tablespoon orange flower water
ground cinnamon

Peel oranges with serrated knife, removing all traces of white pith and membrane from outside of oranges. Segment by cutting between visible membranes, catching juices in bowl. Squeeze any remains of oranges over juice bowl and reserve juice. Keep aside a quarter of orange segments and place remainder in a bowl with the carrots.

Make up 3 tablespoons orange juice using reserved juice and adding freshly squeezed orange as needed. Combine orange juice, lemon juice and sugar in small bowl, and stir until sugar is dissolved. Beat in oil and salt and pepper to taste. Pour over carrots and oranges, toss lightly, cover and chill in refrigerator along with reserved segments.

When ready to serve, transfer to shallow platter and garnish with reserved orange segments and coriander leaves or parsley. Sprinkle with orange flower water and dust lightly with cinnamon.

Orange and Radish Salad Variation: Replace carrots with 15 medium-sized round, red radishes sliced very thinly. Toss together and place in shallow bowl lined with romaine (cos) lettuce leaves.

SHALADA BORTOKAL WA'L'ZAITUN

ORANGE AND OLIVE SALAD (MOROCCO, TUNISIA)   SERVES 6

4 sweet oranges
1 purple onion
3/4 cup (4 oz/125 g) black olives, rinsed and drained
1/4 cup (2 fl oz/60 ml) olive oil
1/8 teaspoon cayenne pepper
1 teaspoon superfine (caster) sugar
1/4 preserved lemon (see page 29) (optional)
fresh coriander leaves (cilantro), to garnish

Peel oranges with serated knife, removing all traces of white pith and outer membrane. Cut into 1/4 in (5 mm) slices on plate to retain juices. Arrange orange slices on shallow serving platter. Slice onion thinly and separate slices into rings. Scatter onion rings and olives over oranges. Pour orange juice from plate into small bowl. Beat in oil, cayenne pepper and sugar and pour over salad.

Discard pulp from preserved lemon, rinse peel and cut into thin strips. Scatter over salad and garnish with coriander leaves.

SALATA THERINI

SUMMER SALAD (GREECE)   SERVES 6

If peeled tomatoes are desired for the salad, place tomatoes in a bowl and pour boiling water over. Leave for 20 seconds, drain and peel.

4 medium tomatoes

2 slender, young green cucumbers (see page 14)

2 green bell peppers (capsicums)

1 medium purple onion, sliced

4 oz (125 g) feta cheese, diced

12 to 18 black olives

Dressing:

1/2 cup (4 fl oz/125 ml) olive oil

2 tablespoons white wine vinegar

salt and freshly ground black pepper

Cut tomatoes into wedges. Wash cucumbers and only peel if necessary. Trim ends, quarter lengthwise and cut into 1/2 in (1 cm) chunks. Discard core, seed and white membrane from bell peppers. Halve and cut into thick strips. Separate onion slices into rings.

Place prepared ingredients in serving bowl, sprinkle with feta cheese and olives. Beat dressing ingredients lightly together in jug and pour over salad just before serving.

INSALATA DI FINNOCHIO

FENNEL SALAD (ITALY)   SERVES 6

Fennel bulbs are a winter vegetable, and are usually braised to accompany roast pork or added to tomato sauce. However they are delicious served raw as a salad. Serve this recipe as a separate course and try it with 1/2 cup chopped new-season walnuts instead of prosciutto and parmesan. The simplest way to serve the fennel is to simply dress it with olive oil, salt and pepper.

3 bulbs fennel

2 tablespoons lemon juice

salt and freshly ground black pepper

1/2 cup (4 fl oz/125 ml) extra virgin olive oil

6 oz (180 g) prosciutto crudo, sliced paper-thin

shaved parmesan cheese

2 tablespoons finely chopped parsley

Wash fennel bulbs and remove 2 outer leaves from each bulb. Trim tops and bases and halve each bulb lengthwise. Place flat side of halved fennel on board and slice very thinly lengthwise using sharp knife. Place fennel into bowl and add lemon juice, and salt and pepper to taste. Add oil and toss well to coat.

Spread fennel in shallow serving dish. Curl slices of prosciutto softly in middle of fennel. Scatter shaved parmesan on top and sprinkle with parsley.

Insalata di Finnocchio e Olive Variation: Instead of prosciutto and parmesan, sprinkle salad with finely sliced red and green bell pepper (capsicum) and add a handful of black olives.

Shalada bil Matesha Basila w'l'Hamad m'Rakad

TOMATO, ONION AND PRESERVED LEMON SALAD (MOROCCO)   SERVES 6

Preserved lemons are essential for this salad and cannot be substituted. You can make your own (see page 29) or purchase them from a gourmet delicatessen or Middle Eastern market.

2 lb (1 kg) firm ripe tomatoes, peeled and seeded

1 small purple onion

1/2 preserved lemon (see page 29)

1/3 cup (3 fl oz/80 ml) olive oil

1 tablespoon lemon juice

1 clove garlic, pressed (crushed)

2 tablespoons chopped flat-leaf (Italian) parsley

2 tablespoons chopped fresh coriander leaves (cilantro)

1/4 teaspoon ground cumin

1/4 teaspoon paprika

salt and freshly ground black pepper

Cut tomatoes into small cubes. Slice onion as thinly as possible and separate into rings. Place tomatoes and onion rings in bowl.

Discard pulp from preserved lemon and rinse peel well. Dry with paper towels, and cut into fine strips crosswise. Add to tomatoes and onion.

Beat olive oil, lemon juice, garlic, herbs, spices, and salt and pepper to taste in jug. Pour over salad, toss lightly, cover and let stand 30 minutes. Serve at room temperature.

Slata Mechouia

ROASTED TOMATO AND PEPPER SALAD (TUNISIA)   SERVES 6

Vegetables roasted on a fire are often cut up or pounded and mixed into a salad for serving as an appetizer. This version, however, is excellent served with broiled (grilled) or barbecued meats, poultry or fish. If you do not like food to be too spicy, omit the chili peppers and add a pinch of cayenne pepper.

6 large, firm red tomatoes

2 green bell peppers (capsicums)

2 red bell peppers (capsicums)

2 fresh, hot red or green chili peppers

2 small brown onions, whole and unpeeled

4 tablespoons olive oil

2 cloves garlic, pressed (crushed)

salt and freshly ground pepper

1 tablespoon finely chopped flat-leaf (Italian) parsley

black olives, to serve

Preheat oven to 425–450°F (220–230°C/Gas 7). Place tomatoes, bell peppers and onions on baking sheet and roast in oven 15 minutes. Turn, add chili peppers and roast 15 minutes more. Remove from oven, place bell peppers in plastic bag, close and let steam 15 minutes. Peel tomatoes and cut into small pieces, draining juice and loose seeds. Halve chili peppers, remove seeds and scrape flesh from skin. Peel and slice onions. When peppers are steamed, peel, halve and remove seeds and membranes. Cut into small squares.

Beat chili pulp, oil and garlic in bowl. Add roasted vegetables and salt and pepper to taste, and mix lightly. Cool to room temperature. Transfer to shallow serving dish, sprinkle with parsley and arrange olives around edge or scatter over top.

Shalada bil Matesha Basila w'l'Hamad m'Rakad

FATTOUSH

TOASTED BREAD SALAD (LEBANON/SYRIA)   SERVES 6

Khoubiz or khobz is the proper name for the flat breads of most of the Arab world, but in the Western kitchen we have adopted them under the name of pita breads, from the Turkish "pide". This salad makes excellent use of stale pita bread, but fresh bread may be used. Purslane (portulaca), while it is essential to the character of the salad, can be substituted with the similar, peppery flavor of watercress if unavailable.

1 large or 2 small pita breads

8 leaves romaine (cos) lettuce

1 small green (Lebanese) cucumber or 1/2 seedless hot-house cucumber

1 cup (11/2 oz/45 g) purslane (portulaca) leaves

2 medium-sized ripe tomatoes, diced

1 green bell pepper (capsicum), seeded and chopped

4 scallions (spring onions/ green onions), chopped

1 cup (2 oz/60 g) chopped flat-leaf (Italian) parsley, packed

3 tablespoons chopped fresh mint

Dressing:

1 clove garlic

1 teaspoon salt

1/2 cup (4 fl oz/125 ml) fresh lemon juice

1/2 cup (4 fl oz/125 ml) extra virgin olive oil

freshly ground black pepper

Toast pita bread under hot broiler (grill) until golden brown, about 1 minute each side. Break into small pieces or cut into small squares using kitchen shears.

Wash lettuce and dry in a salad spinner or roll in a clean cloth. Tear into small pieces. Wash cucumber, quarter lengthwise and cut into chunks. Pick green tender leaves from stalks and leafy tips of purslane.

For dressing: Crush garlic onto plate and mix with salt to smooth paste using tip of knife. Place in bowl with remaining dressing ingredients and beat well with fork.

Combine all salad ingredients in large serving bowl. Just before serving, pour over dressing and toss well.

grapes

LÉGUMES CHAUDS A L'AÏOLI

HOT BEANS AND VEGETABLES WITH AIOLI (FRANCE) SERVES 6

A delicious combination from Provence, ideal for an informal lunch. Use canned beans for convenience, or cook dried beans from scratch, but you will have to cook them separately as the cooking times vary and flavors should not be allowed to mingle. To eat the dish, each diner takes a portion of vegetables and blends in aioli to taste. The eggs are shelled at the table. Serve with plenty of crusty bread and a chilled white wine for a complete meal.

6 globe artichokes

1 lemon, halved

salt

3 small beets (beetroot)

8 oz (250 g) young green beans

8 oz (250 g) baby carrots, scraped

15 oz (425 g) can chickpeas (garbanzos), undrained

15 oz (425 g) can lima (butter) beans, undrained

15 oz (425 g) can red kidney beans, drained

6 to 12 hard-cooked (boiled) eggs, still warm

1 quantity aioli (see page 36)

crusty bread, to serve

Discard 3 to 4 layers of leaves from artichokes, cut off stems and trim carefully around bases. Cut 1 in (2.5 cm) from tops. Halve, remove chokes with spoon and rub with lemon. Cook in saucepan of boiling, salted water until tender, about 20 minutes. Drain and set aside.

Meanwhile, scrub beets and cook in saucepan of boiling, salted water until tender, about 30 minutes. Peel and keep warm.

Top and tail green beans, string only if necessary and leave whole. Cook green beans and carrots in saucepan of boiling salted water until just tender, about 5 minutes. Drain in colander and rinse briefly under cold running water to arrest cooking. Place in deep, oval dish, add artichokes and keep warm.

Place chickpeas and lima beans with their liquid in saucepan. Add kidney beans and heat until boiling. Drain, add to vegetables in dish and toss lightly.

Cut beets into quarters and arrange around edge of dish. Pile hot unshelled eggs in another bowl. Spoon aioli into separate bowl. Serve with crusty bread.

SPAGHETTI ALLA CARBONARA

SPAGHETTI WITH PANCETTA AND EGGS (ITALY)   SERVES 4 TO 6

Speed is necessary in the final assembly of this dish — while the water comes to the boil and the pasta is cooking, prepare the other ingredients. Unlike normal bacon, green bacon is unsmoked. If you cannot obtain it or pancetta, use smoked bacon but boil in water 2 minutes, then drain and dry before use.

1 lb (500 g) spaghetti

8 oz (250 g) pancetta or green bacon, cut in thick slices

2 tablespoons olive oil

2 tablespoons butter

2 cloves garlic, bruised

3 large eggs

2 tablespoons chopped flat-leaf (Italian) parsley

1/2 cup (2 oz/60 g) grated parmesan cheese

freshly ground black pepper

extra grated parmesan cheese, to serve

Add pasta to large saucepan of lightly salted boiling water and boil uncovered until tender (al dente).

Meanwhile, cut pancetta into narrow strips, less than 1/4 in (5 mm) wide. Heat oil and butter in frying pan. Add garlic and cook until lightly browned; discard. Add pancetta to oil in pan and cook over medium heat until lightly browned and fat melts.

Beat eggs lightly in bowl in which spaghetti is to be served. Add parsley, parmesan, and pepper to taste, stir well and set aside. When spaghetti is cooked, drain and add immediately to egg mixture. Toss until well-coated — the heat of the pasta cooks the egg. Add pancetta and oil from pan and toss well. Serve immediately with parmesan.

FETTUCCINE CON PROSCIUTTO E RUCOLA

FETTUCCINE WITH PROSCIUTTO AND ARUGULA (ITALY)   SERVES 4

Arugula is a slightly bitter green with a peppery flavor. It is often used in salads but is excellent cooked this way. Buy fresh pasta or make your own (see page 30) and cut into 1/2 inch (5 mm) wide strips.

8 oz (250 g) arugula (rocket)

1/2 cup (4 fl oz/125 ml) extra virgin olive oil

1 medium onion, finely chopped

4 oz (125 g) prosciutto crudo, sliced 1/4 in (5 mm) thick then cut into matchstick strips

2 cloves garlic, finely chopped

1/4 cup (2 fl oz/60 ml) dry white wine

salt and freshly ground black pepper

1 lb (500 g) fresh fettuccine

grated parmesan cheese, to serve (optional)

Trim stalk ends of arugola and wash leaves well. Spin dry in salad spinner or wrap in clean cloth and set aside to dry.

Warm oil in large frying pan. Add onion and cook gently until transparent, about 10 minutes. Add prosciutto and garlic and cook, stirring, 1 to 2 minutes until prosciutto turns pink. Add wine and salt and pepper to taste and simmer until most of wine has evaporated. Add arugula and cook until just wilted, tossing often.

Meanwhile, add pasta to large saucepan of lightly salted boiling water and boil uncovered until just tender (al dente). Drain and transfer to warm bowl. Add arugula mixture and toss well. Serve immediately. Parmesan is not needed, but may be sprinkled over pasta, if desired.

Fettuccine con Prosciutto e Rucola

210

Pansotti in Salsa di Noci

PANSOTTI WITH WALNUT SAUCE (ITALY)   SERVES 6

A specialty of the Italian Riviera, pansotti is the Ligurian version of ravioli. They can be triangular, but I like to make them in largish squares as it is much quicker. For the sauce, choose fresh, light-skinned walnuts — stale or dark-skinned nuts make the sauce bitter. Purists blanch and skin the nuts, but this is time-consuming, and if they are sweet, there is no need to do so. This sauce is excellent served over plain pasta such as fettuccine or pappardelle. For the mixed greens, use spinach and two or three of the following: chard (silverbeet) leaves with white ribs and stems removed; escarole (endive) with coarse stems removed; dandelion leaves (do not use if in flower); and Belgian endive (witloof). Wash them well, shake off excess moisture, chop roughly and pack well into the cup measure if scales are not available.

1 quantity pasta all'uovo, containing milk (see page 30)

grated parmesan or pecorino cheese, to serve

Herb Filling:

3 cups (8 oz/250 g) chopped mixed greens (see above)

3 tablespoons chopped parlsey or chervil

1 tablespoon chopped fresh marjoram or oregano

2 scallions (spring onions/green onions), finely chopped

1/2 cup (4 oz/125 g) ricotta cheese

3 tablespoons grated parmesan or pecorino cheese

1/4 cup (1/2 oz/15 g) soft white breadcrumbs

salt and freshly ground black pepper

Walnut Sauce:

1 1/4 cups (4 oz/125 g) walnut pieces

1/3 cup (1 1/2 oz/45 g) pine nuts, toasted

1/4 cup (1/2 oz/15 g) soft white breadcrumbs

2 tablespoons water

1 small clove garlic, chopped

1/2 cup (4 oz/125 g) ricotta cheese

2 tablespoons grated parmesan cheese

1/2 cup (4 fl oz/125 ml) extra virgin olive oil

salt, to taste

Make pasta according to directions. Wrap in plastic wrap and set aside.

For herb filling: Place greens in saucepan with 3 tablespoons water and simmer until tender, stirring occasionally. Transfer to sieve and press out as much moisture as possible with back of wooden spoon. Finely chop greens, herbs and scallions in food processor. Add cheeses, breadcrumbs, and salt and pepper to taste and process until combined.

Roll out half the pasta dough on floured surface until very thin. Cut in half and place heaping teaspoons of herb filling evenly over one half, spacing mounds 2 in (5 cm) apart. If the pasta seems dry after placing the filling on top, brush between the mounds of filling with water. Cover with other half of pasta and press well around each mound to seal. Cut into 2 in (5 cm) squares with fluted pastry wheel or knife. Lift onto clean cloth. Repeat with remaining pasta and filling. (If using pasta machine, pass dough through machine starting on widest setting and finishing on second narrowest, rolling and filling 2 strips at a time so pasta is moist as possible for a good seal.) Set aside, uncovered, 30 minutes. If not to be cooked within 30 minutes, cover with a clean cloth — they must be cooked within 2 hours.

For walnut sauce: Place all ingredients in food processor and process to thick sauce, adding a little more olive oil if too thick. Transfer to bowl.

Bring large saucepan salted water to boil. Add pansotti, about 10 at a time, and boil until just tender, about 8 minutes. Remove with slotted spoon or wire skimmer and place in colander. When last batch is cooked, return all pansotti to saucepan and bring to boil. Drain immediately in colander.

Divide pansotti onto warmed plates and top each serve immediately with 2 heaping tablespoons walnut sauce. Serve remaining sauce at table with cheese.

Lasagne Verde al Salsa di Noci

LARGE HERB PASTA WITH WALNUT SAUCE (ITALY)   SERVES 4

As the pansotti (see page 212) are time-consuming to prepare, this is a modern presentation of fresh herb pasta, simply served with the delicious walnut sauce. The herb flavors of the pansotti are incorporated in the pasta dough itself. If rolling the pasta by hand, wrap in plastic wrap and let stand 30 minutes — this is not necessary if using a pasta machine. See page 24 for more details on making pasta. Cooking and serving up the lasagne is an exercise in timing, so quantities are given for four first-course servings.

Pasta Verde:

8 spinach leaves

1 tablespoon chopped flat-leaf (Italian) parsley

3 fresh basil leaves, chopped

1 teaspoon chopped fresh oregano or marjoram

1 tablespoon chopped fresh chives

1 cup (5 oz/150 g) all-purpose (plain) flour, approximately

2 small eggs (about 1 1/2 oz/50 g each)

1 teaspoon olive oil

To Serve:

1 quantity salsa di noci (walnut sauce) (see page 212)

shaved parmesan cheese

2 tablespoons combined finely chopped fresh basil, parsley and chives

Wash spinach leaves but do not dry. Chop coarsely. Place in saucepan with parsley, basil, oregano and chives. Heat, tossing often, until cooked and liquid evaporates from spinach. Transfer to sieve and press out excess moisture with back of wooden spoon.

Place flour in food processor with steel blade fitted. Add spinach mixture and eggs and process until herbs are finely chopped and well blended. Add extra flour if necessary to form soft dough — amount depends on moisture in herb mixture. Transfer to lightly floured surface and knead gently until smooth. Wrap in plastic wrap and let stand 30 minutes.

Roll pasta out on floured surface until paper-thin, or pass through pasta machine starting at widest setting, and finishing on second narrowest setting. Cut into 4 in (10 cm) squares.

Have large bowl of cold water at the ready. Bring very large saucepan salted water to boil, adding oil. Cook pasta, about 6 sheets at a time until they rise to the surface. Cook 30 seconds more, then remove with large skimmer and place in cold water. When all pasta is cooked, drain in colander and return to boiling water in saucepan. When water returns to the boil, check pasta is cooked and boil a little longer if necessary. Remove pan from heat and add 1 cup cold water. Remove pasta with large skimmer, about 6 sheets at a time, and place directly onto warm serving plates in a rough pile.

Thin walnut sauce if necessary with a little pasta water and place large spoonful on each serving. Add shaved parmesan and sprinkle with herbs. Serve immediately with remaining sauce in separate bowl.

CONCHIGLIE MARINARA BIANCO

SHELL PASTA WITH WHITE SEAFOOD SAUCE (ITALY)   SERVES 4

8 oz (250 g) uncooked shrimp (prawns), peeled and deveined

4 oz (125 g) shelled sea scallops

6 oz (180 g) small squid (calamari), cleaned (see page 20)

8 mussels in their shells, cleaned (see page 20)

12 oz (375 g) conchiglie rigate (medium-sized ridged shell pasta)

3 teaspoons olive oil

2 tablespoons butter

8 oz (250 g) boneless white-fleshed fish fillets, cut into 1 in (2.5 cm) pieces

1/4 cup (2 fl oz/60 ml) dry white wine

1 cup (8 fl oz/250 ml) whipping cream

1 tablespoon chopped flat-leaf (Italian) parsley

Rinse shrimp and pat dry. Remove veins from scallops but retain coral (roe) if present. Clean squid, cut bodies into rings, leave tentacles. Place mussels in dry saucepan, cover and cook over medium heat until they open, about 5 minutes; discard any that do not open. Let cool. Drain and reserve cooking liquid. Set mussels and liquid aside.

Add pasta to large saucepan of lightly salted boiling water and boil, uncovered, until tender (al dente).

Meanwhile, heat large frying pan over medium-high heat. Add oil and butter and heat until sizzling, but not browned. Add shrimp and fish, and cook 2 minutes, stirring often. Add scallops and squid and fry until just cooked, about 2 to 3 minutes. Remove seafood to dish. Add wine, cream, parsley and mussel liquid to pan and boil vigorously until lightly thickened, about 2 to 3 minutes. Return seafood to sauce with mussels and heat through gently without boiling.

Drain pasta and divide into plates. Spoon over seafood sauce, arrange 2 mussels in shells on top of each. Serve immediately.

SPAGETTI BIZ-ZALZA TAL-BRUNGIEL

SPAGHETTI WITH EGGPLANT SAUCE (MALTA)   SERVES 6

1 lb (500 g) oval eggplants (aubergines)

salt

4 tablespoons olive oil

1 medium onion, finely chopped

2 cloves garlic, pressed (crushed)

15 oz (425 g) can tomatoes, chopped but undrained

2 tablespoons tomato paste

2 tablespoons finely chopped parsley

1 bay leaf

1/2 cup (4 fl oz/125 ml) water

1 teaspoon sugar

salt and freshly ground black pepper

1 lb (500 g) spaghetti

grated parmesan cheese

Trim stems from eggplant. Cut into 3/4 in (2 cm) cubes. Place in colander, sprinkle well with salt and let stand 30 minutes to dégorge juices. Rinse and pat dry with cloth.

Heat 3 tablespoons oil in large frying pan with lid to fit. Add eggplant and fry over high heat until lightly browned, tossing often. Remove with slotted spoon. Reduce heat, add remaining oil and onion to pan and cook gently until transparent, about 10 minutes. Add garlic and cook 1 minute. Stir in tomatoes with their liquid, tomato paste, parsley, bay leaf, water, sugar, eggplant and salt and pepper to taste. Cover and simmer gently over low heat 30 minutes.

Meanwhile, cook spaghetti in boiling, salted water until al dente. Drain and transfer to large warm bowl. Discard bay leaf from sauce. Toss half the sauce and 2 to 3 tablespoons parmesan through pasta. Divide among plates. Serve with more sauce spooned over, accompanied by extra parmesan.

Conchiglie Marinara Bianco

CANNELLONIS À LA CORSE AUX HERBES ET BROCCIO

CORSICAN CANNELLONI WITH HERBS AND FRESH CHEESE (FRANCE)   SERVES 6

Corsican cuisine is redolent with the many wild herbs that grow in the island's mountainous terrain. Much of Corsican cooking is similar to Italian, and this dish is a case in point. In fact, I "borrowed" the herb pasta for the cannelloni from the lasagne verde al salsa di noci (see page 213), as it is similar to the one used in Corsica. Broccio, a fresh farmhouse sheep's milk cheese, is traditionally used but ricotta is a suitable substitute, as is farmer cheese or the Greek mizithra, both made from whole milk.

1 quantity pasta verde using herbs
(see page 213)

Filling:

1 lb (500 g) fresh spinach

2 cups (1 lb/500 g) ricotta cheese

1 egg

1 egg yolk

2 tablespoons chopped
mixed fresh herbs
(e.g. flat-leaf parsley, basil, mint,
marjoram, oregano, savory, chives)

2 tablespoons grated parmesan
cheese

salt and freshly ground black pepper

Sauce:

3 tablespoons olive oil

1 medium onion, finely chopped

3 cloves garlic, pressed (crushed)

2 x 15 oz (425 g) cans tomatoes,
chopped but undrained

1 tablespoon chopped flat-leaf
(Italian) parsley

2 teaspoons chopped fresh
marjoram

salt and freshly ground black pepper

To Serve:

grated parmesan cheese

Make and cook pasta as directed on page 213. A few seconds after sheets rise to the surface, remove with skimmer to bowl of cold water. Lift out and spread pasta on large, slightly moist cloth, and cover with another cloth until required.

For filling: Trim roots from spinach and discard any damaged stems and leaves. Wash well in several changes of water, drain and chop roughly, including stems. Place in large saucepan, cover and heat until wilted, tossing occasionally with fork. Drain in colander, pressing well with back of wooden spoon to extract as much moisture as possible. Chop finely, and place on paper towels to drain thoroughly and cool. Mash ricotta in bowl. Add spinach and remaining filling ingredients and mix thoroughly. Season to taste with salt and pepper. Set aside.

For sauce: Warm oil in saucepan. Add onion and cook gently until transparent, about 10 minutes. Add garlic and cook several seconds. Add tomatoes with their liquid, herbs, and salt and pepper to taste. Bring to boil, partly cover and simmer until thick, 30 minutes. Puree in food processor or in pan with hand-held blender.

Preheat oven to 325–350°F (160–180°C/Gas 3). Spread about 1 cup sauce in base of shallow oven-proof dish. Place 2 heaping tablespoons filling along one edge of a pasta sheet and roll up. Place rolls, with edge facing down, onto sauce in dish. Repeat with remaining pasta, positioning rolls close together in a single layer. Spoon remaining sauce over and bake 30 minutes.

Serve directly from dish with extra grated parmesan.

Spaghetti Aglio e Olio

SPAGHETTI WITH GARLIC AND OIL (ITALY)   SERVES 4 TO 6

This has to be one of the easiest pasta dishes you can make — it uses a minimum of ingredients. The breadcrumbs need not be used, but as the dish is served without cheese, they do add interest to the pasta; fried or toasted breadcrumbs are often used in southern Italy and Sicily in place of cheese. Chilies can be omitted, but as this dish is regarded as a hangover cure, their inclusion is a must for this purpose — or if you simply like chili! The exact quantity depends on the size of the chilies and your own taste.

1 cup (2 oz/60 g) coarse soft white breadcrumbs

3 tablespoons olive oil

1 lb (500 g) spaghetti

1 to 2 fresh hot red chilies (optional)

6 cloves garlic

1/2 cup (4 fl oz/125 ml) extra virgin olive oil

3 tablespoons finely chopped parsley

freshly ground black pepper (optional)

Toss breadcrumbs with olive oil in heavy frying pan over medium heat and cook until crisp and golden brown, stirring often. Remove to a bowl and set aside. Clean pan.

Cook spaghetti in large saucepan of lightly salted boiling water until just tender (al dente). Meanwhile, halve chilies and remove seeds and white membranes. Chop finely. Peel garlic and slice thinly.

When spaghetti is cooked, drain and return to pan. Toss with 2 tablespoons extra virgin olive oil, cover and set aside (so it is ready to use immediately after next step).

Heat remaining extra virgin olive oil in cleaned frying pan. Add garlic and chili and cook gently until garlic is just golden — do not overcook. Pour immediately into pan of spaghetti. Add parsley and freshly ground pepper (if no chili is used). Toss well, transfer to warm bowl and serve immediately with the bowl of toasted breadcrumbs.

Pennette all'Arrabbiata

PENNETTE WITH TOMATO CHILI SAUCE (ITALY)   SERVES 4 TO 6

1/4 cup (2 fl oz/60 ml) olive oil

2 onions, chopped

1 to 2 teaspoons dried hot chili flakes or crushed dried chilies

3 cloves garlic, finely chopped

2 lb (1 kg) ripe tomatoes, peeled, seeded and chopped

1 tablespoon tomato paste

1 teaspoon sugar

1 tablespoon chopped flat-leaf (Italian) parsley

salt and freshly ground black pepper

1 lb (500 g) pennette or penne

grated parmesan cheese, to serve

Warm oil in saucepan. Add onions and chili to taste and cook gently until onion is transparent, about 10 minutes. Add garlic and cook several seconds. Stir in tomatoes, tomato paste, sugar, parsley, and salt and pepper to taste. Cover and simmer until tomatoes are soft and sauce fairly thick, about 10 minutes, stirring occasionally. Break up tomatoes with wooden spoon.

Add pasta to large saucepan of lightly salted boiling water and boil uncovered until just tender (al dente). Drain, reserving a little cooking water. Transfer pasta to warm serving dish. Add sauce and toss well. If sauce is too thick to coat pasta, add a little pasta water to bowl and toss again. Serve with parmesan.

BULGAR PILAVI

BURGHUL PILAF (TURKEY)   SERVES 6

In Cyprus, burghul or bulgar is called pourgouri, and used for making a plain pilaf. This Turkish recipe is more flavorful, and while meat or chicken stock is traditional, water may be used for vegetarian cooking.

1 long green sweet pepper or bell pepper (capsicum)

1 large ripe tomato, peeled

2 oz (60 g) butter

1 medium onion, finely chopped

2 cups (12 oz/375 g) coarse burghul (steamed cracked wheat)

3 cups (24 fl oz/750 ml) chicken stock (see page 31) or water

1 tablespoon chopped fresh mint

salt and freshly ground black pepper

plain (natural) yogurt, to serve

Seed and chop pepper and tomato.

Melt butter in deep frying pan. Add onion and cook gently until transparent, about 10 minutes, stirring often. Add pepper and cook 2 to 3 minutes. Add burghul and cook 4 minutes, stirring often. Add tomato, stock, mint, and salt and black pepper to taste and bring to boil. Stir, then reduce heat, cover and simmer gently until liquid is absorbed, about 20 minutes. Remove lid, place two paper towels over rim of pan, replace lid and let stand 10 minutes.

Fluff up burghul mixture with fork. Serve with bowl of yogurt, if desired.

FIDEUA

NOODLE AND SEAFOOD PAELLA (SPAIN)   SERVES 6

Pasta does feature in Spanish cuisine; fideos are fine noodles coiled into "nests". In this Valencian dish, they are normally cooked in the sauce but, if using pasta other than fideo, it is better to cook it separately.

1 lb (500 g) firm white-fleshed fish fillets, skin removed

1 lb (500 g) medium uncooked shrimp (prawns)

24 small mussels, cleaned (see page 20)

1 lb (500 g) fideo, capelli d'angelo or vermicelli noodles

1/2 cup (4 fl oz/125 ml) olive oil

2 cloves garlic, pressed (crushed)

1 1/2 teaspoons paprika

1/8 teaspoon cayenne pepper

2 large ripe tomatoes, peeled and chopped

pinch of saffron threads

1 1/2 cups (12 fl oz/375 ml) basic fish stock (see page 31)

salt and freshly ground black pepper

Cut fish into 1 1/2 in (4 cm) pieces. Peel and devein shrimp, leaving 6 unpeeled. Clean mussels as directed. Lightly crumble noodles into a large saucepan of lightly salted boiling water, stir well and return to boil. Boil 3 minutes. Drain and rinse under cold running water. Set aside in colander.

Heat oil in paella pan, large frying pan or wok. Add all shrimp and cook until pink, about 5 minutes, stirring often. Remove with slotted spoon. Add fish and cook briefly, turning once. Add garlic and cook several seconds. Add paprika, cayenne pepper, tomatoes, saffron and fish stock and bring to boil over medium heat. Add salt and pepper to taste, stir well, and simmer 10 minutes. Add mussels and simmer until they open, about 4 to 5 minutes, stirring often; discard any that do not open. Stir in peeled shrimp and noodles and heat through. Smooth surface of mixture until flat and place under hot broiler (grill) just until light brown crust forms on noodles. During last stages of browning, arrange unpeeled shrimp on top.

Bulgar Pilavi

PAELLA MARINERA

SEAFOOD PAELLA (SPAIN)   SERVES 6

8 oz (250 g) shelled uncooked
shrimp (prawns)

8 oz (250 g) small squid (calamari),
cleaned (see page 20)

12 mussels, cleaned (see page 20)

1 lb (500 g) firm white-fleshed
fish fillets

1/2 cup (4 fl oz/125 ml) olive oil

1 large onion, finely chopped

2 cloves garlic, pressed (crushed)

1 green bell pepper (capsicum),
cut into strips

2 large ripe tomatoes,
peeled, seeded and chopped

3 cups (1 lb 5 oz/630 g) Valencia or
arborio rice

pinch saffron threads, crumbled

6 cups (48 fl oz/1.5 L)
basic fish stock (see page 31)

salt and ground black pepper

6 unshelled cooked shrimp
(prawns), to garnish

Preheat oven to 325–350°F (160–180°C/Gas 3). If shrimp are large, cut in half. Cut squid into rings; leave tentacles joined together and trim feelers. Clean mussels. Remove skin from fish and cut into 3/4 in (2 cm) pieces.

Heat oil in paella pan or large, flame-proof casserole dish. Add onion and cook gently until transparent, about 10 minutes. Add garlic and cook 1 minute. Add bell pepper and tomatoes, and cook over medium heat 5 minutes. Stir in rice, saffron, half the stock and salt and pepper to taste, and bring to boil. Reduce heat and cook until liquid is absorbed, about 8 minutes, stirring occasionally.

Remove pan from heat and stir in remaining stock. Press prepared seafood into rice mixture, placing mussels on top. Loosely cover pan with foil and bake until liquid is absorbed and seafood is cooked, about 20 minutes. Discard any mussels that have not opened. Remove foil, cover with cloth, and let stand 10 minutes. Gently fluff rice with fork; do not disturb mussels. Garnish with cooked shrimp and serve directly from pan.

SESKOULORIZO

CHARD PILAF (CYPRUS)   SERVES 6

The cooking of Cyprus has both Greek Cypriot and Turkish Cypriot influences, and a touch of Lebanese, and the use of yogurt to accompany this dish is more Turkish and Lebanese than Greek. Serve the pilaf as a light meal, or as an accompaniment to plainly cooked fish, meat or chicken.

8 to 10 chard (silverbeet) leaves

11/2 cups (11 oz/330 g)
long-grain rice

1/3 cup (3 fl oz/80 ml) olive oil

1 large onion, chopped

2 large ripe tomatoes,
peeled and chopped

2 tablespoons chopped parsley

3 cups (24 fl oz/750 ml) water

salt and freshly ground black pepper

plain (natural) yogurt, to serve

crusty bread, to serve

Cut white ribs and stems from chard; discard or store in refrigerator for later use (see page 188). Wash leaves well and tear into large pieces. Rinse rice in sieve until water runs clear; drain.

Warm oil in large, heavy saucepan. Add onion and cook gently until transparent, about 10 minutes. Add rice, tomatoes, parsley, water, and salt and pepper to taste and bring to boil. Stir in chard, cover tightly and cook gently over low heat until rice is just tender, about 15 minutes. Remove from heat and let stand, covered, 5 minutes. Fluff up with fork and serve with yogurt and bread.

RISOTTO DI SCAMPI

RISOTTO WITH SCAMPI (ITALY)   SERVES 6

In Venice, they make all kinds of risotto but are particularly fond of seafood risotto. Scampi are highly favored. If you cannot obtain fresh scampi, then use uncooked whole shrimp (prawns) in their place. If you don't want to mold the rice as specified in this recipe, simply add all the tomato puree to the risotto, and mix the sautéed scampi through the rice with a fork at the end of cooking time. Let stand as directed before serving.

2 lb (1 kg) whole uncooked scampi
(Dublin Bay prawns)
1/2 cup (4 fl oz/125 ml)
dry white wine
1 1/2 teaspoons salt
2 tablespoons olive oil
2 oz (60 g) butter
1 onion, finely chopped
1 clove garlic, finely chopped
2 cups (14 oz/420 g) arborio rice
15 oz (425 g) can tomatoes, pureed
1 bay leaf, broken into small pieces
freshly ground black pepper

Rinse scampi and remove heads and shells. Set scampi aside. Place heads and shells in saucepan with white wine and water to cover, add salt and boil 10 minutes. Strain through sieve into bowl, pressing heads and shells to remove moisture. Discard these, clean pan and measure liquid back into it. Add water to make up 4 cups (32 fl oz/ 1 L). Cover and simmer gently over low heat until required.

Add oil and half the butter to large flame-proof casserole dish or Dutch oven. Add onion and cook gently over low heat until transparent, about 10 minutes. Add garlic and cook several seconds. Add rice and stir over low heat 3 to 4 minutes. Stir in half the simmering stock and half the pureed tomatoes. Add broken bay leaf and pepper to taste. Cover and cook over low heat 12 minutes. Add remaining hot stock, stir gently, cover and cook 8 minutes more. Remove pan from heat and let stand 5 minutes.

Melt remaining butter in pan used for stock. Add scampi and cook over medium heat until just cooked, stirring often. Remove pan from heat.

Heat remaining pureed tomatoes in small pan until thickened. Add salt and pepper to taste.

Oil a fluted ring mold and press risotto into it. Turn onto warm serving platter. Fill middle with most of hot scampi and spoon hot tomato puree over top of mold. Garnish edge of dish with remaining scampi if desired.

Risotto con gli Asparagi

RISOTTO WITH GREEN ASPARAGUS (ITALY)   SERVES 6

Risotto is one of those dishes that can be a triumph for the cook, or a culinary disaster. It should be moist and creamy, with the grains plump and intact. It can also turn out dry and gluey because of the frequent stirring and constant attention required in its cooking. The following method should assist those cooks who haven't mastered the art of risotto cooking — not conventional, but certainly more than satisfactory! Choose slender green asparagus if possible, as these are the closest to the wild asparagus mostly used for this dish.

1 lb (500 g) fresh slender green asparagus spears

2 cups (16 fl oz/500 ml) water

1/2 teaspoon salt

1/2 teaspoon sugar

2 cups (16 fl oz/500 ml) strong chicken stock (see page 31)

2 cups (14 oz/420 g) arborio rice

2 tablespoons extra light olive oil

3 oz (90 g) butter

1 large onion, finely chopped

freshly ground black pepper

2 tablespoons chopped flat-leaf (Italian) parsley

1/2 cup (2 oz/60 g) freshly grated parmesan cheese

Snap off woody ends from asparagus. Wash and cut into 3/4 in (2 cm) lengths, setting tips aside. Bring 2 cups water to boil in saucepan. Add salt, sugar and asparagus, return to boil and cook, uncovered, 4 minutes. Add tips and cook 1 minute. Drain cooking water into measuring jug. Transfer asparagus to colander, rinse under cold running water and set aside.

Make up cooking water in jug to 2 cups and return to saucepan. Add chicken stock and simmer slowly, partly covered, over low heat.

Heat oil and two-thirds of butter in large heavy saucepan. Add onion and cook gently until transparent, about 10 minutes. Add rice and stir over low heat 3 to 4 minutes. Stir in half the simmering stock, cover and simmer over low heat 12 minutes. Add remaining stock and asparagus, stir gently, cover and simmer gently 8 minutes. Remove from heat, cover and let stand 2 to 3 minutes. Add remaining butter, pepper to taste, parsley and parmesan, and mix gently though rice with fork. Serve immediately.

Risotto con gli Asparagi

RISOTTO ALLA MILANESE

RICE WITH SAFFRON AND PARMESAN (ITALY)   SERVES 6

Usually this risotto contains bone marrow; this recipe is a less complicated version — an excellent accompaniment to rich casseroles and stews.

generous pinch of saffron threads
1/4 cup (2 fl oz/60 ml) boiling water
3 oz (90 g) unsalted butter
1 medium onion, finely chopped
2 cups (14 oz/420 g) arborio rice
4 cups (32 fl oz/1 L) chicken stock
(see page 31)
1/2 cup (2 oz/60 g) grated
parmesan cheese

Place saffron in bowl, pour on boiling water and leave to infuse until required. Melt butter in heavy saucepan. Add onion and cook gently until transparent, about 10 minutes. Add rice and stir over low heat 3 to 4 minutes.

Heat stock in another saucepan, covered, until simmering. Stir half the hot stock into rice, cover and simmer 12 minutes. Stir in remaining stock and saffron with its liquid and simmer, covered, until rice is just tender, about 8 to 10 minutes. Stir in parmesan. Let stand, covered, 3 to 4 minutes before serving.

GNOCCHI DI SEMOLINO

SEMOLINA GNOCCHI (ITALY)   SERVES 6

Also known as gnocchi alla romana, this is a popular dish in Rome and throughout Lazio where it is usually served as a first course at lunch, although its popularity has spread even further afield. Unlike other gnocchi, it cannot be described as a dumpling as it is finished in the oven, not boiled.

4 cups (32 fl oz/1 L) milk
1 tablespoon butter
1 cup (6 oz/180 g) fine semolina
1 teaspoon salt
freshly ground black pepper
freshly grated nutmeg
2 egg yolks
1/2 cup (2 oz/60 g) freshly grated
parmesan cheese
4 oz (125 g) butter, melted

Place milk and 1 tablespoon butter in heavy-based saucepan and bring to boil. When almost boiling, remove from heat and pour in semolina in steady stream, stirring constantly with wooden spoon. Add salt, and pepper and nutmeg to taste, return to heat and stir constantly until bubbling. Reduce heat and cook semolina over low heat until thick enough to support a spoon upright, about 5 minutes, stirring often. Remove from heat and stir in egg yolks and half the parmesan. Transfer to greased baking sheet and spread into rectangle 1/2 in (1 cm) thick, smoothing top with wet spatula. Let stand until cool and firm, about 40 minutes. Cut into 1 1/2 in (4 cm) rounds with pastry cutter. Trimmings can be remolded and also cut into rounds.

Preheat oven to 350–375°F (180–190°C/Gas 4). Grease shallow 8 in x 11 in (20 cm x 28 cm) oven-proof dish and arrange layer of rounds slightly overlapping. Drizzle with half the butter and half the remaining parmesan. Arrange remaining rounds on top. Drizzle with remaining butter and cheese. Bake until top is golden and bubbling, about 20 to 25 minutes. Serve hot from dish.

Gnocchi di Ricotta e Spinaci

SPINACH AND RICOTTA DUMPLINGS (ITALY)   SERVES 4 TO 6

Fresh spinach is recommended, and you can use the tender stalks as well as the leaves; however, frozen leaf spinach is a viable alternative and does save considerable effort. The secret to the success of this dish is to remove as much moisture as possible afterwards. No water should be added when cooking spinach. If using frozen spinach, defrost a 8 oz (250 g) package, drain and extract moisture in the same way as if using fresh; if the spinach is already chopped, press between doubled layers of paper towels, replacing with fresh towels as they become saturated. Serve this dish as a first course.

1¹/₂ lb (750 g) spinach

1¹/₂ cups (12 oz/375 g) ricotta cheese

4 tablespoons grated parmesan cheese

2 eggs, beaten

¹/₄ teaspoon grated nutmeg

salt and freshly ground black pepper

3 to 5 tablespoons all-purpose (plain) flour

extra all-purpose (plain) flour

To Serve:

4 oz (125 g) butter

4 tablespoons grated parmesan cheese

Trim roots from spinach and discard any damaged leaves. Wash in several changes of water. Chop leaves and stems roughly and place in large saucepan. Cover and heat until wilted, tossing often to distribute heat. Drain in colander, pressing well with back of wooden spoon, then squeezing handfuls at a time to remove remaining moisture. Process drained spinach in food processor until finely chopped.

Transfer spinach to bowl. Add ricotta and parmesan and mix thoroughly with fork. Stir in eggs, nutmeg, and salt and pepper to taste. Add enough flour to make a fairly stiff paste.

Spread some extra flour in shallow dish. Take heaping tablespoons of spinach mixture and shape into ovals with moistened hands. Drop into flour to coat lightly. Lift onto tray.

Bring large saucepan of lightly salted water to boil. Drop in gnocchi, about 10 at a time, and boil gently until they rise to surface. Remove with slotted spoon or wire skimmer and place in greased shallow gratin or other oven-proof dish. Keep warm.

When all gnocchi are cooked, melt butter in small saucepan until nut-brown and fragrant. Pour over gnocchi and sprinkle with parmesan. Place under moderately hot broiler (grill) until parmesan begins to brown. Serve immediately.

GNOCCHI DI PATATE

POTATO DUMPLINGS (ITALY)   SERVES 6

Gnocchi are served with various sauces, according to the region where prepared. In Liguria, they are served with pesto (see page 35). In this recipe, I have included a gorgonzola sauce variation, even though it is from Italy's north, as it is delicious and so easy to make. Choose potatoes that are suitable for baking or mashing — floury rather than waxy. Do not puree the potatoes in a food processor as this will create the wrong texture. Use a fork with rounded tines to give characteristic markings on dumplings.

2 lb (1 kg) baking potatoes
1 teaspoon salt
2 cups (10 oz/300 g) all-purpose (plain) flour, sifted
grated parmesan cheese, to serve

Tomato Sauce:

2 x 15 oz (425 g) cans tomatoes
1 large onion, quartered
3 tablespoons olive oil
$1/2$ teaspoon sugar
salt and freshly ground black pepper

Gorgonzola Sauce Variation:

4 oz (125 g) gorgonzola cheese
$1/2$ cup (4 fl oz/125 ml) milk
3 tablespoons butter
$1/4$ cup (4 fl oz/125 ml) heavy (double) cream

Peel potatoes and cut into thick slices. Place in saucepan with water to cover and 1 teaspoon salt. Boil until tender. Drain water from saucepan and return to low heat to evaporate any moisture and dry potatoes.

Puree potatoes in food mill placed over bowl, using disk with medium hoes. Alternatively, mash thoroughly in bowl while hot. Lightly mix in enough flour to make soft dough. Do not over-mix.

Take small handful of dough, covering bowl with folded cloth. Roll into long sausage shape about thumb thickness on lightly floured board. Cut into 1 in (2.5 cm) lengths. Dip into flour and press each piece with thumb or index finger onto fork tines to give grooves on one side and indent on the other. Place on lightly floured cloth. Repeat until all dough is used.

For tomato sauce: Puree tomatoes with food mill or press through sieve. Combine tomatoes, onion, oil, sugar and salt and pepper to taste in small saucepan and bring to boil. Simmer until thick, about 40 minutes.

Meanwhile, bring large saucepan of lightly salted water to boil. Drop in gnocchi, about 20 at a time, and boil until they rise to surface then cook 30 seconds more — about 3 to 4 minutes cooking time in all. Remove cooked gnocchi with slotted spoon and layer in warm serving dish. Remove onions from sauce and spoon a little over each layer of gnocchi. To finish, spoon over remaining sauce and sprinkle with parmesan. Serve immediately with extra parmesan in a separate bowl.

Gorgonzola Sauce Variation: Mash cheese with fork. Heat milk in wide pan. Stir in cheese and butter and bring to boil. Just before serving, whisk in cream and heat through without boiling. Pour over gnocchi.

Gnocchi di Patate (with tomato sauce)

ARANCINI DI RISO

RICE CROQUETTES (ITALY)   MAKES 24

Sicilian in origin, these rice croquettes were named for their resemblance to oranges. Their popularity now extends to the mainland, where they are known as suppli with variations to the name according to the fillings. One name is suppli al telefono, as the mozzarella filling melts and parts in long strands like telephone wires when you bite into it. The croquettes can be coated in breadcrumbs and refrigerated for 2 to 3 hours before deep frying. Serve hot croquettes as an appetizer, or as an accompaniment to veal or poultry.

2 oz (60 g) butter

1 small onion, finely chopped

1 1/2 cups (10 oz/300 g) arborio or medium-grain rice

3 cups (24 fl oz/750 ml) hot chicken stock (see page 31)

1/3 cup (1 1/2 oz/45 g) grated parmesan cheese

salt and freshly ground black pepper

1 egg yolk

To Assemble:

2 oz (60 g) mortadella sausage, thinly sliced

1 1/2 cups (6 oz/180 g) shredded mozzarella cheese

1 egg

1 egg white

salt

1 1/2 cups (5 oz/150 g) dried breadcrumbs

oil, for deep frying

Melt butter in heavy saucepan. Add onion and cook gently until transparent, about 10 minutes. Add rice and cook over medium heat 2 to 3 minutes, stirring often. Add 2 cups hot stock and bring to boil. Cover and simmer over low heat 12 minutes. Stir in remaining stock, cover and simmer until liquid is absorbed, about 8 to 10 minutes.

Remove from heat and stir in parmesan, and salt and pepper to taste. Transfer mixture to baking dish and spread evenly to cool. When cool, stir in egg yolk and mix well.

To assemble croquettes: Finely chop mortadella and mix with mozzarella. Place a heaping tablespoon of rice mixture in moistened palm of your hand. Place a heaping teaspoon of mozzarella mixture in middle and mold rice into a ball to completely enclose filling. Place on tray. Repeat with remaining mixture.

Beat egg and egg white in shallow dish, adding pinch of salt. Place breadcrumbs in another dish. Coat rice balls with egg, then roll in breadcrumbs to coat. Place on tray.

Heat oil in deep fryer to 375°F (190°C) — not quite smoking point — and deep fry croquettes, 4 to 5 at a time, until golden brown, about 3 minutes. Drain on paper towels. Serve hot.

INFARINATA

POLENTA WITH VEGETABLES (ITALY)   SERVES 8 TO 10

Polenta is a popular food in the northern and central regions of Italy, accompanying meats, game and wild mushrooms, even fried eggs. In the Veneto it is also served in grilled slices alongside fried fish. It really is warming, stick-to-the-ribs food, once a staple for the impoverished, who adopted it with enthusiasm when corn was introduced from the New World.

Preparing polenta in the traditional manner takes a lot of patience, particularly when the polenta is added to the hot liquid as it can become lumpy very easily. It also requires up to an hour's cooking, with almost constant stirring. My method would not meet with approval in Italy, but it is much easier. The recipe is from Tuscany, using olive oil instead of the usual butter. Serve as an accompaniment to grilled meats, sausages, game dishes, fried eggs, or sliced mushrooms cooked in olive oil with garlic and parsley.

4 tablespoons olive oil

1 medium onion, chopped

3 cups (12 oz/375 g) chopped vegetables (eg carrot, celery, broccoli with stems)

2 cups (16 fl oz/500 ml) cold water

2 cups (12 oz/375 g) polenta (yellow cornmeal)

1 teaspoon salt

3 1/2 cups (28 fl oz/875 ml) boiling water

Heat 1 tablespoon oil in frying pan. Add onion and cook gently until beginning to soften, about 6 to 7 minutes. Add vegetables, cover, and cook over low heat until tender, about 15 minutes, stirring occasionally. Remove from heat, uncover and set aside.

Meanwhile, pour cold water into large, heavy saucepan, add polenta and stir well. Place over medium-high heat, add salt and boiling water and stir until beginning to bubble. Reduce heat and cook 10 minutes, stirring occasionally. Partly cover pan with lid to prevent polenta spitting over stove, and cook 10 minutes, stirring occasionally. Add vegetables and cook 10 minutes more.

Lightly oil 7 in x 10 in (15 cm x 25 cm) loaf pan. Pack hot polenta mixture into pan, smoothing surface. Turn polenta loaf onto flat platter. Cut half the loaf into 1/2 in (1 cm) thick slices and sprinkle with remaining olive oil before serving. Cut any remaining polenta loaf as required, or cover and store in refrigerator. Serve leftover polenta loaf by slicing and frying in olive oil.

Breads, Pastries and Baking

Of all the wonderful aromas that assail the senses wherever food is prepared in the Mediterranean, that of fresh-baked bread would have to be one of the most memorable. From ancient times, bread has been the region's most important food. It is on the table to accompany appetizers; it is there with soups, with fish, meat, poultry, and vegetable dishes. It is not considered bad manners to dunk bread into the succulent juices from a flavorsome stew, or to use it to soak up the last of the dressing from a salad; in fact it is almost mandatory. It is proper to scoop up hummus and baba ghannouj with bite-sized pieces of pita bread — but not pieces from which you have just taken a bite. Once you get used to the dunking, dipping and soaking, you are eating the Mediterranean way — unpretentious and relaxed.

But the use of bread dough goes beyond the daily loaf. There are the Italian pizzas (the fastest growing of the fast food industries), the calzoni and the focaccias which have surged in popularity. From Catalonia and the Balearic Islands comes coca, a flat bread baked with a savory or sweet topping. Breads are flavored with herbs, onions, olives, leafy greens or garlic, or a combination. Entering any Mediterranean bakery is sheer delight.

Recognizing that today's cook may not have time to make yeast doughs from scratch, I have kept bread recipes rather basic, and in quantities that can make use of frozen bread dough if it is available in your area. If you do make your own dough, an electric mixer fitted with a dough hook saves time and effort.

Savory pastries make use of shortcrust pastry, a Spanish version of a hot water pastry, and fillo and oil pastries from Greece and the eastern regions. In the Maghreb, they use a pastry that is difficult to make without practice, but fillo pastry or egg roll skins (spring roll wrappers) can substitute. You will find recipes using these pastries are user-friendly.

A range of cakes, sweet pastries and cookies are also included, representative of the wide range prepared in Mediterranean cuisines. Nuts feature strongly in Mediterranean baking, giving them special appeal.

The joy of visiting a patisserie and similar establishments in the region is paradise for anyone with a sweet tooth; the displays are legendary. The recipes in this chapter will introduce you to some of the best the region has to offer.

Foundoukopita (page 252)

PÂTE BRISÉE

SHORTCRUST PASTRY (FRANCE)

MAKES ENOUGH PASTRY TO LINE
9 IN (23 CM) PIE PAN (FLAN TIN)

Thanks to the food processor, making shortcrust pastry is a breeze. It may not quite achieve the texture of pastry made by hand, but it takes the pain out of pastry-making. Process the dough as briefly as possible so it does not become warm through friction — pulse the processor as needed to prevent this. Refrigerate pastry for 30 minutes before using — this rests the pastry and helps prevent shrinkage.

1 cup (5 oz/150 g) all-purpose (plain) flour

3 oz (90 g) firm butter, roughly chopped

1 egg yolk

1/4 teaspoon lemon juice

1 to 2 tablespoons ice-cold water

Place flour and salt in bowl of food processor fitted with steel blade and process 5 seconds to remove any lumps. Add butter and process until mixture resembles coarse crumbs, about 20 seconds. Add egg yolk and lemon juice. With motor operating, gradually add enough water to form soft dough on blades.

Turn pastry onto work surface, knead lightly until just smooth and flatten into thick disc. Wrap in plastic wrap and refrigerate 30 minutes. Use as directed in recipes.

Pâte Sucrée (Sweet Shortcrust Pastry) Variation: Add 3 tablespoons superfine (caster) sugar to flour, use unsalted butter and omit lemon juice.

FILLO HORIATIKO

OIL PASTRY (GREECE)

MAKES ENOUGH PASTRY FOR A 10 IN X 12 IN
(25 CM X 30 CM) COVERED PIE

4 cups (20 oz/600 g) all-purpose (plain) flour

1/2 teaspoon salt

3/4 cup (6 fl oz/180 ml) light olive oil

1/2 cup (4 fl oz/125 ml) cold water

3 teaspoons lemon juice

Sift flour and salt into bowl. Add oil and rub in with fingertips until evenly distributed. Add water and lemon juice and mix with hands to soft dough. Knead lightly in bowl to form a ball, wrap in plastic wrap and let stand 30 minutes before using.

When required roll out on lightly floured board.

Food Processor Method: Place flour in food processor bowl. Add oil and process until evenly distributed. Add water and lemon juice and process to soft dough — it will look crumbly. Turn onto work surface and knead into ball. Wrap and let stand as above.

BREAD DOUGH

MAKES ABOUT 2 LB (1 KG) BREAD DOUGH

This basic recipe can be used for many breads and pies of the region. Follow the directions and you will find the dough rises in an hour or less. Yield is equivalent to two 1 lb (500 g) packages of frozen bread dough, which can be thawed, according to directions, and used in place of this dough in recipes, if preferred. The dough can be mixed in the bowl of an electric mixer with dough hook attachment, beating for 5 minutes.

4 cups (20 oz/600 g) all-purpose (plain) flour

1/2 teaspoon salt

1 oz (30 g) fresh compressed yeast or 2 1/2 teaspoons (1 x 1/4 oz/7 g sachet) active dry yeast

1 3/4 cups (14 fl oz/440 ml) lukewarm water

1 tablespoon olive oil

Sift 3 cups flour with salt into large, warm bowl. Make well in middle of flour.

Put yeast into small bowl; for fresh yeast, cream with wooden spoon then stir in 4 tablespoons of the lukewarm water; for dry yeast, just stir in 4 tablespoons water. When yeast is dissolved, pour into well and stir in a little flour to make light batter. Flick a little flour on top of batter, cover bowl with cloth and leave until batter is spongy, about 10 minutes.

Add remaining water and gradually mix flour into liquid, adding oil gradually. Mix to soft dough, adding reserved flour as required — it may be necessary to add a little more than amount specified but dough should be a little sticky.

Knead dough in bowl until smooth and elastic and no longer sticky, about 10 minutes. Remove from bowl and shape into ball. Place 1/2 teaspoon oil in bowl, add dough and turn to coat with oil. Stretch plastic wrap over bowl, cover with thick cloth, and let stand in warm place until doubled in bulk, about 1 hour. Use as directed in recipes.

233

BISTEEYA

CHICKEN AND ALMOND PIE (MOROCCO)   SERVES 6

Bisteeya is traditionally made with pigeon (chicken is a popular substitute) and warkha, a special paper thin pastry (fillo is a ready alternative). While it is fried in Morocco, it is is easier to bake if using fillo.

3 oz (90 g) butter

1 large onion, grated

2 cloves garlic, finely chopped

1 teaspoon ground ginger

1/4 teaspoon turmeric

1/4 teaspoon cayenne pepper

pinch of saffron powder (optional)

3 in (8 cm) cinnamon stick

3 lb (1.5 kg) chicken breasts,
on the bone, halved

2 tablespoons chopped flat-leaf
(Italian) parsley

2 tablespoons chopped fresh
coriander leaves (cilantro)

salt

2 cups (16 fl oz/500 ml) hot water

3 tablespoons lemon juice

6 egg yolks

3/4 cup (4 oz/125 g) whole blanched
almonds, chopped

1 1/2 teaspoons ground cinnamon

1/4 cup (1 1/2 oz/45 g) powdered
(icing) sugar, sifted

extra 4 oz (125 g) butter, clarified
(see page 9)

12 sheets fillo pastry (see page 23)

extra powdered (icing) sugar

ground cinnamon

Melt 2 oz (60 g) butter in large saucepan. Add onion, garlic and spices and cook gently over low heat 5 minutes, stirring. Increase heat to medium, add chicken and cook until no longer pink, about 10 minutes, turning occasionally. Add chopped herbs, 1 teaspoon salt and hot water. Cover and simmer over low heat until tender, about 1 hour. Let stand 30 minutes. Remove chicken using slotted spoon and discard cinnamon stick. Return pan to heat and boil liquid rapidly until reduced to 1 1/2 cups (12 fl oz/375 ml). Meanwhile, discard skin and bones from chicken and shred meat into thick strips about 1 1/2 in (4 cm) long. Set aside. Stir lemon juice into reduced liquid and more salt if necessary. Reduce heat. Beat egg yolks in bowl with whisk. Beat in half the hot liquid and pour back into pan. Stir over low heat until sauce is thick and coats back of wooden spoon, about 2 to 3 minutes. Stir in chicken meat and remove from heat.

Preheat oven to 325–350°F (160–180°C/Gas 3). Melt remaining 1 oz (30 g) butter in small frying pan. Add almonds and cook, stirring, until lightly browned, about 2 minutes. Transfer to bowl and stir in cinnamon and powdered sugar. Set aside. Keep clarified butter warm by standing bowl in pan of hot water. Brush 12 to 14 in (30 to 35 cm) metal pizza pan with melted clarified butter. Stack 6 sheets fillo pastry on board, keeping remainder covered. Brush top sheet with butter and place on pizza pan with two ends overhanging. Brush next sheet and place at an angle to first sheet. Repeat with remaining sheets, fanning so there is an even overhang of pastry around pan. Spread chicken filling evenly in pan, patting flat with spatula. Top with fillo sheet, folded so it covers chicken. Brush with butter and sprinkle almond mixture evenly over top. Bring overhanging pastry over top all around, and brush with butter. Stack remaining 5 sheets fillo, butter and place on pie in same way as base, leaving top sheet unbuttered. Trim overhanging pastry with scissors to give even edge. Using rubber spatula to lift edge of pie, tuck overhang underneath. Brush top with butter and bake until golden brown, about 40 minutes. Remove and immediately sift powdered sugar on top. Lift onto serving platter. Use cinnamon to make lattice design. Serve hot.

Focaccia con la Cipolla e Salvia

ONION AND SAGE BREAD (ITALY)   MAKES 2 BREADS

This bread is tasty enough to eat on its own, warm and fragrant from the oven, but portions can be split and filled with whatever takes your fancy. Some suggestions are given below. Frozen bread dough may be used in place of the prepared dough.

Suggested fillings for focaccia:
• Thinly sliced prosciutto with drained and chopped sun-dried tomatoes and sliced mozzarella cheese or bocconcini cheese (also known as fresh buffalo mozzarella).
• Thinly sliced onions cooked slowly in olive oil in frying pan for 45 minutes until caramelized, with drained and chopped canned anchovy fillets and strips of roasted red and yellow bell pepper (capsicum) (see page 27).
• Freshly boiled asparagus spears seasoned with salt, freshly ground black pepper and a squeeze of lemon juice and shaved parmesan cheese.
• Peperonata (see page 197), with paper-thin slices of prosciutto.
• Marinated eggplant (aubergine) (see page 56), with drained and chopped sun-dried tomatoes and sliced mozzarella cheese or mild provolone cheese.

To assemble and cook: Cut wedges or squares of focaccia, slit horizontally and add choice of filling to middle. Place on baking sheet and warm in preheated oven at 350–375°F (180–190°C/Gas 4) until filling has warmed through, 6 to 8 minutes. They can also be heated about 20 seconds per portion on full power in microwave oven.

1 quantity bread dough
(see page 233)

5 tablespoons olive oil

2 large onions, thinly sliced

3 teaspoons chopped fresh sage

salt and freshly ground black pepper

Make bread dough according to recipe on page 233 and leave to rise as directed. Warm 2 tablespoons oil in frying pan. Add onions and cook gently until transparent, about 10 minutes, stirring often. Let cool.

Punch down dough, sprinkle with sage and knead into dough. Halve dough and shape each half into ball. Oil two 7 in x 11 in (18 cm x 28 cm) shallow cake pans liberally, or use two 9 in (23 cm) layer cake pans (sandwich tins). Roll each dough ball into thick rectangles or circles, lift into pans and push dough into shape of pans. Press tops to even.

Divide cooked, cooled onion over top of dough and press in with fingers. Drizzle over remaining oil, particularly over sides, and sprinkle with salt and pepper. Cover with folded clean cloth and let stand in warm place until doubled in bulk, about 30 minutes.

Preheat oven to 425–450°F (220–230°C/Gas 7). When bread has risen, bake on middle shelf in oven 20 minutes, covering top loosely with foil if onion begins to burn towards end of cooking time. To test if bread is cooked, it should sound hollow when base of pan is tapped. Let stand 3 minutes before removing from pan. Serve warm.

FOCACCIA ALLE OLIVE E ROSMARINO

FOCACCIA WITH OLIVES AND ROSEMARY (ITALY)   MAKES 1 LARGE BREAD

1 quantity bread dough
(see page 233)

²/₃ cup (4 oz/125 g) black olives,
pitted (stoned) and halved

3 teaspoons chopped fresh
rosemary leaves

3 tablespoons olive oil

Make bread dough according to recipe on page 233, cover and let stand in warm place until doubled in bulk, about 1 to 1½ hours. After dough has risen, punch down, knead lightly and shape into ball. Roll out to thick rectangle.

Lightly oil large baking sheet. Lift partly rolled dough onto baking sheet and roll and stretch into rectangle about 10 in x 12 in (25 cm x 30 cm), using rolling pin and then fingers. Spread olives and rosemary over top, and lightly press into dough with rolling pin. Cover with folded clean cloth and let stand in warm place until risen to almost doubled in thickness, about 30 minutes.

Preheat oven to 425–450°F (220–230°C/Gas 7). Drizzle focaccia with oil and bake until base sounds hollow when tapped, about 20 minutes. Serve warm or cold.

COCA MALLORQUINA

MAJORCAN FLAT BREAD (SPAIN)   MAKES 2 COCAS

Coca is Catalonia's version of pizza. Toppings vary greatly, ranging from savory to sweet. In Majorca, one of the Balearic islands, the coca is one of the most popular snack foods, with bakers producing their own specialties. The following is one of the more elaborate versions. You can use two 1 lb (500 g) packages of frozen bread dough, thawed according to directions, for the bread dough recipe, if preferred.

4 tablespoons olive oil

2 large onions, thinly sliced

4 cloves garlic, chopped

1 green bell pepper (capsicum),
cut into strips

1 red bell pepper (capsicum),
cut into strips

2 large tomatoes,
peeled and chopped

1 teaspoon salt

freshly ground black pepper

1 quantity bread dough
(see page 233)

3 tablespoons pine nuts, toasted

Heat oil in frying pan. Add onions and cook gently 7 to 8 minutes, stirring often. Add garlic and bell pepper strips and cook 1 minute. Add tomatoes, increase heat and cook until tomatoes soften and most moisture has evaporated. Season with salt and pepper to taste. Let cool.

After bread dough has risen, punch down, divide in half and roll out into ovals about ½ in (1 cm) thick. Place each oval onto oiled baking sheet and press middle out a little to give thicker rim.

Spread cooled tomato mixture evenly over dough, leaving edges uncovered and top with pine nuts. Cover with cloth and leave in a warm place until almost doubled in thickness, about 30 minutes. Preheat oven to 425–450°F (220–230°C/Gas 7). Bake until crust is golden, about 12 to 15 minutes. Tap base of baking sheet and if it sounds hollow, coca is cooked. Serve hot, warm or cold.

SPANAKOTIROPITA

SPINACH AND CHEESE PIE (GREECE)   SERVES 6 TO 9

This popular Greek pie has many variations; firstly spinach must be used, although chard (silverbeet) can be substituted providing the white ribs are discarded. At times of fasting, only olive oil is used, even for the fillo, and cheese is not used as dairy foods are not allowed. However, more flavorings may be added, such as leeks and additional herbs. The following is just one of the many versions using cheese. Butter brushed on the fillo gives it a better flavor, but a good olive oil may be substituted — do not use a butter substitute. This pie will serve six as a main course and nine as a first course.

If the pie is to be served cold, or cut into smaller portions for appetizers, it is better to use a shortcrust pastry in place of fillo: use pastry recipe for pissaladière (see page 238) but make up 1¹/₂ times quantity. Glaze top of pie with beaten egg and bake for 15 minutes in oven preheated to 375–400°F (190–200°C/Gas 5), then reduce heat to 325–350°F (160–180°C/Gas 3) and bake 30 minutes.

2 lb (1 kg) spinach
¹/₂ cup (4 fl oz/125 ml) olive oil
1 large onion, finely chopped
10 scallions
(spring onions/green onions),
including some green tops, chopped
¹/₂ cup (1 oz/30 g) finely chopped
flat-leaf (Italian) parsley
1 tablespoon chopped fresh dill
¹/₄ teaspoon grated nutmeg
6 oz (180 g) feta cheese
1 cup (8 oz/250 g) ricotta cheese
5 eggs, lightly beaten
salt and freshly ground black pepper
20 sheets fillo pastry
4 oz (125 g) butter, melted

Trim roots from spinach and remove damaged leaves. Retain stems on leaves as they are tender. Wash in several changes of water, drain and chop roughly. Place in large saucepan, cover and cook until wilted, about 5 to 6 minutes, tossing occasionally to heat evenly. Transfer to colander and press well with wooden spoon to extract as much moisture as possible. Chop coarsely and place in large bowl.

Heat oil in frying pan. Add onion and cook gently until transparent, about 10 minutes. Add scallions and cook 2 to 3 minutes until soft. Add to spinach with herbs and nutmeg. Mash cheeses together in bowl with fork and add to spinach with eggs. Mix well and season with salt and pepper to taste.

Preheat oven to 325–350°F (160–180°C/Gas 3).

Grease metal baking dish, base size 9 in x 11 in (23 cm x 28 cm). Stack 10 sheets fillo on work surface, keeping remainder covered. Brush top sheet lightly with butter, lift up and turn upside down onto stack. Brush top with butter and turn 2 buttered sheets upside down. Continue in this way until stack is buttered, picking up extra sheet each time. Leave top sheet unbuttered. Place in dish and brush top sheet with butter. Spread spinach filling in dish.

Stack and butter remaining fillo and place on top of spinach, pressing top and bottom pastry layers together around edges. Trim evenly and tuck edges in around pie. Brush top with butter, then score through top 2 to 3 sheets with sharp knife or razor blade into serving-size squares. Sprinkle top lightly with water to prevent pastry curling and brush lightly to spread evenly. Bake until puffed and golden, about 45 minutes. Let stand 5 minutes. Cut into serving portions as marked and serve immediately.

CALZONI PUGLIESI

ONION PASTIES (ITALY)   MAKES 6

Originally a calzone was a large envelope of bread dough filled with various ingredients and baked. Now it can be made of bread dough or pastry, large or small, baked or fried. The following recipe is from Apulia; the filling can have other ingredients added, such as anchovies, olives and capers.

1/2 quantity bread dough
(see page 233), or 1 lb (500 g) frozen
bread dough, thawed

3 tablespoons olive oil

2 large white onions, thinly sliced

2 medium tomatoes,
peeled, seeded and chopped

3 tablespoons raisins

1/2 cup (2 oz/60 g) grated pecorino
cheese

freshly ground black pepper

extra olive oil

Make bread dough according to recipe on page 233 and leave to rise, or thaw frozen dough according to directions.

Heat oil in frying pan. Add onions and cook until soft and transparent, about 15 minutes. Add tomatoes and raisins and cook 10 minutes. Let cool completely.

When dough has risen, punch down and roll out on lightly floured surface until just under 1/2 in (1 cm) thick. Cut into 4 in (10 cm) squares. Spread cooked onion mixture on one side of each square, 1/2 in (1 cm) from sides. Top each with 1 tablespoon cheese and season with pepper. Fold dough over to enclose filling, pressing edges with tines of fork to seal. Place on greased baking sheet, cover with clean cloth and let stand in warm place until well risen, about 25 to 30 minutes. Preheat oven to 425–450°F (220–230°C/Gas 7). Brush calzoni lightly with extra oil and bake until golden brown, about 15 minutes. Serve hot.

TARTE NIÇOISE

TOMATO AND OLIVE FLAN (FRANCE)   SERVES 4 TO 6

unbaked 9 in (23 cm) pie (flan) shell
(see shortcrust pastry page 232)

6 small tomatoes

1/2 cup (2 oz/60 g) shredded
gruyère cheese

1 tablespoon grated parmesan cheese

1/4 cup (1/2 oz/15 g) soft breadcrumbs

1 tablespoon chopped fresh basil

salt and freshly ground black pepper

2 tablespoons butter

3 large eggs

1/4 cup (2 fl oz/60 ml) milk

1/2 cup (4 fl oz/125 ml)
light (single) cream

1/4 teaspoon grated nutmeg

6 small black Niçoise or kalamata
olives, pitted and halved

Preheat oven to 375–400°F (190–200°C/Gas 5).

Prick pie shell with fork, line with greased foil (greased-side down) or parchment (baking paper), and fill with baking beans or weights. Bake until sides are cooked, about 12 minutes. Remove baking beans and foil or paper and bake 5 minutes to dry pastry. Remove from oven and reduce temperature to 325–350°F (160–180°C/Gas 3).

Halve tomatoes and remove seeds with teaspoon. Arrange tomatoes cut-side up in pie crust. Combine cheeses, breadcrumbs, basil, and salt and pepper to taste in bowl. Sprinkle mixture over tomatoes and dot with pieces of butter. Beat eggs, milk, cream, and nutmeg, and salt and pepper to taste in jug and pour carefully around tomatoes. Arrange olives decoratively on top. Bake until set, about 30 to 35 minutes. Let stand 5 minutes before cutting into wedges to serve.

KOLOKITHOPITA

SAVORY PUMPKIN PIE (GREECE)   SERVES 6 TO 8

4 cups (1 lb/500 g) shredded butternut pumpkin (squash)

2 tablespoons uncooked medium-grain rice

1 medium onion, grated

4 scallions (spring onions/ green onions), finely chopped

1/2 teaspoon salt

1/4 teaspoon grated nutmeg

1/2 teaspoon ground cinnamon

4 oz (125 g) feta cheese, crumbled

3 eggs, beaten

1 quantity fillo horiatiko (see page 232)

beaten egg or milk, to glaze

Combine pumpkin, rice, onion, scallions, salt, nutmeg, and cinnamon in bowl. Let stand 3 hours, stirring occasionally. Add feta cheese and eggs, and mix well.

Preheat oven to 350–375°F (180–190°F/Gas 4).

Roll out half the pastry to form 12 in x 14 in (30 cm x 35 cm) rectangle. Lift into buttered shallow 10 in x 12 in (25 cm x 30 cm) ovenproof dish. Spread filling evenly into pastry. Roll out remaining pastry and place on top. Press edges to seal and brush with beaten egg or milk. Prick top of pie evenly with fork.

Bake until top is lightly browned and filling is cooked, about 45 to 50 minutes. Let stand 10 minutes before cutting into squares or diamonds to serve. Serve hot or cold.

ELIOTI

OLIVE BREAD (CYPRUS)   MAKES 1 LOAF

This delicious bread is now available at many small bakeries and delicatessens, but it can be easily made at home. This version is one Cypriot cooks make when there isn't time to prepare a yeast dough. Use ordinary black olives, not the kalamata as these are flavored with vinegar and are not suitable.

3 tablespoons olive oil

1 medium onion, finely chopped

2 cups (10 oz/300 g) all-purpose (plain) flour

5 teaspoons baking powder

2/3 cup (4 oz/125 g) black olives, pitted and roughly chopped

1/2 cup (4 fl oz/125 ml) milk

1/4 cup (2 fl oz/60 ml) water

beaten egg and milk, to glaze

Preheat oven to 400–425°F (200–220°C/Gas 6).

Heat oil in frying pan. Add onion and cook gently until transparent, about 10 minutes. Remove from heat.

Sift flour and baking powder into bowl. Stir in olives and make well in middle. Combine milk, water and warm onion mixture and pour into flour. Mix to form soft dough with round-bladed knife. Turn onto greased baking sheet and shape into round using spatula, leaving texture fairly rough. Glaze top with beaten egg and milk and cut a deep cross in top of dough. Bake until bread sounds hollow when tapped, about 35 to 40 minutes — reduce temperature to 375°F (190°C/Gas 5) after 20 minutes if browning too quickly. Remove to rack and serve warm or cold on same day.

EMPANADILLAS DE ATÚN

LITTLE TUNA TURNOVERS (SPAIN)   MAKES ABOUT 36

Popular as a tapa, these little pastries can also be filled with a ground (minced) veal or beef mixture. Their popularity in Spain is such that the pastry dough is sold cut into rounds and packaged. When using any pastry for frying, the fat content should be relatively low; if the dough is high in fat, the pastry absorbs too much oil.

Pastry:

2 cups (10 oz/300 g) all-purpose (plain) flour

3/4 cup (6 fl oz/180 ml) water

2 oz (60 g) butter

1 tablespoon sunflower or corn (maize) oil

1/4 teaspoon salt

1 medium egg, beaten

oil, for shallow frying

Tuna Filling:

1 tablespoon olive oil

1 medium onion, finely chopped

2 medium tomatoes, peeled and chopped

6 to 7 oz (180 to 200 g) can tuna chunks packed in brine

3 tablespoons chopped drained canned pimiento

2 tablespoons chopped flat-leaf (Italian) parsley

salt and freshly ground black pepper

Sift flour into bowl and set aside. Heat water, butter, oil and salt in saucepan until butter melts. Remove from heat and pour in flour all at once. Stir thoroughly with wooden spoon to mix to stiff dough. Gradually stir in egg until dough is smooth. Turn onto lightly floured work surface, dust top with flour and knead until no longer sticky, adding more flour if necessary. Divide into two balls and cover with folded clean cloth. Let stand 30 minutes.

For tuna filling: Heat oil in saucepan. Add onion and cook gently until transparent, about 10 minutes. Add tomatoes, cover and simmer until tomatoes are soft, about 10 minutes, stirring occasionally. Drain tuna and add to saucepan with pimiento, parsley and salt and pepper to taste. Stir well to break up tuna and simmer, uncovered, until little moisture remains, about 5 to 8 minutes. Let cool.

To make turnovers, knead one dough ball on floured surface about 5 to 6 turns. Roll out until fairly thin. Cut into 3 1/2 in (9 cm) rounds with floured cutter, twisting cutter to separate each round from rest of pastry. Lift off pastry trimmings and place under cloth. Brush edge of each round with water and place generous teaspoon of tuna filling in middle. Fold over and press edges together. Press with tines of fork, or use thimble or tip of coffee spoon to give scalloped edges. Place on cloth-lined tray. Use remaining ball of dough, pastry trimmings and filling to complete turnovers.

Pour oil into large frying pan until 3/4 in (2 cm) deep. Heat well until scrap of dough dropped in sizzles immediately. Shallow fry 5 to 7 turnovers at a time, turning to brown evenly, and cook until golden brown, about 3 minutes. Drain on paper towels and serve hot.

Empanadillas de Atun

BURMA BÖREK

BAKED FILLO ROLLS (TURKEY)   MAKES 30

Turkey is famous for its börekler, with similar recipes appearing in Greek and Cypriot cuisine. While a simple home-made pastry is usually used, fillo pastry — called yufka in Turkish — is also popular. For the cheese filling, a home-made, cottage-style cheese called beyaz panir is usually used. It is very similar to ricotta in flavor; however, when salted, it is somewhat akin to feta. Use one of the fillings given in this recipe, or double the amount of fillo and butter and make both fillings. If desired, uncooked pastries, brushed with butter, may be frozen on baking sheets, then lifted carefully into a rigid container, sealed and frozen for later use. Separate each layer with waxed (greaseproof) paper. When required, thaw on baking sheets and cook.

20 sheets fillo pastry (see page 23)
6 oz (180 g) butter,
clarified (see page 9)

Cheese Filling:

6 oz (180 g) feta cheese
6 oz (180 g) ricotta or cottage cheese
4 tablespoons finely chopped
flat-leaf (Italian) parsley
1 egg, beaten
freshly ground black pepper

Meat Filling:

2 tablespoons butter
2 tablespoons pine nuts
1 large onion, finely chopped
1 lb (500 g) ground (minced)
lamb or beef
2 tablespoons chopped flat-leaf
(Italian) parsley
1/2 teaspoon ground cinnamon
salt and freshly ground black pepper

Leave fillo pastry in its wrapping at room temperature for 2 hours before unfolding. Stack sheets of fillo pastry and cut into three even sections, using ruler and sharp knife or razor blade. Width of pastry becomes length of strips; strips should be approximately 6 in (15 cm) wide and 12 to 14 in (30 to 35 cm) long. Stack strips and cover with folded clean cloth topped with a moistened one.

Preheat oven to 350–375°F (180–190°C/Gas 4).

For cheese filling: Mash cheeses together in bowl and add parsley, egg and pepper to taste.

For meat filling: Melt butter in frying pan. Add pine nuts and cook until golden, about 2 to 3 minutes. Remove to plate with slotted spoon. Add onion to pan and cook gently until soft, about 10 minutes. Increase heat, add meat, and cook until juices evaporate and meat begins to brown, about 10 minutes, stirring often to break up lumps. Add pine nuts, parsley, cinnamon, and salt and pepper to taste. Let cool.

To make fillo rolls, take 2 fillo strips at a time, brush one strip with melted clarified butter and top with second strip. Butter top of strip, and with narrow end towards you, place about 1 tablespoon filling along end, 3/4 in (2 cm) in from base and sides. Fold fillo over filling, fold in sides and brush side folds with butter. Roll up in cigar shape to end and place seam-side down on greased baking sheet. Brush top with butter. Repeat with remaining fillo strips and filling. Bake until golden, about 20 minutes. Serve hot.

Brik bil Anchouwa

FRIED PASTRIES WITH EGG AND ANCHOVIES (TUNISIA)   MAKES 4

In Tunisia, brik is made with a special pastry called malsouqua, more widely known as the warka or ouarka of Moroccan cuisine. Whereas fillo can be used as a substitute in dishes such as oven-baked bisteeya, egg roll skins (spring roll wrappers) made with wheat flour and prepared in a similar way to the North African pastry leaves, are a better substitute for this recipe. The skins fry crisply and stay crisp, unlike fillo which softens quickly with the moist filling. Do not assemble all the briks at the same time, or the filling will soak through the skins, tearing them.

To eat in the traditional manner, the brik is held by two corners, with fold uppermost. Bite into egg yolk — any runny yolk should flow down into the brik, not onto you. Otherwise use a knife and fork.

Other fillings may be used in place of anchovies, such as a 3 oz (90 g) can of oil-packed tuna, drained and flaked, or 3 tablespoons chopped, cooked chicken; omit the capers if using chicken.

4 x 8 in (20 cm) square egg roll skins
(spring roll wrappers)

1 tablespoon olive oil

1 large onion, finely chopped

1¹/2 tablespoons finely chopped
drained canned anchovy fillets

2 tablespoons chopped parsley

3 teaspoons capers,
drained and chopped if large

freshly ground black pepper

olive or other oil, for shallow frying

1 egg white, lightly beaten

4 small fresh eggs
(each 1¹/2 oz/45 g)

Place separated egg roll skins in stack on 8 in (20 cm) side plate, and cut corners with scissors to give roundish shapes. Remove to board, cover with folded clean cloth and set aside.

Heat olive oil in small frying pan. Add onion and cook gently until very soft and transparent, about 12 to 15 minutes, stirring often. Mash in anchovies, remove from heat, and stir in parsley, capers and pepper to taste. Let cool. Divide into four portions in pan.

Pour oil for shallow frying into 10 in (25 cm) frying pan until 1/4 in (5 mm) deep and heat well over medium heat.

Place egg roll skin on side plate and brush around edge with beaten egg white. Place a portion of onion filling in heap on one side, with edge of filling just touching middle. Make indent in filling with soup spoon and break 1 egg into it. Fold egg roll skin over filling to meet other side and press edges to seal. Slide immediately into hot oil and shallow fry until golden brown and crisp, about 45 seconds on each side, turning brik over using two egg lifters or pancake turners. Lift out and drain on paper towels. Prepare and cook remaining briks in same way. Serve hot.

CHURROS

SUGARED FRITTERS (SPAIN)   MAKES ABOUT 18

Fried dough, drizzled with honey or sprinkled with sugar, features in the cuisines of many Mediterranean countries as it was a quick way to satisfy a sweet tooth when ovens were not part of the domestic kitchens. Churros are a popular breakfast item in Spain, and are also eaten with coffee or strong, hot chocolate later in the day. Churros must be eaten as soon as they are made, although they can be reheated briefly in a microwave.

1¼ cups (10 fl oz/310 ml) water
½ teaspoon salt
1 tablespoon light olive oil
1 cup (5 oz/150 g) all-purpose (plain) flour
1 to 2 large eggs
oil, for deep frying
1 cup (7½ oz/220 g) superfine (caster) sugar

Combine water, salt and olive oil in heavy saucepan and bring to boil. Sift flour into bowl and as soon as water is boiling, pour in flour all at once and stir over heat with wooden spoon until dough forms a ball. Remove from heat and let cool a little. Beat in egg. If dough is too stiff, beat another egg in small bowl and gradually add to dough until it is soft enough to pipe yet can hold its shape.

Heat oil for deep frying in saucepan until almost smoking. Spoon dough into pastry (piping) bag fitted with large fluted (star) nozzle. Pipe dough into hot oil in approximately 3 to 4 in (8 to 10 cm) lengths, letting them curve slightly at each end if possible. Deep fry four to five at a time until golden brown and cooked through, about 5 to 6 minutes, turning to brown evenly. Remove with slotted spoon and drain on crumpled paper towels. Dip into sugar to coat, pile onto dish and serve hot.

Churros

FOUNDOUKOPITA

HAZELNUT CAKE (GREECE)

A cake for the health conscious! It uses extra light olive oil instead of the usual butter, and is delicious. Serve as is, just with a dusting of powdered sugar, or make it sinfully delicious with sugar syrup for a dessert cake. Greek nut cakes are traditionally made in slabs in baking dishes but the modern Greek cook may use a European-style cake pan.

melted butter, for greasing

flour, for coating

3/4 cup (6 fl oz/180 ml) extra light olive oil or maize oil

1¼ cups (9 oz/275 g) superfine (caster) sugar

4 x 2 oz (60 g) eggs, separated

½ cup (4 fl oz/125 ml) fresh orange juice

1 cup (5 oz/150 g) coarsely ground toasted hazelnuts

1½ cups (7½ oz/225 g) all-purpose (plain) flour

4 teaspoons baking powder

½ teaspoon ground cinnamon

pinch ground cloves

¼ teaspoon salt

powdered (icing) sugar, to serve (optional)

whipped cream, to serve (optional)

Syrup (optional):

3/4 cup (5½ oz/165 g) sugar

½ cup (4 fl oz/125 ml) water

thin strip of orange rind

1 teaspoon lemon juice

1 tablespoon brandy

Preheat oven to 325–350°F(160–180°C/Gas 4). Grease a 9 in (23 cm) gugelhopf or tube cake pan with melted butter and refrigerate to set coating. Dust with flour and shake out excess.

Combine oil, sugar, egg yolks and orange juice in bowl and beat with electric mixer until thick and creamy and sugar is dissolved. Stir in hazelnuts. Sift flour with baking powder and spices and fold into egg mixture. Beat egg whites with salt in separate bowl until stiff, using clean beaters, and fold into cake batter with metal spoon.

Pour mixture into prepared pan and bake 1 to 1¼ hours until cooked when tested. Let stand 10 minutes, then turn onto wire rack to cool. Sieve powdered sugar on top just before serving.

Alternatively, make syrup while cake is cooling by placing sugar, water, orange rind and lemon juice in small, heavy pan. Stir over heat until sugar is dissolved, bring to boil and boil over medium heat 5 minutes. Stir in brandy. Remove from heat and discard orange rind. Place warm cake on plate and gradually pour over boiling hot syrup. When cold, place cake on serving plate and serve as dessert cake with whipped cream, if desired.

TAHINOPITA

TAHINI CAKE (GREECE)

Often prepared by Greeks during Lent, this cake contains no animal products. I have cooked it often, but found the secret of success by accident. Having prepared the batter, cooking was delayed for some reason, and when I could finally bake it, I found that the cake batter had risen in the pan while standing. The result was so much lighter and less crumbly than previous efforts, and this is the way I now make it.

1 tablespoon vegetable margarine, melted

1 cup (8 fl oz/250 ml) tahini (sesame paste)

1 cup (7½ oz/220 g) superfine (caster) sugar

grated rind of 1 orange

¾ cup (6 fl oz/180 ml) strained fresh orange juice

2¼ cups (11 oz/330 g) all-purpose (plain) flour

pinch of salt

3 teaspoons baking powder

½ teaspoon baking soda (bicarbonate of soda)

½ teaspoon ground allspice

½ cup (2 oz/60 g) finely chopped walnuts

½ cup (3 oz/90 g) golden raisins (sultanas)

Brush 8 in (20 cm) tube or ring cake pan with melted margarine. Cut circle of waxed (greaseproof) paper to fit base and place in pan, brushing with margarine. Refrigerate to set margarine. Dust with flour, shaking out excess.

Beat tahini with sugar and orange rind in large bowl of electric mixer 10 minutes, then gradually beat in orange juice. Sift dry ingredients twice and fold into tahini mixture. Stir in walnuts and sultanas. Transfer to prepared pan and let stand at room temperature until cake has almost doubled in bulk, about 30 to 40 minutes. Meanwhile, preheat oven to 325–350°F (160–180°C/Gas 3).

Bake until golden brown and cooked when tested with fine skewer, about 55 to 60 minutes. Invert onto wire cake rack and let stand 3 minutes before removing pan and lining paper. Let cool on rack. Can be stored in sealed container until required.

grapes

SHTRUDEL PEYROT YIVEHSHIM

DRIED FRUIT STRUDEL (ISRAEL)

This strudel, of Austrian origin, takes on an unmistakable Israeli flavor when packed with the excellent dried fruit and nuts of the region. Use dessert figs as they are softer than the usual dried figs.

6 sheets fillo pastry (see page 23)

6 oz (180 g) butter or vegetable margarine

1/2 cup (3 oz/90 g) raisins

1/2 cup (3 oz/90 g) chopped, pitted, dried dates

4 dried dessert figs, chopped

1/2 cup (2 oz/60 g) chopped walnuts

grated rind of 1 lemon

2 tablespoons superfine (caster) sugar

1/2 teaspoon ground cinnamon

12 to 16 red candied (glacé) cherries

3 tablespoons soft white breadcrumbs

1/2 cup (2 oz/60 g) ground almonds

powdered (icing) sugar

Leave fillo pastry in its wrapping at room temperature for 2 hours before unfolding.

Melt butter or margarine. Set aside. Preheat oven to 350–375°F (180–190°C/Gas 4).

Combine raisins, dates, figs and walnuts in bowl. Combine lemon rind with sugar and cinnamon in another small bowl. Leave cherries whole.

Stack fillo sheets. Brush top sheet with melted butter, turn it upside down on stack and brush again with butter. Repeat until stack is buttered, lifting an extra sheet each time, and butter top of stack.

Sprinkle breadcrumbs over fillo stack, leaving 2 in (5 cm) border clear of crumbs on 3 sides, with 3 in (8 cm) strip clear of crumbs at top. Top with even layer of almonds and drizzle with 3 tablespoons melted butter. Spread dried fruit and nut mixture evenly on top. Place row of cherries along middle of filling. Sprinkle sugar mixture evenly over filling and drizzle with 3 tablespoons melted butter.

Turn end of pastry over filling, and fold in sides. Brush side folds with butter, and roll strudel up firmly. Place fold-side down on greased baking sheet and brush top with butter. Using sharp knife, make shallow diagonal slashes across top, spacing them 1 1/2 in (4 cm) apart. Bake until golden brown, about 30 to 35 minutes. Leave on tray and dust with sieved powdered sugar while hot. Let cool on tray.

Remove to serving platter, or store in sealed container at room temperature. Use slashes as guide to cut strudel into slices on angle.

Shtrudel Peyrot Yivehshim

BAKLAWA

ALMOND PASTRY (LEBANON, SYRIA)   MAKES ABOUT 40 PIECES

The baklawas of Lebanon and Syrian patisserie are cooked to a pale golden color; they take great care not to brown the pastries too much, and not to overcook the nuts. To achieve the latter, they add flour to the nut mixture, according to my favorite supplier of Levantine pastries.

25 sheets fillo pastry (see page 23)
6 oz (180 g) butter, clarified
(see page 9)

Syrup:
2 cups (15 oz/440 g) sugar
1¹/2 cups (12 fl oz/375 ml) water
1 teaspoon strained lemon juice
1 tablespoon rose water
1 tablespoon orange flower water

Almond Filling:
2 cups (10 oz/300 g) finely chopped
blanched almonds
1 cup (4 oz/125 g) ground almonds
¹/2 cup (2¹/2 oz/75 g) all-purpose
(plain) flour
¹/4 cup (2 oz/60 g) superfine
(caster) sugar
2 oz (60 g) unsalted butter, melted
1 tablespoon rose water

Let fillo pastry stand in its wrapping at room temperature 2 hours.

For syrup: Combine sugar, water and lemon juice in heavy saucepan and heat, stirring occasionally, until sugar is dissolved, brushing down sugar from sides of pan with wet brush. Bring to boil and boil 10 minutes over medium heat. Stir in rose water and orange flower water and pour into jug. Let cool, then refrigerate until cold.

Preheat oven to 325–350°F (160–180°C/Gas 3).

Stand container of clarified butter in pan of hot water to keep melted. Brush 9 in x 11 in (23 cm x 28 cm) metal baking dish with melted clarified butter.

For almond filling: Mix almond filling ingredients together in bowl until thoroughly combined.

To make baklawa, open out fillo. Stack 11 sheets and cover remainder to prevent drying. Brush top sheet of stack with melted butter, turn it upside down onto stack and brush again with butter. Pick up top 2 fillo sheets and turn over. Continue in this way until stack is buttered, leaving top and bottom unbuttered. Place in prepared dish and brush top with butter. Spread half the filling evenly over fillo.

Butter 3 more fillo sheets using the same method. Place in dish, brush with butter and spread with remaining filling. Butter remaining 11 sheets, place on top and press all fillo edges together to seal. With razor blade, trim pastry 3/4 in (2 cm) above top of baklawa to give raised edge. Brush top with butter. Using sharp knife, cut through pastry in straight, evenly-spaced lines along length of dish, about 1¹/2 in (4 cm) apart. Cut through diagonally to give diamond shapes. Sprinkle top with cold water and brush evenly over pastry to prevent curling during cooking. Bake on middle shelf until lightly golden, about 40 minutes.

Remove from oven and immediately pour chilled syrup evenly over hot pastry. Let cool. Cut through pastry and lift out pieces with metal spatula. Store at room temperature in sealed container.

Floyeres me Loukoumia

FILLO ROLLS WITH TURKISH DELIGHT (GREECE)   MAKES 18 PIECES

"Floyeres" is a variation of the Greek for "flute", which indicates the shape of these pastries. Make sure you use real Turkish delight, loukoumi in Greek, not the home-made version set with gelatin — that would certainly not work. Choose a rose water or vanilla Turkish delight with almonds, or use a combination. Of course other flavors may be used. Some of the filling might ooze out of the rolls at ends — do not be concerned if this happens, but remove from oven if it does. The rolls are excellent served with after-dinner coffee.

18 pieces Turkish delight

6 sheets fillo pastry

$1/2$ cup (4 oz/125 g) butter, clarified (see page 9)

4 to 5 tablespoons finely chopped, toasted almonds

powdered (icing) sugar, sieved

Preheat oven to 350–375°F (180–190°C/Gas 4).

Brush off excess icing sugar from Turkish delight and cut each piece into 3 equal strips.

Stack fillo sheets and cut crosswise into 3 or 4 equal strips, with width of pastry becoming length of strips. Size should be about 5 in (12.5 cm) wide by 12 to 14 in (30 to 35 cm) long. Cover with folded dry cloth topped with moistened one while you work.

Place strip of fillo on work surface with narrow end towards you. Brush with melted butter. Place Turkish delight strips end to end, $3/4$ in (2 cm) in from end and sides of fillo, and sprinkle with scant teaspoon of almonds. Fold end over filling and roll firmly and evenly to other end. Place on greased baking sheet, seam-side down, and brush top with melted butter. Repeat with remaining ingredients, placing rolls about 1 in (2.5 cm) apart on baking sheet.

Bake until lightly golden, about 12 to 15 minutes. Remove from oven and sprinkle with powdered sugar immediately. Let cool. Store in sealed container at room temperature.

Poura me Tsokolata

CHOCOLATE AND NUT "CIGARS" (GREECE)   MAKES 20

These delicious nut rolls are normally finished in a syrup, but I prefer to dust them with powdered sugar. Another innovation is to use egg white instead of melted butter to brush the pastry layers. Not only does this reduce calories, it also stops the pastry flaking; they store well too. Have the fillo pastry at room temperature for 2 hours before opening the pack and counting out the sheets.

Filling:

1 egg yolk

1/4 cup (2 oz/60 g) superfine (caster) sugar

1/2 cup (2 1/2 oz/75 g) finely chopped walnuts

1/2 cup (2 1/2 oz/75 g) finely chopped almonds

1 oz (30 g) semi-sweet (dark) chocolate, chopped

1/4 teaspoon ground cinnamon

To Assemble:

14 sheets fillo pastry (see page 23)

1 egg white, lightly beaten

unsalted butter, melted

powdered (icing) sugar, sieved

Preheat oven to 325–350°F (160–180°C).

For filling: Beat egg yolk in bowl with sugar until light and creamy. Stir in nuts, chocolate and cinnamon and mix to stiff paste.

To assemble: Stack fillo sheets on board and cut into strips about 6 in (15 cm) wide and 12 in (30 cm) long. Stack onto cloth and cover with folded dry cloth or heavy plastic.

Take 2 fillo strips and place on work surface with narrow end towards you. Brush one strip lightly with egg white and top with second strip. Place about 3 teaspoons of filling 1/2 in (1 cm) in from lower and side edges in an even strip. Fold in base and sides of pastry, brush uncovered pastry lightly with egg white and roll up firmly to end of strip in cigar shape. Place seam-side down on greased baking sheet. Repeat with remaining ingredients.

Brush tops and sides of rolls with melted butter and bake until golden, about 15 minutes. Leave rolls on baking sheet and sieve powdered sugar over them while still hot. Let cool. Store in sealed container.

Poura me Tsokolata

Panforte di Siena

SIENA FRUIT AND NUT CAKE (ITALY)

A speciality of Siena, panforte has attained international fame and is exported to many countries. It is said a similar cake was carried by the crusaders as a sustaining snack. Traditionally candied or glacé citron, orange and lemon peel are used, but you can add glacé apricots, pineapple and/or figs if you wish, particularly if candied or glacé citron is not available. Serve the cake cut in thin wedges as it is very rich. It goes beautifully with coffee after dinner.

3/4 cup (4 oz/125 g) whole blanched almonds

3/4 cup (4 oz/125 g) shelled hazelnuts

1 cup (6 oz/180 g) chopped mixed candied (glacé) fruits and peel

1/2 cup (2 1/2 oz/75 g) all-purpose (plain) flour

2 tablespoons cocoa powder

1 teaspoon ground cinnamon

1/4 teaspoon ground allspice

2 oz (60 g) semi-sweet (dark) chocolate, chopped

1/2 cup (3 1/2 oz/110 g) superfine (caster) sugar

1/3 cup (3 fl oz/80 ml) honey

powdered (icing) sugar, to serve

Preheat oven to 300°F (150°C/Gas 2).

Line 8 in (20 cm) layer cake pan (sandwich tin) with foil and grease lightly.

Toast almonds and hazelnuts in oven 10 minutes. Combine nuts with candied fruits in bowl. Sift flour, cocoa, cinnamon and allspice together and mix well with fruit and nuts.

Place chocolate in bowl and stand bowl in hot water until chocolate is melted. Combine sugar and honey in large heavy saucepan and place over low heat until sugar dissolves, stirring occasionally and brushing any sugar from side of pan using wet brush. Bring to boil and boil gently 5 minutes, without stirring.

Remove from heat, stir in melted chocolate and add fruit and nut mixture immediately. Stir well until combined. Transfer to prepared pan and smooth top by pressing with spatula.

Cut 4 sheets newspaper into 10 in (25 cm) square. Place newspaper pad on baking sheet — this acts as insulation to prevent base from overcooking. Place cake pan on middle of paper and bake 30 minutes — cake will appear moist but becomes firm when cooled. Let cool in pan, turn out cake and remove foil. Store in sealed container for at least one day before using.

To serve, place on serving plate, dust with sieved powdered sugar and cut into slender wedges.

CROISSANTS AUX PIGNONS

PINE NUT CRESCENTS (FRANCE)   MAKES ABOUT 40

While the patisseries of Mediterranean France reflect French patisserie in general, there are a few local delicacies such as these pine nut cookies. Pine nuts are very much a part of the region.

$^{1}/_{2}$ cup ($2^{1}/_{2}$ oz/75 g) pine nuts

8 oz (250 g) unsalted butter

$^{2}/_{3}$ cup (5 oz/150 g) superfine (caster) sugar

grated rind of 1 orange

$^{1}/_{2}$ teaspoon vanilla extract

3 teaspoons orange flower water

2 egg yolks

$2^{1}/_{2}$ cups ($12^{1}/_{2}$ oz/375 g) all-purpose (plain) flour

3 tablespoons honey

Toast half the pine nuts and chop coarsely. Beat butter, sugar, orange rind, vanilla and 1 teaspoon orange flower water in large bowl of electric mixer until light and fluffy. Beat in egg yolks. Remove bowl from mixer and fold in flour and chopped, toasted pine nuts to make dough.

Combine honey in small bowl with remaining orange flower water and stand in shallow pan of boiling water. Stir until liquid and leave in pan, off heat, to keep hot.

Preheat oven to 325–350°F (160–180°C/Gas 3).

Roll dough into walnut-sized balls. Spread remaining pine nuts on board. Roll ball of dough between palms of hands into sausage shape, press one side into pine nuts so a few stick into dough, then bend into crescent. Place on greased baking sheet with pine nuts facing up. Repeat with remaining dough and pine nuts.

Using small brush, lightly brush tops of crescents with honey mixture, taking care not to dislodge pine nuts or to drip honey onto baking sheet as it will scorch. Bake crescents until golden, about 20 minutes. Leave on sheet 5 minutes. Using a metal spatula, lift onto wire rack to cool. Store in sealed container.

KAAB EL GHZAL

GAZELLE'S HORNS (MOROCCO, ALGERIA, TUNISIA)   MAKES ABOUT 30

Instead of orange flower water and powdered sugar coating, uncooked pastries may be glazed with beaten egg and a little milk. Cut slits in pastry after glazing then bake as described below.

Pastry:

2 cups (10 oz/300 g) all-purpose (plain) flour

1 tablespoon butter, melted

1 egg yolk

2 tablespoons orange flower water

1/2 cup (4 fl oz/125 ml) cold water, approximately

Almond Filling:

2 1/2 cups (12 oz/375 g) whole blanched almonds

3/4 cup (3 oz/90 g) powdered (icing) sugar

1 tablespoon orange flower water

1 egg white

2 tablespoons butter, melted

1/2 teaspoon ground cinnamon

1/4 teaspoon almond extract

Coating:

1/3 cup (3 fl oz/80 ml) orange flower water

1 cup (4 oz/125 g) powdered (icing) sugar, sifted

For pastry: Process flour with melted butter, egg yolk, orange flower water and half the cold water in food processor until dough forms on blades. If still crumbly, gradually add remaining water. Process 1 minute more to make elastic. Turn out and knead until smooth. Divide in half and wrap in plastic wrap. Let stand 15 minutes at least.

For almond filling: Process almonds in clean food processor bowl with powdered sugar until almonds are finely ground. Add remaining ingredients and process until stiff paste forms. Mold 3 level teaspoons of paste into a ball. Make all remaining balls this size. Shape balls of paste into almond shapes, tapering slightly at each end, and about 3 in (7.5 cm) long. Place on tray.

Preheat oven to 325–350°F (160–180°C/Gas 3).

To assemble pastries, roll out half the dough on floured surface into rectangle about 12 in x 16 in (30 cm x 46 cm), with longer edge towards you. Place three almond shapes 2 in (5 cm) up from lower edge, 1 1/2 in (4 cm) apart, and same distance from each end. Lightly brush pastry at lower edge and between almond shapes with water and fold bottom section over filling, molding and pressing pastry around filling to seal. With fluted pastry wheel, cut around top of each shape in crescent shape, about 3/4 in (2 cm) away from filling to give border of pastry. Remove each crescent and press cut edge again to make firm seal. Pick up each pastry, with filling-side up, and bend up into crescent shape. Place on greased baking tray and make 3 tiny diagonal slits in top of each pastry with point of sharp knife. Straighten edge of remaining pastry on board with knife, fill and shape again. Repeat with remaining ingredients, using pastry trimmings after second ball of pastry is used.

Bake until lightly colored, about 15 minutes. Place orange flower water in small bowl and sieved powdered sugar in deep bowl. Work quickly while pastries are hot. Dip each hot pastry immediately into orange flower water and drop into bowl of icing sugar. Using dry hand, coat pastry with powdered sugar and place on wire rack. Let cool. Sift more powdered sugar over cooled pastries and store in sealed container at room temperature.

BURMA TEL-KATAYIF

SHREDDED PASTRIES WITH PISTACHIOS (TURKEY)   MAKES 30

Shredded pastry is usually sold under the Greek name kataifi at Middle Eastern markets. It is made with a thin dough poured through a perforated screen onto a hotplate, dried briefly, then scooped off. Make sure you have unsalted nuts for this recipe. I have found that pistachios in their shell are far better than shelled nuts; they seem to be plumper. It is unnecessary and tedious to blanch the nuts for the filling but do blanch a few to sprinkle on top. A bamboo sushi mat can be used to assist in rolling the pastries.

12 oz (375 g) kataifi pastry

6 oz (180 g) butter,
clarified (see page 9)

3 tablespoons finely chopped,
blanched pistachio nuts

Syrup:

1 cup (8 fl oz/250 ml) water

1¹/₂ cups (12 oz/375 g) sugar

1 teaspoon strained lemon juice

3 teaspoons rose water or
orange flower water

Pistachio Filling:

1 egg white

¹/₄ cup (2 oz/60 g) superfine
(caster) sugar

1¹/₂ cups (6 oz/180 g) finely
chopped pistachio nuts

1 teaspoon rose water or
orange flower water

Remove package of pastry from refrigerator 2 hours before required to bring it to room temperature. Clarify butter and place in bowl in pan of hot water to keep warm.

For syrup: Place water, sugar and lemon juice in heavy pan over medium heat and stir until sugar is dissolved. Bring to boil and boil over medium heat 12 minutes. Add rose or orange flower water, stir and remove from heat. Let cool completely.

For filling: Beat egg white in bowl until stiff. Gradually beat in sugar. Fold in nuts and rose or orange flower water.

Preheat oven to 325–350°F (160–180°C/Gas 3).

To assemble pastries: With kataifi still in plastic bag, squeeze and knead to loosen strands. Remove a sixth of kataifi and spread onto board, roughly with strands running away from you. Shape into 7 in x 11 in (18 cm x 28 cm) rectangle with shorter edge in front of you. Dab strands with brush dipped in melted clarified butter. Place about one-sixth of filling along lower edge and roll up firmly into neat roll. Make another 5 rolls in same way.

Grease 7 in x 11 in (18 cm x 28 cm) shallow cake pan or baking dish with butter and place rolls over base, spacing a little apart. Brush remaining butter over rolls. Bake towards top of oven, until golden and crisp, about 40 minutes.

Remove from oven and pour cold syrup evenly over hot rolls. Cover with folded white paper towels and let stand until syrup has been absorbed and rolls are cold. To serve, cut each roll diagonally into 4 pieces and sprinkle tops with chopped blanched pistachio nuts. Store rolls in sealed container at room temperature.

Ma'Amoul

DATE AND NUT-FILLED COOKIES (LEBANON, SYRIA)   MAKES ABOUT 45

These deliciously different cookies usually contain a walnut filling, but a date and nut filling such as this one is also used. If you prefer only walnuts, increase nuts to 1½ cups and mix with ¼ cup superfine (caster) sugar and 1 teaspoon ground cinnamon. You can purchase a tabi for molding the cookies from Middle Eastern food stores, otherwise make them as directed in method.

4½ cups (1½ lb/750 g) fine semolina

½ cup (3½ oz/110 g) superfine (caster) sugar

8 oz (250 g) unsalted butter

1 cup (8 fl oz/250 ml) milk

½ teaspoon baking soda (bicarbonate of soda)

powdered (icing) sugar

Date and Walnut Filling:

2 tablespoons butter

8 oz (250 g) dried dates, pitted and chopped

½ cup (2½ oz/75 g) chopped walnuts

2 teaspoons rose water

Combine semolina and sugar in large bowl. Melt butter in saucepan and heat until bubbling. Add to semolina mixture and mix with wooden spoon to distribute evenly. Heat milk in same saucepan, and when bubbles begin to rise, remove from heat and stir in soda. Add to semolina mixture and mix well to soft dough. Let cool a little, then knead lightly. Cover bowl tightly with plastic wrap and let stand 5 hours at least, or overnight.

For date and walnut filling: Melt butter in saucepan. Add dates and heat until dates soften to a paste, stirring often. Remove from heat and stir in walnuts and rose water.

Preheat oven to 350–375°F (180–190°C/Gas 4).

To assemble cookies, knead dough to make pliable. Shape into large walnut-sized balls. Press a ball in palm of hand and push up sides to make cup shape. Fill hollow with heaping teaspoon of date and walnut filling, and mold dough over filling, sealing joins. Roll into ball again.

If you have a decorative mold (tabi), press ball into tabi and tap out onto board then place on ungreased baking sheet. Alternatively, place ball on baking sheet, flatten slightly and press tines of fork around sides obliquely, to give slightly conical shape. Bake until lightly colored, about 20 to 25 minutes. Remove and let cool 10 minutes on baking sheets.

Sift powdered sugar onto large sheet of waxed (greaseproof) paper. Place still warm cookies on sugar, spacing a little apart, then sift more powdered sugar on top to coat thickly. Let cool completely. Store in sealed container at room temperature.

KOURAMBIETHES

BUTTER SHORTBREADS WITH ALMONDS (GREECE)   MAKES 40

These powdered sugar-coated shortbread cookies are traditionally made at Christmas time; the aromatic clove usually inserted into the middle represents the frankincense and myrrh brought to the infant Jesus. There are many versions of the recipe, but the common factors are using unsalted butter, creaming it until very fluffy to give the right texture, and using very little sugar so that a thick shape is retained when baked. In hot weather it is advisable to refrigerate the dough for 20 minutes before adding extra flour, if needed, or shaping dough. The shortbreads taste best the day after baking, but will keep for 2 weeks.

8 oz (250 g) unsalted butter

1/4 cup (1 oz/30g) powdered (icing) sugar, sifted

1 egg yolk

1 tablespoon brandy or ouzo

1/2 cup (4 oz/125 g) finely chopped toasted almonds

2 1/2 cups (12 oz/375 g) all-purpose (plain) flour

1 teaspoon baking powder

whole cloves (optional)

extra powdered (icing) sugar, to coat

Cream butter and powdered sugar in bowl until very light and fluffy. Beat in egg yolk and brandy or ouzo. Stir in almonds. Sift flour with baking powder and fold into butter mixture to form soft dough. Press with finger — dough is ready if it does not stick, otherwise mix in a little more flour.

Preheat oven to 300–325°F (150–160°C/Gas 3).

Take walnut-sized ball of dough and roll between palms into sausage shape, tapering at ends, and bend into crescent. Repeat with remaining dough. Insert whole clove into middle of each crescent, if desired. Place on lightly greased baking sheets, spacing them apart to allow for spreading. Bake until only lightly browned, about 15 to 20 minutes — do not over-brown or flavor will be altered. Let cool on baking sheets 5 minutes.

Sift thick layer of powdered sugar onto large sheet of waxed (greaseproof) paper. Carefully lift shortbreads onto sugar using metal spatula, leaving a little space between each. Sift more powdered sugar on top. Let cool. Pack into container, sifting more powdered sugar onto each layer. Store at room temperature.

Kourambiethes

GHORAYEBAH

NUT SHORTBREAD COOKIES (MIDDLE EAST, NORTH AFRICA)　　　　　MAKES ABOUT 40

8 oz (250 g) unsalted butter

1 cup (4 oz/125 g) powdered (icing) sugar

1 egg yolk

1 tablespoon orange flower water

1/2 cup (21/2 oz/75 g) finely chopped skinned toasted hazelnuts, walnuts or almonds (optional)

21/2 cups (12 oz/375 g) all-purpose (plain) flour

1 teaspoon baking powder

about 40 whole blanched almonds (optional)

Cream butter and powdered sugar until very light and fluffy. Beat in egg yolk and orange flower water, then fold in nuts if used. Sift flour with baking powder and fold into butter mixture to form soft dough. Press with finger — it is ready if it does not stick, otherwise mix in more flour.

Preheat oven to 300–325°F (150–160°C/Gas 3).

Roll dough into walnut-sized balls and place on lightly greased baking sheets, spacing apart to allow for spreading. Press thumb in middle of each ball to flatten slightly and to make indent. Place almond in middle, if chopped nuts were not included. Bake until only lightly browned, about 15 to 20 minutes — do not over-brown or flavor will be altered. Let cool completely on baking sheets. Remove carefully with metal spatula and store in sealed container.

NEPITELLE

FIG AND NUT PASTRIES (ITALY)　　　　　MAKES ABOUT 36

Pastry:

3 cups (15 oz/450 g) all-purpose (plain) flour

1/2 cup (31/2 oz/110 g) superfine (caster) sugar

6 oz (180 g) butter, chopped

2 large eggs

1 egg, to glaze

Filling:

4 oz (125 g) dried figs

1/2 cup (2 oz/60 g) finely chopped walnuts

1/2 cup (21/2 oz/75 g) finely chopped toasted almonds

1/2 cup (3 oz/90 g) raisins, chopped

2 teaspoons grated orange rind

1/2 teaspoon ground allspice

about 3 tablespoons orange marmalade

For pastry: Process flour, sugar and butter in food processor until mixture resembles coarse crumbs. Add 2 eggs and process until dough forms on blades. Turn onto floured surface and knead until smooth, adding more flour if dough is sticky. Wrap in plastic wrap and refrigerate 30 minutes.

For filling: Simmer figs in water to cover in saucepan until just soft, about 10 minutes. Drain, dry and chop coarsely. Combine figs with nuts, raisins, grated rind and allspice in bowl. Add enough marmalade to make stiff, coarse paste.

Preheat oven to 325–350°F (160–180°C/Gas 3).

To assemble: Roll out pastry on floured surface until 1/4 in (5 mm) thick. Cut into rounds using 4 in (10 cm) cutter, using trimmings as well. Separate egg and beat egg white in bowl until frothy. Place a heaping teaspoon of filling in middle of each round, brush edges lightly with egg white and fold pastry over filling in half-moon shape. Press edges to seal and place on greased baking sheets. Add yolk to remaining white and beat well. Brush pastries with egg glaze and cut 3 small slits in top of each with point of knife. Bake until golden brown, about 20 to 25 minutes. Let cool on baking sheets. Store in sealed container at room temperature.

AMARETTI

BITTER ALMOND MACAROONS (ITALY)   MAKES ABOUT 20

These crunchy almond macaroons are available in gourmet food stores, each individually wrapped. They can sometimes be difficult to find, but are easy to make. Although bitter almonds are traditionally used, almond extract adds the desired flavor. In Italy, these are often served with dessert wine, in which the macaroons are dunked to soften them slightly, and are also used in desserts. The amaretti made with bitter almonds are also crumbled over boiled greens.

1 cup (5 oz/150 g) whole blanched almonds

3/4 cup (51/2 oz/165 g) superfine (caster) sugar

2 egg whites

1/2 teaspoon vanilla extract (essence)

1/4 teaspoon almond extract (essence)

blanched, split almonds, to decorate (optional)

Preheat oven to 325–350°F (160–180°C/Gas 3). Grease baking sheet and dust completely with flour, shaking off excess.

Place almonds in food processor bowl with steel blade and process until coarsely ground, adding about 1/4 cup of the sugar to prevent almonds becoming oily.

Beat egg whites, ground almonds, remaining sugar, and vanilla and almond extracts in small bowl with electric mixer, 3 minutes. Set aside 5 minutes for sugar to dissolve. Place mixture in pastry (piping) bag fitted with plain 1/2 in (1 cm) nozzle. Pipe almond mixture into neat mounds on baking sheet about 11/4 in (3 cm) in diameter. Place split almond in middle of each, if desired. Bake until golden brown, about 20 minutes. Let stand 5 minutes on baking sheet. Using metal spatula, remove to wire rack to let cool completely. Store in sealed container when cold.

LENGUAS DE GATO

CATS' TONGUES (SPAIN)   MAKES ABOUT 24

Originally French, these cookies are also prepared in Spain to serve with ice cream and other creamy desserts. They often accompany a bowl of fresh strawberries or caramelized oranges (see page 293) and can also be served with coffee.

2 oz (60 g) unsalted butter

1/2 cup (31/2 oz/110 g) superfine (caster) sugar

1/4 teaspoon grated lemon rind (optional)

1/2 teaspoon vanilla extract (essence)

2 egg whites

1/2 cup (21/2 oz/75 g) all-purpose (plain) flour

Preheat oven to 350–375°F (180–190°C/Gas 4). Grease baking sheets. Cream butter and sugar until light and fluffy in small bowl with electric mixer, adding lemon rind and vanilla extract. Beat in egg whites until just combined. Sift in flour and stir until smooth. Spoon mixture into pastry (piping) bag fitted with plain 1/4 in (5 mm) nozzle.

Pipe mixture onto baking sheets in thin strips 21/2 in (6 cm) long, spacing them well apart to allow for spreading. Bake until golden brown around edges, about 5 to 6 minutes. Using metal spatula, remove to wire rack to cool. Store in sealed container at room temperature. Serve with desserts.

DESSERTS

I n the Mediterranean, a meal is not complete until fresh fruit is served — another healthy
food habit and one we all would do well to adopt. In France and Italy, the fruit is usually
accompanied by cheese. Elsewhere, fruit alone, in all its glory, is sufficient. The sun
works its magic, especially in summer, giving stone fruits, figs, grapes and melons that extra
sweetness, succulence and perfume.

However, the region offers rich pickings for those with a sweet tooth. Fine desserts do
exist. Mediterranean France has a varied repertoire, using fruit in compotes and for the flat
tarts typical of Provençal cooking; but you are just as likely to encounter feather-light
soufflés made with local ingredients such as chestnut or fruit purees, or a wickedly rich
chocolate mousse.

A favorite Italian dessert is sweetened fruit with rich mascarpone cheese. Fresh, low-fat
ricotta cheese, originally a by-product of mozzarella cheese-making in the south, is enjoyed
as a dessert, simply drizzled with honey, or used in southern Italian and Sicilian desserts and
pastries that are served on special occasions. Sicily is also famous for its ice creams or
gelatos, sorbets and granitas using fruit and nuts for flavoring. Ice cream is popular throughout much of the region, although it is rarely made at home, rather it is enjoyed while out and
about during the day or evening.

Many Spanish desserts have been adopted and adapted from other cuisines, such as pears
cooked in a wine syrup, "burnt" cream or crème brulée (although the Catalonians claim this
as their own creation) and the popular flan, crème caramel, that is made throughout Spain,
either plain, with apples or flavored with orange.

Rice puddings, or puddings thickened with cornstarch, ground rice or almonds, are
favored in Greece, the Levant and North Africa, flavored in various ways, including fragrant
orange flower water or rose water. Turkish and Arabic versions are served with a sprinkling
of chopped almonds, pistachios, or, when in season, pomegranate seeds.

In Turkey, Greece and Cyprus, they are very fond of halva, a pudding or type of sweetmeat (depending on how thick it is) made with semolina or browned flour, syrup and flavorings. Fruit compotes are also popular, especially using dried fruit in winter.

You will find a dessert to finish off any Mediterranean dinner or lunch, served in the
tradition of the region. If in doubt, serve fresh fruit of the best quality. For everyday meals,
make it a habit; if fruit is cut up and presented attractively, it will soon disappear.

Tartes aux Figues Fraîches (page 272)

Tartes aux Figues Fraîches

FRESH FIG TARTS (FRANCE)   SERVES 6

Provençal tarts are usually flat discs of pastry topped with fruit. However, I like to crimp the edge to give a shallow tart shape. Sliced apples or pears can be used when figs are not available.

Pastry:

2 cups (10 oz/300 g) all-purpose (plain) flour

1/4 cup (2 oz/60 g) superfine (caster) sugar

2 tablespoons ground almonds

6 oz (180 g) butter, chopped

1 egg

Fig Topping:

9 to 12 ripe figs, depending on size

6 teaspoons sugar or lavender honey

To Serve:

heavy (double) cream or crème fraîche (see page 35) (optional)

For pastry: Process flour, sugar and almonds in food processor briefly to mix. Add butter and process until mixture resembles coarse breadcrumbs. Add egg and process just enough to form a dough, adding a little cold water if necessary. Remove dough, smooth into a square, wrap in plastic wrap and refrigerate 30 minutes.

Preheat oven to 375–400°F (190–200°C/Gas 5). Roll pastry on lightly floured surface until 1/4 in (5 mm) thick. Cut into 6 rounds of 5 in (13 cm) diameter. Lift onto greased baking sheet and pinch edges with fingertips to give shallow tart shapes. Refrigerate at least 15 minutes. Bake 12 minutes; do not allow to brown. Remove and set aside. Reduce oven heat to 325–350°F (160–180°C/Gas 3).

For fig topping: Peel figs thinly with a sharp knife or vegetable peeler. Cut into 1/4 in (5 mm) slices. Overlap fig slices on pastry bases. Sprinkle each tart with 1 teaspoon sugar or a light drizzle of honey. Return to oven and bake further 15 minutes.

Serve warm, with cream or crème fraîche, if desired.

grapes

Tarte au Citron

LEMON TART (FRANCE)   SERVES 8

This tart is made in the style most often used in Provence, with a similar ratio of filling to pastry. This filling is very much like the lemon curd of English cuisine, but with care, can be more quickly prepared in a saucepan over direct heat, rather than the usual double boiler method. Do not allow the mixture to boil. If it begins to curdle, place base of pan immediately into cold water and stir well with balloon whisk.

1 quantity pâté sucrée pastry (see page 232)

1/2 cup (31/2 oz/110 g) sugar

1 teaspoon grated lemon rind

1/4 cup (2 fl oz/60 ml) strained fresh lemon juice

2 oz (60 g) butter, chopped

1 large egg

1 egg yolk

heavy (double) cream or crème fraîche (see page 35), to serve

Preheat oven to 375–400°F (190–200°C/Gas 5).

After chilling pastry, roll out on lightly floured board into a 10 in (25 cm) round and lift onto greased baking sheet. Crimp edge with fingertips to give shallow tart shape. Prick well with fork and bake until lightly golden brown and cooked, about 15 to 18 minutes. Let cool on baking sheet.

Combine sugar, lemon rind, juice and butter in small, heavy saucepan. Beat egg and egg yolk in bowl with balloon whisk and strain into pan. Mix well with wooden spoon. Place over medium-low heat and stir constantly until mixture thickens and coats back of spoon, leaving a track when a finger is run across it. Place pan in cold water to arrest cooking, and let cool until lukewarm, stirring occasionally.

Place pastry on flat serving platter and spread filling over. Let cool. Serve cut into wedges with cream or crème fraîche.

Tarte aux Pruneaux

PRUNE TART (FRANCE)   SERVES 6 TO 8

Other fruit may be used in place of the prunes in this tart, such as peeled and cored slices of ripe pear, pitted cherries, and quince slices poached in a sugar syrup and drained.

1 quantity pâté sucrée pastry (see page 232)

2 tablespoons cognac or good brandy

8 oz (250 g) prunes, pitted

3 large eggs

1/4 cup (2 oz/60 g) superfine (caster) sugar

1/2 cup (4 fl oz/125 ml) heavy (double) cream

3/4 cup (3 oz/90 g) ground almonds

2 tablespoons orange flower water

2 tablespoons butter, melted

1/2 teaspoon vanilla extract (essence)

whipped cream or crème fraîche (see page 35), to serve (optional)

Preheat oven to 375–400°F (190–200°C/Gas 5).

After pastry is chilled, roll it out on lightly floured board to fit greased 9 in (23 cm) tart pan (flan tin) with removable base. Lift into pan, trim edge and refrigerate 10 minutes.

If prunes feel firm, cover with hot water and soak 15 minutes, drain and pat dry with paper towels. Beat eggs lightly with balloon whisk in bowl. Add sugar, cream, almonds, orange flower water, butter and vanilla and beat well until smooth.

Place prunes on base of pastry and pour egg mixture on top. Bake until golden brown and firm in middle, about 25 to 30 minutes. Sprinkle top with cognac as soon as tart is removed from oven and let cool on wire rack. Serve plain or with cream or crème fraîche.

Sformato di Aranci

ORANGE AND ALMOND CAKE (ITALY)   SERVES 8 TO 10

This dessert cake is rather similar to a cake which contains no flour or breadcrumbs made by the Sephardic Jews for Passover. The Italian cake dates from the Renaissance and the original recipe has a mousse-like texture which does not hold its shape well when cooled. I have combined the two recipes, both of which contain boiled orange pulp, to give a cake which turns out perfectly every time. Buy the almonds already ground; if you grind them yourself and use a cup measure, the weight will differ. Use orange blossom honey if it is available. Don't beat the eggs until thick — if you incorporate too much air the cake will sink. Orange segments macerated in a little orange blossom honey and Grand Marnier liqueur may be arranged alongside each serving, if desired.

2 sweet oranges
(total weight 13 oz/400 g)

1/2 teaspoon salt

melted butter, to grease

flour, to coat

6 medium eggs

1 cup (7 1/2 oz/220 g) superfine
(caster) sugar

2 1/4 cups (8 oz/250 g) ground
almonds

2 tablespoons dried breadcrumbs

2 tablespoons orange flower water

1 teaspoon baking powder

4 tablespoons finely chopped,
toasted, unblanched almonds

3 tablespoons honey

whipped cream, to serve

Wash oranges and place in saucepan with water to cover. Add salt and bring to boil. Cover and boil gently 30 minutes. Pour off water, replace with fresh water and boil until oranges are soft, about 30 minutes. Drain, thinly slice off skin from each end only, cut oranges into quarters and discard any seeds. Process to pulp in food processor and let cool.

Preheat oven to 325–350°F (160–180°C/Gas 3). Grease 8 in (20 cm) springform pan with melted butter and refrigerate until set. Dust pan with flour, shaking out excess.

Beat eggs and sugar in bowl with electric mixer just until light in color — do not beat until thick. Remove bowl from mixer and fold in ground almonds, breadcrumbs and orange flower water. Add baking powder to orange pulp in food processor, process briefly to mix, and fold into cake batter.

Pour batter into prepared pan and bake until cooked, about 1 hour — a fine skewer inserted in the middle will come out clean. Let cool in pan. Remove sides from pan and lift cake carefully onto wire rack.

On long strip of waxed (greaseproof) paper, spread toasted almonds in strip a little wider than side of cake. Warm honey and brush most of it over side of cake. Lift cake carefully with one hand on base and one on top. Roll cake along almonds so they cling to side. Reserve any that do not cling.

Place cake on serving plate. Brush top with remaining honey and sprinkle with reserved almonds. Serve cut in wedges with whipped cream.

Sformato di Aranci

Monte Bianco

CHESTNUT DESSERT (ITALY)   SERVES 6

When fresh chestnuts are in season, make this simple but delicious dessert. You can use a 15 oz (425 g) can unsweetened chestnut puree: dissolve sugar in milk over heat, mix into puree and add vanilla and brandy before finishing as directed. Monte Bianco, or Monte Blanc, is also popular in France and Greece.

1 lb (500 g) fresh chestnuts, shelled and skinned (see page 22)

3 tablespoons milk

1/4 cup (2 oz/60 g) sugar

1 teaspoon vanilla extract (essence)

1 tablespoon brandy

1 cup (8 fl oz/250 ml) whipping cream, whipped

grated semi-sweet (dark) chocolate, to serve

Place shelled and skinned chestnuts in saucepan, cover with water and bring to boil. Cover and boil gently until very soft, about 30 minutes. Drain well. Return to saucepan, stir in milk and sugar and heat until moisture evaporates. Add more sugar to taste if necessary. Let cool. Puree in food mill with finest screen or in food processor. Transfer to bowl, stir in vanilla and brandy, and chill.

Pile mixture in mounds in small dessert glasses and pipe a swirl of whipped cream on top of each. Sprinkle cream with chocolate and serve immediately.

Soufflés aux Marrons et Chocolat

CHESTNUT AND CHOCOLATE SOUFFLÉS (FRANCE)   SERVES 8

Soufflés look spectacular but are really quite easy to make. Use canned, unsweetened chestnut puree for convenience. Choose large eggs, each 2 oz (60 g) or slightly more in weight; eggs must be at room temperature. The egg yolk mixture can be set aside, covered, and finished with the beaten whites about 25 minutes before serving. Have the whites ready in another bowl at room temperature. If serving the soufflés with cream, a hole is made in the middle of the soufflé at the table and the cream poured in.

butter, for greasing

1/2 cup (31/2 oz/110 g) superfine (caster) sugar

4 egg yolks

15 oz (425 g) can unsweetened chestnut puree

2 oz (60 g) chopped semi-sweet (dark) chocolate

1 tablespoon cognac or brandy

8 egg whites

pinch of salt

powdered (icing) sugar, to serve

light (single) cream, to serve (optional)

Grease 8 x 1 cup (8 fl oz/250 ml) soufflé dishes with butter and dust lightly with some of the sugar, shaking out excess. Place on baking sheet. Beat egg yolks and 2 tablespoons sugar in large bowl until thick and creamy. Stir in chestnut puree, chocolate and cognac or brandy, cover and set aside until 25 minutes before serving.

Preheat oven 375–400°F (190–200°C/Gas 5). Beat egg whites with salt in another large bowl until stiff. Gradually beat in remaining sugar. When glossy, fold 2 heaped tablespoons egg white into chestnut mixture. Fold in remaining egg white using large metal spoon. Fill soufflé dishes with mixture and level with spatula. Run finger around inside edge of each dish so that soufflé forms a "cap" when cooked. Bake until well-risen and golden brown, about 15 minutes. Dust with sieved powdered sugar. Transfer dishes to small plates. Serve immediately with jug of cream.

MEMBRILLO

QUINCE PASTE (SPAIN)   MAKES ABOUT 2½ LB (1.2 KG)

In Spain, membrillo is molded into a loaf or slab and served as a popular accompaniment to cheeses and cold meats. In France it is known as pâte de coigns, set in a slab, cut into lozenges and coated with fine sugar to serve with soft cheeses. The Greek kithonopasto is similarly shaped and coated and stored with bay leaves to add flavor; it is served as a sweetmeat.

While the quinces are usually cooked with the skin on, I like to peel and core the fruit and boil the trimmings separately to extract the pectin; the fruit can then be pureed more easily without the need to press through a sieve to separate fruit from peels. Do not worry about any discoloration of the quinces as this disappears in the cooking. The cinnamon and lemon rind are typical flavorings for membrillo, but the cinnamon can be omitted if making the French or Greek version.

2 lb (1 kg) quinces

3 cups (24 fl oz/750 ml) water

2-inch (5 cm) cinnamon stick (optional)

thinly peeled rind of 1 lemon

3 cups (24 oz/660 g) sugar

Peel quinces, quarter and remove cores. Place cores and peels in a saucepan with 3 cups water, crumbled cinnamon stick, and lemon rind. Cover and boil gently 45 minutes.

Cut each quince quarter in half and place in heavy-based pan. Strain liquid from peels through seive into pan, pressing to extract moisture. Discard peels and cores. Cover pan and simmer gently 1 hour or until quinces are very soft and rosy pink — add a little more water if necessary so that they do not stick to pan.

Puree quinces and liquid in food processor or food mill. Return to pan, add sugar and stir over heat until sugar is dissolved, scraping down sides of pan. Bring to boil and boil gently, stirring often, 45 minutes or until paste is very thick and reddish — take care as hot paste can spatter and watch that it does not stick to base of pan. Remove pan from heat and let stand 10 minutes.

Line round-based loaf pan or slab cake pan with plastic wrap and pour in paste. Spread evenly and let stand 24 hours. Unmold onto baking sheet and remove plastic. Cover with gauze and let stand at room temperature 1 week. Store in sealed container in refrigerator, using as required; it keeps for several months.

Serve the loaf on a plate, to be sliced as required. Cut slab into squares or lozenges. Use as an accompaniment to cold meats and cheeses, or serve on bread as a snack.

Cassata Siciliana

SICILIAN CASSATA WITH RICOTTA (ITALY)   SERVES 8 TO 10

A cassata must be made in a bombe shape if it is to bear the name as the word comes from the Arabic kasi, meaning bowl. Arabic influence in Sicilian cooking is very strong and still lingers centuries after the Arab presence on the island. For the candied fruits, choose a selection such as citron and orange peel, apricots, figs and cherries. Choose large savoiardi, at least 4 in (10 cm) long. If you do not have a food processor, rub the ricotta cheese through a sieve into a mixing bowl and beat with other ingredients. You can place savoiardi or cake into lined loaf pan or 8 in (20 cm) springform pan if desired, but the bombe shape is traditional. Lining the basin with plastic wrap helps savoiardi or cake to stay in place.

3 cups (1¹/2 lb/750 g) ricotta cheese

¹/4 cup (2 fl oz/60 ml) heavy (double) cream

¹/2 cup (4 oz/125 g) superfine (caster) sugar

1 teaspoon vanilla extract (essence)

1 tablespoon dark rum

1 teaspoon grated orange rind

¹/2 teaspoon ground cinnamon

3 to 4 tablespoons finely chopped semi-sweet (dark) chocolate

1 cup (6 oz/175 g) chopped mixed candied (glacé) fruits

12 to 15 savoiardi (sponge fingers) or 2 x 7 in (18 cm) sponge cakes

¹/2 cup (4 fl oz/125 ml) sweet dessert wine eg. sauternes or amber-colored Italian dessert wine

To Serve:

powdered (icing) sugar

whipped cream

extra candied (glacé) fruits

Place ricotta in food processor with cream, sugar, vanilla, rum, orange rind and cinnamon and process until smooth. Transfer to bowl and stir in chocolate and candied fruits.

Line 8-cup (64 fl oz/2 L) jelly mold or pudding basin with plastic wrap, draping enough over sides so that it will cover top when needed. Slit savoiardi in half through middle, using fine-bladed serrated knife. If using sponge cake, slit in half. Pour wine into shallow dish and skim each savoiardi half across surface, slightly dampening each side. Line base and sides of mold with savoiardi, browned-side facing outwards — they will soften more and mold into shape when filling is added.

Alternatively, cut sponge cake to fit base and sides, dip in wine and place with browned surface outwards.

Spoon in ricotta filling and tap mold on work surface to help filling settle. Cover top with savoiardi or sponge scraps and trim excess cake from around edge. Bring plastic wrap over top, cover basin and refrigerate at least 3 hours.

Open plastic wrap and invert serving plate on top of cake. Turn out cassata and remove wrap. Cover and return to refrigerator if not to be served immediately. Decorate as desired with dusting of sieved powdered sugar, piped whipped cream and extra candied fruits.

Cassata Siciliana

RIZOGALO

CREAMED RICE (GREECE, CRYPRUS)   SERVES 6

Rice puddings are popular throughout the eastern Mediterranean; in Middle Eastern countries they are usually flavored with orange flower or rose waters. In Greece and Cyprus, various flavorings are used according to the cook's preference — vanilla, lemon rind or cinnamon are used alone or in combination. I prefer vanilla and like nutmeg on top instead of the usual cinnamon.

1 cup (8 fl oz/250 ml) water

1/2 cup (31/2 oz/110 g) medium-grain rice

4 cups (32 fl oz/1 L) milk

pinch of salt

3 egg yolks

extra milk

2 to 3 tablespoons sugar

11/2 teaspoons vanilla extract (essence)

ground cinnamon or freshly grated nutmeg

Bring 1 cup water to boil in heavy-based saucepan. Stir in dry, unrinsed rice and cook gently, stirring often, until water is absorbed, about 8 minutes. Add milk and salt and bring to boil, stirring occasionally. Cook gently, uncovered, 25 minutes, until rice is very soft (a grain should disintegrate when pressed), stirring occasionally to prevent it boiling over.

Beat egg yolks with a little cold milk in bowl. Mix in 1/2 cup hot creamed rice and return to saucepan, stirring over gentle heat just long enough to thicken and begin to bubble. Add sugar to taste and vanilla, and pour into serving dish or individual bowls. Dust with cinnamon or nutmeg and serve warm or chilled.

MOUSSE AU CHOCOLAT

CHOCOLATE MOUSSE (FRANCE)   SERVES 6

Chocolate is another of the contributions to the Old World from the New. Its development into the block chocolate we know today took some 300 years from the time the cocoa bean was brought to Spain in the 16th century. While chocolate is not used a great deal in Mediterranean cooking, chocolate mousse is as popular in the region as elsewhere.

4 oz (125 g) semi-sweet (dark) chocolate, chopped

4 eggs, separated

1/4 cup (2 oz/60 g) superfine (caster) sugar

1 tablespoon brandy

1/2 teaspoon vanilla extract (essence)

1 cup (8 fl oz/250 ml) whipping cream, whipped

grated semi-sweet (dark) chocolate or chocolate curls, to serve

Melt chocolate in heat-proof bowl, set over saucepan of simmering water. Meanwhile, combine egg yolks with half the sugar in heat-proof bowl over another saucepan of simmering water and beat until thick. Stir in chocolate, brandy and vanilla until smooth and remove from heat. Let cool.

Beat egg whites in bowl until stiff. Beat in remaining sugar. Fold into chocolate mixture using metal spoon, adding 2 tablespoons whipped cream. Pour into small mousse pots or into individual dessert glasses and refrigerate until set, about 6 hours.

Using remaining cream, pipe large rosettes onto each mousse and decorate with chocolate.

TIRAMISU

TUSCAN TRIFLE (ITALY)   SERVES 8

This originally began as an Italian-style trifle called zuppa del duca, using sponge cake, espresso coffee, zabaglione, mascarpone and whipped cream. It became known as zuppa inglese in Florence as it was a favorite of the resident English population in the 1800s. Today tiramisu is made in a variety of ways, and the following is a simplified version much favored by restaurateurs as it is easy to serve.

2 eggs, separated

1/3 cup (2 1/2 oz/75 g) superfine (caster) sugar

1 lb (500 g) mascarpone cheese

1 1/2 cups (12 fl oz/375 g) whipping cream, whipped

1 cup (8 fl oz/250 ml) strong espresso coffee, cooled

1 tablespoon rum

1/2 cup (4 fl oz/125 ml) sweet marsala

1 lb (500 g) savoiardi (sponge fingers)

2 oz (60 g) semi-sweet (dark) chocolate, grated

Beat egg yolks and sugar in bowl with electric mixer until light. Beat in mascarpone. Beat egg whites until stiff in another bowl with clean beater and fold into mascarpone mixture using wooden spoon. Fold in two-thirds whipped cream and reserve remaining cream.

Choose rectangular glass or ceramic dish, about 9 in x 12 in (23 cm x 30 cm), that will take 2 rows of savoiardi — you may not need all of them. Combine cooled coffee, rum and marsala in shallow bowl. Dip savoiardi, one at a time, into coffee mixture and place close together on base of dish. Brush with more coffee mixture and cover with half the mascarpone mixture. Repeat with remaining savoiardi and remaining mascarpone mixture. Smooth top. Cover and refrigerate several hours or overnight.

Just before serving, cover top thickly with grated chocolate and decorate with rosettes of reserved whipped cream. Serve cut into squares.

ZABAGLIONE

MARSALA CUSTARD (ITALY)   SERVES 6

Sweet marsala wine from Sicily is used for this rich dessert; there is also a dry marsala served as an aperitif. Zabaglione is Venetian in origin, not Sicilian, but is popular throughout Italy. Other dessert wines may be used in place of the marsala. In France, it is known as Sabayon and is made with local wines or champagne, depending on the region. The beating of the egg yolk mixture takes about 10 minutes; it may be necessary to scrape the sides and base of the bowl occasionally — remove the bowl from pan of water when you do this. Hot or cold zabaglione goes well with fresh fruit such as strawberries.

6 egg yolks

4 tablespoons superfine (caster) sugar

1 teaspoon vanilla extract (essence)

1/2 cup (4 fl oz/125 ml) sweet marsala

savoiardi or dessert cookies, to serve (optional)

Beat egg yolks, sugar and vanilla until thick and light in heat-proof bowl. Place over saucepan of simmering water and continue to beat with rotary beater or hand-held electric mixer, about 10 minutes, gradually adding marsala. When mixture is thick enough to hold its shape on beaters when lifted, it is ready. Pour into individual stemmed dessert glasses. Serve hot with savoiardi or other dessert cookies, or refrigerate and serve cold.

Gelato alla Nocciola

HAZELNUT ICE CREAM (ITALY)   SERVES 6 TO 8

To make hazelnut ice cream in the proper way, the roasted nuts are pounded to a paste, steeped in hot milk, then strained through muslin to give a hazelnut-flavored milk. Pistachio ice cream is made in the same manner, and both methods use a lot of nuts to achieve sufficient flavor. I prefer a simpler method — it may not have the smoothness of the traditional but it is a method used in Sicily, home of these iced delights, and it still makes a delicious ice cream. Adding sugar during the processing prevents the nuts from becoming oily.

3/4 cup (4 oz/125 g) shelled hazelnuts (see page 22)

1/2 cup (3 1/3 oz/110 g) sugar

2 cups (16 fl oz/500 ml) milk

1 cup (8 fl oz/250 ml) heavy cream (35% milk fat)

4 egg yolks

2 teaspoons cornflour (cornstarch)

1/2 teaspoon vanilla extract (essence)

Toast hazelnuts and remove skins as directed on page 22. Let cool. Process in food processor with 2 tablespoons sugar until a fine powder.

Place milk in small saucepan and bring almost to boiling point. Stir in nuts, remove from heat and let stand, covered, 30 minutes. Add cream, return to heat and heat, uncovered, until almost boiling.

Beat egg yolks in bowl with remaining sugar and cornflour until thick and light, gradually adding about 1 cup hot milk mixture. Pour back into pan and place over medium-low heat, stirring constantly with wooden spoon, until custard thickens and coats back of spoon. Remove from heat and place pan in cold water. Let cool, stirring occasionally.

Add vanilla. Transfer to bowl, cover, and refrigerate several hours.

Process in ice cream churn according to manufacturer's instructions. For alternative method, see notes on page 285. Transfer ice cream to freezer-proof container, seal and freeze. Transfer to refrigerator 30 minutes before required to let soften sufficiently. Serve scooped into dessert glasses.

Gelato al Pistacchio (Pistachio Ice Cream) Variation: Use shelled, unsalted pistachios instead of hazelnuts. Blanch if you have the time (see page 21), otherwise leave skins on. Process two-thirds of pistachios to a powder with sugar; chop remainder coarsely by hand. Steep ground pistachios in hot milk and continue as above, using 1 tablespoon orange flower water instead of vanilla. Add chopped pistachios while churning ice cream. Add 1 to 2 drops green coloring, if desired.

Pages 282 to 283: Burma Tel-Katayif (page 264),
Compote de Coigns (page 297), Cassata Siciliana (page 278)

HELADO DE CANELA

CINNAMON ICE CREAM (SPAIN)   SERVES 6 TO 8

Ice cream or iced confections are made in some Spanish domestic kitchens, but it is in restaurants and cafes that many imaginative offerings are created. Cinnamon ice cream usually appears on menus as leche merengada (cinnamon milk ice), as cream is a relatively new addition to Spain's table. The ice cream is excellent served alongside apple pie or peres al vi negre (see page 292).

If you do not have an ice cream churn, refrigerate bowl and beaters of electric mixer in freezer. Pour custard into a shallow container and place in freezer until it is frozen halfway to middle. Break up and place in refrigerated bowl. Beat until thick and light and transfer to refrigerated container, seal and freeze.

2 cups (16 fl oz/500 ml) whole milk

2 x 2 in (5 cm) cinnamon sticks

thinly peeled rind of 1 lemon

1 cup (8 fl oz/250 ml) heavy (double) cream

4 egg yolks

1/2 cup (3 1/2 oz/110 g) sugar

pinch of salt

3 teaspoons cornstarch (cornflour)

1 teaspoon vanilla extract (essence)

To Serve:

ground cinnamon (optional)

lenguas de gato (see page 269) or dessert cookies (optional)

Combine milk, cinnamon sticks and lemon rind in heavy saucepan and bring to a simmer, partly covered with lid. Simmer over low heat 20 minutes. Remove from heat, cover and let stand 1 hour. Strain into jug, discarding cinnamon and rind, and wash saucepan. Return milk to saucepan, stir in cream and bring to simmering point.

Beat egg yolks with sugar, salt and cornstarch in bowl until light and creamy using balloon whisk. Stir in about one-third of hot milk mixture, then return to saucepan. Stir constantly over medium-low heat until thickened and just beginning to bubble (cornstarch prevents it curdling). Remove from heat, stir in vanilla and stand pan in cold water. Stir occasionally until cool. Cover and refrigerate 2 hours or overnight. Place container in which ice cream is to be stored in freezer to chill well.

Pour custard into ice cream churn and process according to manufacturer's instructions. Transfer to chilled container, seal and freeze at least 24 hours.

Place in refrigerator 30 minutes before serving to soften a little. Serve with light dusting of cinnamon and lenguas de gato or other dessert cookies.

FLAN DE NARANJA

ORANGE CARAMEL CREAM (SPAIN)   SERVES 6

Baked caramel custard or crème caramel is claimed by the French as their invention but it is so popular in Spain that its inclusion in their cuisine is compulsory. This version is flavored with orange which makes it very Spanish. The custards may be cooked in small custard molds: pour a little toffee into each mold and swirl around to cover base and partly cover sides. Cook in a water bath at the same temperature as for large one for 30 minutes.

3/4 cup (5¹/2 oz/165 g) sugar
1 orange
2¹/2 cups (20 fl oz/625 ml) milk
1 cup (8 fl oz/250 ml) heavy (double) cream
1¹/2 in (4 cm) piece cinnamon stick
pinch of salt
¹/3 cup (2¹/2oz/75 g) sugar, extra
3 eggs
3 egg yolks
¹/2 teaspoon vanilla extract (essence)

Preheat oven to 325–350°F (160–180°C/Gas 3).

Have ring cake pan or fluted ring pan on hand, with capacity of at least 5 cups (42 fl oz/1.25 L). Place sugar in small heavy frying pan over medium heat and stir occasionally at the start to warm evenly, brushing sugar from sides of pan using wet brush. As sugar melts, tip pan back and forth to mix unmelted sugar with melted sugar (do not stir). Heat until an amber-colored toffee is formed. Pour into cake pan, holding pan with cloth and rotating so toffee coats base and part way up sides. Set aside.

Using fine grater, lightly scratch surface around circumference of orange so that flavor can be released easily, then thinly peel this strip of rind from orange with swivel peeler. Heat milk in saucepan with cream, orange rind, broken up cinnamon stick and salt and bring slowly to boil, stirring occasionally. Remove from heat, stir in extra sugar, cover and let stand 15 minutes. Beat eggs and egg yolks lightly in bowl — do not beat until frothy. Stir into warm milk with vanilla extract. Pour through fine strainer into toffee-lined pan. Place pan in baking dish of warm water and bake until knife tip inserted in middle comes out clean, about 45 to 50 minutes.

Remove custard from water bath and let cool. Refrigerate, covered, several hours or overnight.

When ready to serve, run tip of knife around outer and inner edges of custard, place serving plate over top of pan and invert custard onto plate. Serve cut in thick slices, spooning some caramel onto each plate.

Flan de Naranja

CREMA CATALANA

CATALAN 'BURNT' CREAM (SPAIN)   SERVES 4

Catalonia claims this popular dessert as its own, predating its entry into French cuisine as crème brûlée, but there is strong evidence that the dessert actually originated in England. The flavorings, however, are very Mediterranean.

The professional way to caramelize the sugar topping on this dessert is to use a very well-heated salamander, a thick metal disc with a handle. However, a small heavy saucepan, preferably of aluminum or cast iron, can be used. Add some used olive oil to a depth of 1/2 in (1 cm) to prevent buckling and to hold the heat; it will be extremely hot and you need to take care when handling this, or the salamander.

Fold a piece of old terry cloth or towel into a thick pad and place on work surface between the stove and the custards. Heat the pan or salamander over hot flame or very hot hot plate until really hot. Place directly onto the rim of a dish of custard and leave until sugar melts and forms a toffee — check that it isn't burning. Wipe saucepan base or salamander quickly across cloth pad to clean off burnt sugar then reheat for next custard. Put the saucepan of oil at the back of the stove to cool after you have finished, then dispose of oil.

If your broiler (grill) has the capacity to maintain a high, even heat, then place all the custards under the broiler (grill), as long as they do not take too long to caramelize. The idea is to have a hot toffee top with a cold custard. If desired, the custard may be served in a large dish and the top caramelized with a small butane blow torch.

1 lemon

3 cups (24 fl oz/750 ml) milk

1 cup (8 fl oz/250 ml) heavy (double) cream

1 cinnamon stick, broken up

pinch salt

6 egg yolks

1 tablespoon cornstarch (cornflour)

1/3 cup (2 1/2 oz/75 g) sugar

1/2 cup (3 1/2 oz/110 g) superfine (caster) sugar

Lightly scratch surface of lemon on fine side of grater so flavor can be released more readily. Cut peel thinly from lemon. Place in heavy saucepan with milk, cream, cinnamon and salt and bring slowly to boil, stirring occasionally.

Beat egg yolks with cornstarch and 1/3 cup sugar in large bowl using balloon whisk until well mixed. Strain hot milk through fine sieve into jug, discarding peel and cinnamon. Gradually beat into egg yolk mixture. Pour into saucepan and stir constantly over medium heat with wooden spoon until custard thickly coats back of spoon. Return to bowl and cover surface of custard with plastic wrap to prevent skin forming. Cover bowl and refrigerate several hours or overnight.

Just before serving, fill heat-proof soufflé dishes or cazuelas of 3/4 to 1 cup (6 to 8 fl oz/185 to 250 ml) capacity with custard. Level tops with spatula. Sprinkle with thin layer of sieved superfine sugar. Wipe rims of dishes and caramelize sugar (see introductory note above). Serve immediately.

SORBETTO AL LIMONE

LEMON SORBET (ITALY)   SERVES 6 TO 8

The lemons of Sicily are regarded as the best in the region, prized for their particular fragrance. Choose ripe, fragrant lemons for best results. Incidentally, Italy is accredited with having introduced ice creams, sorbets and granitas to Europe.

4 lemons
3 cups (24 fl oz/750 ml) water
1 cup (7$^{1}/_{2}$ oz/220 g) sugar
extra fresh lemon juice
1 egg white

Wash lemons well; scrub under hot water if waxed. Using swivel peeler, cut rind thinly from lemons, with as little white pith as possible. Place rind in saucepan with 3 cups water, bring slowly to boil and boil 10 minutes. Strain through sieve into measuring jug and make up to 2 cups (16 fl oz/500 ml) with extra water if necessary. Return lemon water to saucepan. Add sugar and stir over heat until dissolved. Bring to boil and boil 5 minutes. Let cool.

Squeeze juice from lemons and strain. Add more lemon juice if necessary to give $^{3}/_{4}$ cup (6 fl oz/180 ml) and stir into cooled syrup. Pour into freezer-proof bowl and freeze. When half frozen, stir well to break up ice crystals.

Beat egg white in bowl until stiff but not dry, and mix thoroughly into icy syrup. Cover with foil and freeze until just firm. Break up and beat well with electric mixer until smooth and light. Transfer to suitable freezer container, cover and freeze until firm, about 3 hours or longer.

Alternatively, use an ice cream churn. Refrigerate lemon syrup after cooling. Beat egg white only until frothy and stir into syrup. Place in churn and process according to manufacturer's instructions. Serve straight from churn, or store in freezer container in freezer until required.

LATTE ALLA GROTTA

PISTACHIO CUSTARD WITH MERINGUES (ITALY)   SERVES 6

This delightful custard dessert from Liguria is very much like the oeufs a la neige of French cuisine except that the custard is usually poured over the meringues (which float to the top anyway). The pistachios give the custard a pale green tinge; the fresher the nuts, the better the color. The dessert looks more spectacular served as I have suggested below rather than the traditional way.

6 cups (48 fl oz/1.5 L) water

4 egg whites

pinch of salt

1/2 cup (4 oz/125 g) superfine (caster) sugar

4 cups (32 fl oz/1 L) milk

3 tablespoons ground pistachio nuts

1/4 teaspoon ground cinnamon

6 teaspoons plain (all-purpose) flour

5 egg yolks

1 to 2 drops green food coloring (optional)

1 tablespoon chopped, blanched pistachio nuts (see page 21)

Bring 6 cups water to boil in wide pan (a sauté pan is ideal), and reduce heat to maintain water at simmering point.

Beat egg whites with salt in bowl until stiff. Gradually beat in half the sugar until glossy and meringue holds a peak. Using an oval serving spoon, scoop heaping spoonfuls of meringue and slide five or six at a time into simmering water, using spatula to push meringue off spoon. Simmer 5 minutes, gently turning half way through cooking. Remove using slotted spoon and drain on clean cloth. You should have 12 to 14 meringues. Discard water.

Pour 3 1/2 cup milk into heavy stainless steel or enamelled pan and stir in ground pistachio nuts and cinnamon. Bring to boil and reduce heat to maintain at simmering point.

Combine remaining sugar well with flour. Using balloon whisk, beat egg yolks with sugar and flour mixture until smooth. Gradually beat in remaining 1/2 cup milk. Whisk half the hot milk into egg mixture and pour back into pan, stirring constantly with wooden spoon. Stir over gentle heat until custard coats back of spoon — do not boil. Stir in food coloring, if using. Place saucepan into cold water and let custard cool until just warm, stirring occasionally. Pour into wide glass bowl or individual dessert glasses, top with meringues, cover and chill until required. Sprinkle with pistachios just before serving.

Latte alla Grotta

Granita all'Arancia

ORANGE WATER ICE (ITALY)   SERVES 6 TO 8

While orange is the principle flavoring in this Sicilian recipe, it tastes even better if lemon is included.

2 oranges
1 lemon
3 cups (24 fl oz/750 ml) water
1 cup (7 1/2 oz/220 g) sugar
1 cup (8 fl oz/250 ml) strained fresh orange juice
1/4 cup (2 fl oz/60 ml) strained fresh lemon juice

Wash fruit well; scrub under hot water if waxed. Using swivel peeler, peel rind thinly from fruit, with as little white pith as possible. Place rind in saucepan with 3 cups water, bring slowly to boil and boil, 10 minutes. Strain through sieve into measuring jug and make up to 2 cups (16 fl oz/500 ml) with extra water if necessary.

Return measured liquid to pan. Add sugar and stir over heat until dissolved. Bring to boil and boil 5 minutes. Let cool.

Add orange and lemon juice to syrup and pour into freezer container. Freeze 3 hours until just firm, stirring occasionally as it freezes so that water ice has fine grainy texture rather than large ice crystals. When serving, stir ice well with fork and pile into small chilled dessert glasses.

Peres al vi Negre

PEARS IN RED WINE (SPAIN)   SERVES 6

Popular in Spain, particularly Catalonia, pears are also prepared in similar ways in France and Italy, although the recipes are usually attributed to regions not directly on the Mediterranean Sea. The black pepper in this particular recipe can be omitted, but it is worth trying as it has an affinity to fruit; try some ground onto fresh strawberries. Select pears that are barely ripe for easier handling.

6 medium pears (beurre bosc, bartlett or comice pears)
juice of 1/2 lemon
1 cup (8 fl oz/250 ml) water
1 1/2 cups (12 fl oz/375 ml) red wine
1 cup (7 1/2 oz/220 g) sugar
thinly peeled strips of orange and lemon rind
3 in (8 cm) cinnamon stick
1/4 teaspoon black peppercorns (optional)
helado de canela (cinnamon ice cream) (see page 285) or whipped cream, to serve (optional)

Peel pears right up to stalk. Carefully cut blossom remains from bottom of pears. If pears do not stand upright, trim base slightly. Place in bowl of cold water with lemon juice added.

Combine 1 cup water, wine and sugar in saucepan. Add orange and lemon rind, cinnamon stick and peppercorns and stir over heat until sugar is dissolved. Bring to boil and boil 3 to 4 minutes.

Drain pears and place upright in pan with sugar syrup. Cover and simmer gently until tender when tested with fine skewer, about 25 to 30 minutes, basting with syrup 2 to 3 times. Remove pears to serving bowl. Bring syrup to rapid boil and boil until reduced to light syrupy consistency. Let cool and strain over pears. Cover and refrigerate, spooning syrup occasionally over pears to maintain an even color. Serve pears on individual plates with syrup.

KAYMAKLI KAYISI TATLISI

POACHED APRICOTS WITH CREAM (TURKEY)   SERVES 4 TO 6

You need soft Turkish apricots for this dessert, pitted but left whole — not dried in halves. In Turkey, these would be filled with kaymak, a thick, clotted cream usually made from buffalo milk.

6 oz (180 g) dried whole apricots

1¹/₂ cups (12 fl oz/375 ml) water

thinly peeled strip of lemon rind

¹/₂ cup (3¹/₂ oz/110 g) sugar

1 teaspoon lemon juice

³/₄ cup (6 fl oz/180 ml) clotted or extra thick cream or crème fraîche (see page 35)

2 tablespoons finely chopped, blanched pistachio nuts (see page 21)

Rinse apricots and place in saucepan with water and lemon rind. Cover, slowly bring to a gentle boil and boil 10 minutes until soft. Add sugar and lemon juice and shake pan gently until sugar is dissolved — avoid stirring or apricots could break up. Bring to boil, cover and simmer over low heat 10 minutes. Let cool to lukewarm. Remove apricots to sieve with slotted spoon, allowing excess syrup to strain back into pan. Return syrup to the boil and boil 1 minute. Strain syrup through fine sieve into jug. Let cool and refrigerate until chilled. Meanwhile, gently open each apricot and insert heaping teaspoon of cream. Close a little — cream should be visible. Arrange in serving dish in single layer. Cover and refrigerate until required. To serve, pour cooled syrup around apricots and sprinkle with pistachios.

NARANJAS ACARAMELADAS

CARAMELIZED ORANGES (SPAIN)   SERVES 4 TO 6

Oranges were introduced into Spain by the Moors and have thrived there ever since, particularly in the south-east. This dessert is an excellent end to a rich meal. The toffee melts while the dessert chills.

6 sweet oranges

1³/₄ cups (14 fl oz/435 ml) water

1¹/₂ cups (11 oz/330 g) superfine (caster) sugar

lenguas de gato (see page 269), to serve (optional)

Using a swivel peeler, remove rind thinly from 2 oranges and cut into julienne strips. Alternatively use zester to remove thin strips. Place rind in small saucepan with 1 cup water and boil 10 minutes for julienne, 5 minutes if zester was used. Drain and set aside. Peel all oranges using serrated knife, removing all traces of white pith and outer membrane. Cut oranges into ¹/₄ in (5 mm) slices on a plate to collect juice. Arrange slices in shallow serving dish, slightly overlapping. Collect any juice and set aside. Place sugar and ³/₄ cup water in heavy-based saucepan and stir over medium heat until sugar is dissolved — do not boil. Wipe down sugar crystals from side of pan using wet brush. When dissolved, bring to boil and boil over medium heat without stirring until toffee is golden brown — do not over-brown. Remove immediately from heat and stir in rind and 2 tablespoons juice. Pour over oranges, cover and refrigerate at least 2 hours. Serve chilled, accompanied by lenguas de gato, if desired.

İRMİK HELVASI

SEMOLINA HALVA WITH SAFFRON AND PISTACHIOS (TURKEY)   SERVES 6 TO 8

Halva is Turkey's oldest sweet, and can be made with flour, nuts and grape syrup, or with semolina. Do not confuse this halva with the sesame seed confection of the same name. The saffron in this recipe does not become a powder, but the flavor is released more readily when pounded in a mortar. Take care when adding the milk syrup to the semolina as it may spatter a little.

1/4 teaspoon saffron threads

1 tablespoon hot water

3 cups (24 fl oz/750 ml) milk

3/4 cup (5 1/2 oz/165 g) sugar

3 oz (90 g) unsalted butter

1/3 cup (1 1/2 oz/50 g) pistachio nuts (see page 21)

3/4 cup (4 1/2 oz/140 g) semolina

Pound saffron strands in mortar, add hot water and let stand 10 minutes. Heat milk in saucepan. Add sugar and stir until dissolved. Add saffron water and bring slowly to gentle boil.

Meanwhile, melt a little of the butter in heavy saucepan. Add pistachio nuts and cook over medium heat 2 to 3 minutes — do not brown. Remove and set aside.

Place remaining butter and semolina in saucepan and cook over medium-low heat 10 minutes, stirring often — do not allow to color. Remove pan from heat and stir in boiling milk syrup. Return to heat and stir constantly until thickened and beginning to bubble. Boil gently 2 minutes, stir in nuts and remove from heat. Transfer to bowl and serve warm or at room temperature.

KHOSHAF

COMPOTE OF DRIED FRUIT (MIDDLE EAST)   SERVES 6 TO 8

An excellent dessert, this compote is also good served for breakfast. Two methods are given here: the cooked version does not require planning and I think it has a better flavor. Dried dessert figs are plump and moist, but if using other figs, soak overnight first, even if using the cooked method. As an alternative flavoring to the scented water in the cooked method, add a cinnamon stick and a thinly peeled strip of lemon rind to the fruit at the beginning of cooking — leave these in the bowl while fruit is chilling.

4 oz (125 g) dried apricots

8 oz (250 g) prunes

4 oz (125 g) dried peaches or pears, halved

4 oz (125 g) dried dessert figs, left whole or halved

2 oz (60 g) golden raisins (sultanas)

4 cups (32 fl oz/1 L) water

1/2 cup (3 1/2 oz/110 g) sugar

2 tablespoons orange flower water or rose water

blanched chopped almonds, pistachio nuts or walnuts, or toasted pine nuts, to serve

Soaked method: Rinse fruit and place in large bowl with 4 cups water. Stir in sugar and orange flower or rose water. Cover and refrigerate 2 to 3 days, stirring occasionally during first day to dissolve sugar.

Cooked method: Rinse fruit and place in saucepan with 4 cups water. Bring slowly to boiling point, partly covered. Cover and simmer 5 minutes. Add sugar and shake until dissolved. Cover and simmer over low heat 15 minutes. Let cool. Add scented water. Transfer to bowl, cover and refrigerate.

To serve: Place in large serving dish or individual dishes and sprinkle with choice of nuts, or a combination.

Khoshaf

CHARLOTTE DE POMMES AU MIEL DE LAVANDE

APPLE CHARLOTTE WITH LAVENDER HONEY (FRANCE)   SERVES 8

Originating in neighboring region of Dauphine, this warming winter dessert is also prepared in Provence, using their winter apples in combination with the luscious lavender honey and bread.

6 oz (180 g) butter,
clarified (see page 9)

4 lb (2 kg) golden delicious or
russet apples, peeled, cored and
thinly sliced

1/2 cup (4 fl oz/125 ml)
dry white wine

1/2 teaspoon ground cinnamon

1/4 cup (2 fl oz/60 ml)
lavender honey

1/4 cup (2 oz/60 g) sugar

8 to 10 slices stale white bread,
crusts removed

Lavender Cream:

1 cup (8 fl oz/250 ml)
whipping cream

1 tablespoon superfine (caster) sugar

1 tablespoon lavender honey

1 teaspoon dried edible
lavender flowers,
crushed to powder (optional)

Heat 2 tablespoons clarified butter in large, heavy saucepan. Add apples, wine and cinnamon, cover and cook over low heat until apples are very soft, about 20 minutes, stirring occasionally. Add honey and half the sugar, and cook, uncovered, over medium heat until liquid evaporates and puree is very thick and holds its shape when stirred — stir often to break up the apples. Add more sugar to taste if necessary.

Preheat oven to 400–425°F (200–220°C/Gas 6).

Cut trimmed bread into wide strips to fit charlotte mold or 3 in x 7 in (8 cm x 18 cm) deep round cake pan or soufflé dish and cut triangles for base.

Dip bread into remaining melted clarified butter in shallow dish to coat each side. Place strips of bread close together around sides and triangles over base of mold. Fill with apples, mounding them in the middle, and cover with remaining butter-coated bread strips.

Bake 15 minutes to brown bread. Reduce heat to 350–375°F (180–190°C/Gas 4) and bake until top is golden brown and charlotte feels firm in middle, about 35 to 45 minutes. Remove from oven and let stand 15 minutes.

For lavender cream: Whip cream and stir in honey and dried lavender.

To serve, turn charlotte onto serving dish and serve warm with lavender cream.

Pesche al Mascarpone

PEACHES WITH MASCARPONE (ITALY)   SERVES 6

Poached peaches are a popular dessert in Italy, often filled with crushed amaretti, store-bought or home-made (see page 269). Filled with a mixture of mascarpone and amaretto, they are even more delicious.

3 large or 6 medium-sized, firm,
free-stone peaches

juice of 1/2 lemon

1 cup (7 1/2 oz/220 g) sugar

1/2 cup (4 fl oz/125 ml) water

1/2 cup (4 fl oz/125 ml) white wine

strip of lemon rind

1 tablespoon amaretto or kirsch
liqueur

8 oz (250 g) mascarpone cheese

5 amaretti cookies, crushed

1 tablespoon brandy

Place peaches in large bowl, cover with boiling water and let stand 2 to 3 minutes. Drain and gently pull away skin. Place peaches in bowl of cold water with lemon juice.

Place sugar, 1/2 cup water, wine and lemon rind in wide saucepan and stir over medium heat until sugar is dissolved. Bring to boil and boil 5 minutes.

Drain peaches and cut in halves, removing seeds. Place in pan with syrup in single layer if possible. Cover and simmer gently until peaches are tender, about 8 to 10 minutes, turning carefully during cooking to cook evenly. Remove with slotted spoon to bowl. Boil syrup in saucepan over high heat until about 1 cup remains. Let cool. Stir in liqueur and strain over peaches. Cover and refrigerate several hours.

Place mascarpone in bowl and add all but 2 tablespoons crushed amaretti. Stir in brandy. Place 1 to 2 peach halves on dessert plates, add generous dollop of mascarpone mixture and spoon some peach syrup onto plate. Sprinkle remaining amaretti onto peaches and serve.

Compôte de Coigns

QUINCE COMPOTE (FRANCE)   SERVES 6

Do not worry about discoloration as quinces are prepared, as this actually helps the fruit color during cooking. However, do check quinces often as they simmer; some soften quickly but most will take over an hour to become tender and develop a rosy color. The vanilla bean can be re-used; rinse and dry before storing. Pale pink roses from perfumed roses, carefully rinsed, are a perfect finish for this delicate dessert.

3 to 4 quinces,
peeled, halved and cored

1 1/2 cups (11 oz/330 g) sugar

3 cups (24 fl oz/750 ml) water

1 vanilla bean (pod)

pink rose petals,
to garnish (optional)

lenguas de gato (see page 269),
to serve (optional)

Cut each quince half into 3 to 4 even wedges, depending on size of quinces. Dissolve sugar in water in large saucepan over medium heat. Bring to boil. Add vanilla bean and quinces, cover, and simmer until tender, about 1 hour. Transfer quinces from syrup to bowl using a slotted spoon. Boil syrup, uncovered, until reduced by half, about 10 minutes. Let cool. Place quinces in large glass bowl or individual dessert glasses, and strain syrup over. Serve garnished with rose petals and accompanied by lenguas de gato if desired.

INDEX

ACKNOWLEDGMENTS

The author and publishers would like to thank the following people and organizations
for their assistance in producing this book.
Rowen Fotheringham for his superb food photography; Janet Mitchell for her expert food styling,
assisted by Myles Beaufort. For lending props, Accoutrement (Mosman NSW Australia),
Orson & Blake Collectibles (Woollhara NSW Australia), Tilecraft (Northbridge NSW Australia),
Villaroy & Boch, Appley Hoare Antiques, Kerryn Haig, Redelman Fabrics, Royal Copenhagen,
Country Road, Mokum Fabrics
The author particularly wishes to thank editor Kirsten Tilgals,
who so expertly steered this project through the intricate processes of creating a book.
Also thanks to her sister, Ellen Argyriou, a cookery professional, for assistance in recipe testing;
husband John Mallos for his unwavering help and support; daughter Suzanne Mallos and
Mary Sambaliotis for assistance with the typing.
Thank you also to those who gave freely of their time and expertise in various matters
relating to Mediterranean cooking: Philippa Goodrick and the International Olive Oil Council;
the charming French-born cookbook author, Gabriel Gaté, for some updates on the food of Provence;
Barbara Santich, expert on medieval Mediterranean cuisine; Doreen Badger regarding breads,
Paula Wolfert, Liane Colwell, Said Mouftakir and Jamil Ben Hassine, for answering many queries
on the cooking of the Maghreb; Rosa Rodriguez and John Newtown, for their expertise regarding
Spanish cuisines; Rosie Stevens, Lisa Panucci, Beppi Polese and Antonino and Dominique La Rosa
for advice on Italy; for Malta, Charles Hili; Michael Bailes and Robyn Eager of The Fragrant Garden;
Stirling Macoboy and Colin Olson for things botanical.

BIBLIOGRAPHY

Algar, Ayla, *Classical Turkish Cooking*, Harper Collins Publishers, New York, 1991

Ayto, John, *The Glutton's Glossary*, Routledge, London, 1990

Boni, Ada, *Italian Regional Cooking*, Bonanza Books, USA, 1969

Bugialli, Giuliano, *The Taste of Italy*, Conran Octopus Ltd, London, 1985

Carrier, Robert, *Taste of Morocco*, Century Hutchinson Ltd, London, 1987

Carrier, Robert, *Feasts of Provence*, Allen & Unwin Pty. Ltd, Sydney, 1992

Casas, Penelope, *The Foods and Wines of Spain*, Penguin Books Ltd, England, 1985

Davidson, Alan, *Mediterranean Seafood*, The Penguin Group, England, 1972

Ganor, Avi and Maiberg, Ron, *The Taste of Israel*, Prion, Multimedia Books Ltd, London, 1990

Halici, Nevin, *Turkish Cookbook*, Dorley Kindersley Ltd, London, 1989

Haroutunian, Arto, *North African Cooking*, Century Publishing Co. Ltd, London, 1985

Harris, Valentina, *Italian Regional Cookery*, BBC Books, London, 1990

Hazan, Marcella, *The Classic Italian Cookbook*, MacMillan London Ltd, 1980

Hazan, Marcella, *The Second Classic Italian Cookbook*, Pan Macmillan Publishers Ltd, London, 1983

Hemphill, John and Rosemary, *What Herb is That?*, Lansdowne Publishing Pty Ltd, Sydney, 1995

Manjon, Maite, *The Gastronomy of Spain and Portugal*, Garamond Ltd, London, 1990.

Ortiz, Elizabeth Lambert, *The Foods and Wines of Spain and Portugal*, Headline, London, 1990

Passmore, Jacki, *The Complete Spanish Cookbook*, Lansdowne Publishing Pty. Ltd, Sydney, 1995

Rogers, Jo, *What Food is That?*, Lansdowne Publishing Pty. Ltd, Sydney, 1995

Root, Waverley, *Food*, Simon & Schuster, Inc. New York, 1980

Santich, Barbara, *The Original Mediterranean Cuisine*, Wakefield Press, Australia, 1995

Tannahill, Reay, *Food in History*, Eyre Methuen Ltd, London, 1975

Torres, Marimar, *The Catalan Country Kitchen*, Adison-Wesley Publishing Company, Inc. USA, 1992

Willan, Anne and l'Ecole de Cuisine, *French Regional Cooking*, Marshall Editions Ltd, London, 1981

Vergé, Roger, *Cuisine of the Sun*, edited and adapted by Caroline Conran, Macmillan London Ltd, 1979

Wolfert, Paula, *Couscous & Other Good Food from Morocco*, Harper Row Publishers Inc. USA, 1973